This book is a marvel. And we need it now more than ever. *Teaching LGBTQ+ History in High Schools* is a book *for* and *by* teachers. It features contributions from a wide range of thinkers and practitioners invested in the art and craft of teaching accurate history that also diversifies the voices that we have been told are worth studying. The authors offer personal stories of empowerment and strategy in the classroom, while also laying out a roadmap to help ensure LGBTQ+ history remains a key part of our curricula.

Julio Capo, Jr., *Florida International University, Author of* Welcome to Fairyland: Queer Miami before 1940

Written by teachers, for teachers, *Teaching LGBTQ+ History in High Schools* shares theories of pedagogy, classroom-tested curricular activities, and examples proving the continued relevance of the LGBTQ+ past. Most powerfully, it offers the voices of educators speaking from the perspective of their classrooms and with the wisdom of experience. Brimming with creativity and compassion, the volume combines practical guidance for those who want to introduce or more fully incorporate LGBTQ+ topics in history and social studies classes with inspiring accounts of the positive impact that teachers can make in the lives of their students. And vice versa! At a time when public education in the US seems mired in divisive politics, *Teaching LGBTQ+ History in High Schools* brings a reminder of the transformative possibility of schools.

Anne Valk, *The Graduate Center at the City University of New York & Director of the American Social History Project*

Teaching LGBTQ+ History in High Schools

Teaching LGBTQ+ History in High Schools: Practical Strategies and Voices of Experience offers insights, concrete strategies, and lesson plans for teaching LGBTQ+ history in high schools. With essays from educators, historians, and activists, it speaks to the power and significance of LGBTQ+-inclusive curriculum and its greater necessity at a time when the LGBTQ+ community is both more visible and increasingly targeted.

Across the US, challenges exist that prevent teaching LGBTQ+ history, including curriculum censorship laws prohibiting discussion of the LGBTQ+ community in schools. However, there are also grassroots movements in the US that are generating quality LGBTQ+ history curriculum and implementing them in secondary schools. This book shows how integrating LGBTQ+ content offers myriad benefits for all students, including making history more relevant and representative, and reversing years of silence and erasure in the sources, topics, and narratives that students encounter throughout their education.

Combining insights from changemakers with practical strategies and lesson plans for teaching LGBTQ+ history, this book will equip educators with the rationale and resources they need to effectively integrate this history into the curriculum. It will also be highly valuable for pre-service teachers, particularly within Social Studies Education and Social Justice Education.

Stacie Brensilver Berman is a Clinical Assistant Professor at New York University, USA, and was previously a public school teacher for 10 years. She is the author of *LGBTQ+ History in High School Classrooms in the United States since 1990* and *Project Based Learning in Real World US History Classrooms: Engaging Diverse Learners* (co-authored by Diana B. Turk).

Robert Cohen is a Professor of History and Social Studies at New York University, USA, whose most recent books are *Confronting Jim Crow: Race, Memory and the University of Georgia in the Twentieth Century* and *Rethinking America's Past: Howard Zinn's People's History of the United States in the Classroom and Beyond* (co-authored by Sonia E. Murrow).

Teaching LGBTQ+ History in High Schools

Practical Strategies and Voices of Experience

Stacie Brensilver Berman and Robert Cohen

R Routledge
Taylor & Francis Group

NEW YORK AND LONDON

Designed cover image: FG Trade / Getty Images

First published 2026
by Routledge
605 Third Avenue, New York, NY 10158

and by Routledge
4 Park Square, Milton Park, Abingdon, Oxon, OX14 4RN

Routledge is an imprint of the Taylor & Francis Group, an informa business

Library of Congress Cataloging-in-Publication Data
Names: Berman, Stacie Brensilver, author. |
Cohen, Robert, 1955 May 21– author.
Title: Teaching LGBTQ+ history in high schools : practical strategies and voices of experience / Stacie Brensilver Berman and Robert Cohen.
Description: New York, NY : Routledge, 2025. |
Includes bibliographical references and index.
Identifiers: LCCN 2025005277 (print) |
LCCN 2025005278 (ebook) | ISBN 9781032689661 (hardback) |
ISBN 9781032689647 (paperback) | ISBN 9781032689678 (ebook)
Subjects: LCSH: Gay and lesbian studies–Study and teaching–United States. | Sexual minorities–History–Study and teaching–United States.
Classification: LCC HQ75.16.U6 B47 2025 (print) |
LCC HQ75.16.U6 (ebook) | DDC 306.76071/273–dc23/eng/20250221
LC record available at https://lccn.loc.gov/2025005277
LC ebook record available at https://lccn.loc.gov/2025005278

ISBN: 9781032689661 (hbk)
ISBN: 9781032689647 (pbk)
ISBN: 9781032689678 (ebk)

DOI: 10.4324/9781032689678

Typeset in Palatino
by Newgen Publishing UK

This book is dedicated to the teachers who strive to ensure that all of their students feel seen, valued, and represented. Your work saves lives.

This book is dedicated to students, who deserve teachers and school communities that see and uplift them.

Contents

Meet the Authors

Stacie Brensilver Berman is a Clinical Assistant Professor at New York University. She is the author of *LGBTQ+ History in High School Classes in the United States since 1990* and "Books Have Their Own Stories: LGBTQ History in High School US History Textbooks" in *Nationhood, Citizenship, Gender and Religion – Comparative Perspectives on Textbook Analysis*. She is the co-author of *Project Based Learning in Real-World US History Classrooms: Engaging Diverse Learners* as well as "Teaching War Crimes in a Comparative Perspective" in *Teaching Recent Global History* (2014), "Teaching the Port Huron Statement" in *Inspiring Participatory Democracy* (2012), "The Civil Rights Movement" in *Teaching US History* (2010), and journal articles on using project based learning in social studies classes. She has worked extensively with high school teachers on developing curriculum and navigating the challenges around introducing potentially controversial issues in classrooms, presenting at conferences throughout the United States, and working individually with educators teaching topics including LGBTQ+ history, civil rights, students' rights, constitutional history, and the feminist movement. Prior to earning her doctorate, Brensilver Berman was a New York City Public School teacher for ten years.

Robert Cohen is a professor of History and Social Studies at NYU. His books include *Confronting Jim Crow: Race, Memory and the University of Georgia in the Twentieth Century* (2024); *With Liberty and Justice For All? The Constitution in the Classroom* (2022), co-edited with Maeva Marcus and Steven Steinbach; *Howard Zinn's A People's History of the United States in the Classroom and Beyond* (2021, co-authored by Sonia E. Murrow (2021); *Howard Zinn's Southern Diary: Sit-ins, Civil Rights, and Black Women's*

Student Activism (2018); *Rebellion in Black and White: Southern Student Activism in the 1960s* (2013), co-edited by David J. Snyder; *Freedom's Orator: Mario Savio and the Radical Legacy of the 1960s* (2009); *Dear Mrs; Roosevelt: Letters from Children of the Great Depression (2002); The Free Speech Movement: Reflections on Berkeley in the 1960s* (2002), co-edited by Reginald E. Zelnikl; *When the Old Left Was Young: Student Radicals and America's First Mass Student Movement: 1929-1941* (1993). He is the founder of the NYU Steinhardt-NYU Law School Constitutional History Partnership, which has law students teach lessons on the Constitution in high need public high schools, has written many articles on teaching American history for the National Council for the Social Studies' teachers' magazine, *Social Education*, and serves as consulting editor for the Emma Goldman Papers Project's four volumes on her American years.

Contributors

Bettina Aptheker is Distinguished Professor Emerita, Feminist Studies Department, University of California, Santa Cruz. Her most recent book is *Communists in Closets: Queering this History, 1930s-1990s* (Routledge, 2023).

David Duffield is a teacher in Denver, Colorado. He is the founder of the Colorado LGBTQ History Project, as well as the websites GlobalQueerHeritage.com and TheDenverPrinciples.com. He is a board member of the Committee on LGBTQ History.

Olive Garrison, a non-binary educator, teaches history in the Kern High School District, advises the Pride Club, and is on the PRISM Advisor's Committee. They are also part of the Social Studies Leadership Team, developing curriculum and professional development. Pursuing a doctorate in Educational Leadership, Olive aims to promote LGBTQ+ inclusive curriculum and protect trans youth.

Lil Miss Hot Mess serves on the board of Drag Story Hour and is the author of three picture books: *Make Your Own Rainbow: A Drag Queen's Guide to Color*; *If You're a Drag Queen and You Know It*; and *The Hips on the Drag Queen Go Swish, Swish, Swish*. By day, Lil Miss Hot Mess is a university professor, and has published in numerous academic journals and news outlets, including *Curriculum Inquiry* and *Slate*.

More info: www.lilmisshotmess.com/.

Daniel Hurewitz is an Associate Professor of History at Hunter College in New York City. He is the author of *Stepping Out*, a history of LGBT life across Manhattan, and *Bohemian Los Angeles and the Making of Modern Politics*. His recent work examines American homophobic policies and their implementation at the local level.

Lauren Jensen entered the classroom in 2002 and has been teaching high school English for nearly 20 years. She recently earned her Master's in Educational Leadership from Harvard University while teaching AP Literature for the Fairfax County Public Schools Online Campus and AP Language for Crimson Global Academy.

Justin Martinez is a high school history teacher from the Bronx, NY. His goal as an educator is to empower students with an education that portrays their identities not as the historical other but as a central component to our greater historical narrative. Justin completed his BA at Wheaton College Massachusetts and holds an MAT from NYU.

J.B. Mayo, Jr. is an Associate Professor of Social Studies Education at the University of Minnesota. His research highlights the inclusion of queer histories in standard social studies curriculum, students' identity formation in GSAs, and the intersections of racialized/sexual identities. Mayo's current project focuses on the joys and challenges of queer parenting.

Rick Oculto is a 20-year non-profit veteran specializing in justice, equity, diversity, and inclusion. He has worked to implement LGBTQ+ inclusive practices to create welcoming and inclusive climates for youth and families of diverse backgrounds. Rick has recently spearheaded efforts in California to implement LGBTQ+ inclusive history in schools.

John M. Palella is Lecturer in Education and Director of the Social Studies MAT Cohort at Brown University. His work centers on LGBTQ+ history, anti-racist practices, and media literacy pedagogies. Recently, John coauthored Rhode Island's new

Social Studies State Standards and collaborates with teachers on creating inclusive and standards-aligned curricula.

Don Romesburg is a Visiting Professor of Women's, Gender and Queer Studies at Cal Poly San Luis Obispo. He has authored *Contested Curriculum: LGBTQ History Goes to School* (Rutgers, 2025), edited the *Routledge History of Queer America* (2018), and was the lead scholar working to bring LGBTQ content into California's 2016 K-12 History-Social Science Framework.

Wendy L. Rouse is a Professor of History and coordinator of the Social Science Teacher Preparation Program at San Jose State University. Her research focuses on the history of women, gender, and sexuality. Rouse's most recent book is *Public Faces, Secret Lives: The Queer History of the Women's Suffrage Movement* (NYU Press, 2022).

Sandra Slater is an Associate Professor of History at the College of Charleston in South Carolina and Director of the Carolina Lowcountry in the Atlantic World Program. She has published several journal articles. Her most recent book is *The Pompe and Pride of Man: Pride and Humility in Early New England*, published by Brill Academic Publishers in 2025.

Jinnie Spiegler has been the Director of Curriculum and Training at ADL since 2013. She is responsible for the oversight and creation of K-12 curriculum and training efforts. Jinnie has worked for over 20 years in K-12 education for both NYC-based and national educational organizations. Jinnie has an M.Ed in Education from Lesley University and B.A. from Hampshire College.

Preface

Teaching is hard work. To do it well, one must be an expert in their content area (or several content areas!); build meaningful relationships with students and their families; understand what their students need and how to create circumstances that enable them to learn; have the space to hold all of their students' joys, triumphs, struggles, concerns, and angst, many of which stay with a teacher long after the school day is over; keep up to date with trends, memes, and slang; and be willing to adapt and reinvent oneself on a daily or hourly basis. Then, factor in standards, testing, district policies, state policies, and national political and media figures threatening your academic freedom and telling you what you should or should not teach, thus always wondering if your job and livelihood are at risk. Teaching, as we said, is hard work.

This book is for teachers. It centers teachers' voices as they share their journeys and experiences, providing them with a platform that they do not often have to reflect on and discuss their practice. It offers classroom-tested, teacher-developed resources, lesson plans, activities, and strategies focused on teaching LGBTQ+ history to use in middle and high school classrooms. It includes essays and personal stories meant to remind teachers that your work is valuable, your efforts do not go unnoticed, and you are capable of doing this important work.

You may be wondering how this book on teaching LGBTQ+ history came into existence at a time like ours. In red state America, LGBTQ+-themed books have been banned from school libraries, and teaching this history has been implicitly and explicitly outlawed by law, policy, and/or community norms. Trump's victorious 2024 presidential campaign, which relied on discriminatory language and tropes, devoted more than $20 million to transphobic television ads[1]. It is true, of course, that these are difficult days, when intolerance and censorship abound. But it is also true that there is a very large, really an immense, national constituency for LGBTQ+ rights. America's great prophet of democracy, Martin Luther King, Jr., asserted that "the arc of the moral universe is long, but it bends toward justice."[2] These words ring true when we consider how that long arc of justice has bent on issues like marriage equality.

Gallup polls show that in 1996 only 27% of Americans supported same-sex marriage, while 68% opposed it. In the twenty-first century, though, support for same-sex marriage has skyrocketed, reaching 60% by 2015, paving the way for even Chief Justice John Roberts's conservative Supreme Court to legalize it that year, in its historic *Obergefell* decision. In 2024, nine years after that decision, support for same-sex marriage enjoyed even larger majority support, standing at 69% according to Gallup, while the opposition shrunk to 29%[3]. There is, then, not merely a huge constituency for LGBTQ+ rights, but an obvious need for historians and history teachers to probe the LGBTQ+ experience in the US and explain how a nation that for centuries demonized and discriminated against people who identify as LGBTQ+ finally began to recognize them as equal citizens before the law.

Historians since the 1960s have risen to the challenge of exploring the LGBTQ+ experience in the American past. Such great historians as Martin Duberman, a Pulitzer Prize winner, John D'Emilio, George Chauncey, and Blanche Wiesen Cook, have not only published important works of LGBTQ+ history, but also helped establish interdisciplinary LGBTQ+/ gender studies programs that have educated generations of talented historians who themselves have published path breaking works that made LGBTQ+ history one of the most intellectually stimulating fields of scholarship. There are currently well over 100 colleges and universities that offer gender studies courses, more than 250 LGBTQ+ centers on campuses, and high-quality queer history and gender studies scholarly journals that bring the latest studies to readers. When one considers this rich intellectual milieu, it is not at all surprising that both professors who contribute to it and teachers who have been educated amidst it – both of whom are represented in this book – are eager to link the high school world to the scholarship it has generated. And that some school systems – particularly in the seven states that require the teaching of LGBTQ+ history – have proven eager to have their students learn the history we explore in the pages of this book, with its more inclusive version of the American past. Educators and policymakers in these states, as well as those linked by a similar sense of commitment to this cause in other parts of the country, understand this history's power to improve students' historical literacy and end the marginalization and bullying of LGBTQ+ students by exposing students to the oppressive nature of America's homophobic and transphobic past. Such historical teaching and learning offer many students their first glimpse of the many contributions LGBTQ+ Americans have made in enriching American culture and promoting minority rights. And since middle and high school history education is in part aimed at preparing students for college, it seems high time those schools did more to introduce their students to the field of LGBTQ+ history which, as we have seen, has such an impressive presence on our nation's college and university campuses.[4]

This is a history that, if taught well, has the power to awaken students to what was, in James Baldwin's words, both "terrible" and "beautiful" in the LGBTQ+ experience, in an American past where democracy and bigotry existed side by side. This is evident in the use of pseudo-science to characterize homosexuality as a mental illness, the misuse of religion to treat LGBTQ+ Americans as pariahs, the mobilization of Cold War paranoia to purge gays and lesbians from government service, the military, and the teaching profession, and police harassment of LGBTQ+ social life – leaving even Bayard Rustin, one of the greatest anti-racist organizers in American history, with a police record that such segregationists as Strom Thurmond could use to slander him. Yet along with this ugliness, and overcoming it, were the scholars, activists, the cultural and political leaders who refuted the demonizing myths, and who labored in the courts, the streets, the legislatures, and in universities and schools, struggling for equality and dignity. A long – and still ongoing – struggle that finally achieved recognition from the very top of the American political system when President Barack Obama paid tribute to the gains made for gender equity in the US "from Seneca Falls to Stonewall."

The idea for this book evolved in the spring of 2022 out of a related academic freedom struggle faced by high school teachers, as right-wing think tanks and ideologues sought to ban Critical Race Theory from the nation's schools. In response to this repression, we started a working group for teachers who wanted to learn more about Critical Race Theory (CRT), its strengths, weaknesses, and how to integrate both CRT and the debates it provoked into their curricula. Over the course of that semester, we engaged in powerful discussions about the need to push back against curriculum censorship, support educators who are dedicated to teaching inclusive, representative, and accurate versions of history, and the significance of collaborative environments for teachers who might confront challenges. By that May, the teachers in our group taught lessons on the Emancipation Proclamation, *Brown v. Board of Education*, and the centuries-long struggle for Civil Rights that integrated CRT. They spoke about how transformative these learning experiences were for their students and committed to doing similar work in the future. We were not sure what the outcomes of this project would be; we were invigorated and felt compelled to do more when it went so well. Given our prior work on teaching LGBTQ+ history, and the rising tide of repression against the teaching of that history, recruiting teachers and establishing a working group focused on teaching LGBTQ+ history in high school seemed a logical next step.

We were thrilled when nearly all of the teachers that we invited to join our group on teaching LGBTQ+ history agreed to participate. Listening to their ideas about what they might teach and why it was important for their students, there was no doubt that their efforts would result in powerful, engaging, and inclusive lessons that would be meaningful for their students and also helpful for teachers across the country with whom we would share their plans and resources. The question became, then, how to reach teachers beyond our group and outside of our existing networks. Furthermore, once we did so, how could we let all of these educators know that, despite a challenging (to say the least) national atmosphere around teaching LGBTQ+

history, that bringing this content into classrooms is worth the time, effort, and, in some cases, risk?

To answer that question, we landed on the idea of contributed essays from people with experience teaching or advocating for the inclusion of LGBTQ+ history. These "voices of experience" could share their stories, strategies, experiences, resources, and ideas, giving readers a peek inside their classrooms, processes, journeys, and workplaces. For teachers all over the country who do not have the opportunity to participate in a working group, these essays could provide community and inspiration for educators who want to do this work and understand its significance but may not feel confident or know where to start—common sentiments among teachers considering if and how to integrate LGBTQ+ history. After years of work in this field, we had a network of such voices—teachers, teacher educators, historians, activists, organizers—on whom we could call for this project. All were eager to pass along their expertise and be a small part of what is largely a grassroots effort.

This book is therefore the product and reflection of years of effort and thought around why and how we must and can incorporate LGBTQ+ history into the curriculum and our classes. It offers, as the title says, practical strategies and voices of experience. We hope it will be a guide and a guidepost that readers turn—and return—to on their journeys toward building and sustaining the inclusive classrooms that all students need and deserve. History and social studies education construct a national story. Integrating LGBTQ+ history is one essential aspect of ensuring that the story is accurate.

Teaching is hard work. We hope these strategies and voices make it a little easier.

Notes

1   Kiara Alfonseca and Soo Rin Kim, "Trump and allies are pouring millions into anti-trans election ads as election nears," ABC News, October 21, 2024, https://abcnews.go.com/US/trump-spends-millions-anti-trans-ads-despite-polls/story?id=115001816.

2   This quote, inscribed in the Martin Luther King, Jr. memorial in
     Washington, D.C. is from King's "Remaining Awake Through a
     Great Revolution" sermon, delivered at the National Cathedral in
     Washington, D.C. on March 31, 1968. It draws from a speech by
     abolitionist Theodore Parker at the Massachusetts Anti-Slavery
     Convention in 1858. ("Quote from 'Remaining Awake Through
     a Great Revolution' Sermon," National Park Service, accessed
     December 31, 2024, www.nps.gov/places/quote-from-remaining-
     awake-through-a-great-revolution-sermon.htm.)

3   "LGBTQ+ Rights," Gallup, accessed December 31, 2024, https://
     news.gallup.com/poll/1651/gay-lesbian-rights.aspx#:~:text=
     In%201996%2C%20a%20significant%20majority,%2C%20w
     ith%2053%25%20in%20favor.

4   Though this book focuses on high school teachers and classes,
     it can also support middle school teachers seeking to include
     LGBTQ+ history.

References

Alfonseca, Kiara and Kim, Soo Rin. "Trump and allies are pouring millions
    into anti-trans election ads as election nears." *ABC News*. October
    21, 2024. https://abcnews.go.com/US/trump-spends-millions-
    anti-trans-ads-despite-polls/story?id=115001816.

Gallup. LGBTQ+ Rights." Accessed December 31, 2024. https://news.
    gallup.com/poll/1651/gay-lesbian-rights.aspx#:~:text=In%201
    996%2C%20a%20significant%20majority,%2C%20with%20
    53%25%20in%20favor.

National Park Service. "Quote from 'Remaining Awake Through a Great
    Revolution' Sermon." Accessed December 31, 2024. www.nps.gov/
    places/quote-from-remaining-awake-through-a-great-revolution-
    sermon.htm.

Acknowledgements

This book is a collaborative effort. It would not be possible without the care, community, advocacy, and continuous learning of the people whose work and voices are represented in these pages and many others, who work tirelessly on behalf of students and teachers and in support of those of us who strive to make classrooms more inclusive and representative for all students.

Our priority in editing and writing this book was to provide teachers with the guidance, resources, and tools they needed to integrate LGBTQ+ history into their classes. We could not have done that without the brilliant, committed teachers who worked with us over the course of a year to plan and implement lessons that incorporated individuals, themes, and events relevant to the LGBTQ+ population. Charles, Emma, Kiley, and Lia–all pseudonyms for these incredible teachers–remained fully committed to this project despite chaotic schedules, personal upheaval, the overwhelm that all teachers experience, and mounting challenges to including this history throughout the country. Their work and reflection provide teachers with detailed models that they can bring into their own classrooms. Their open-mindedness and unwavering dedication to inclusivity made them role models for us.

As we developed the idea for this book we compiled a list of dream contributors whose work, history, and experiences we thought would inspire, instruct, and guide readers. We never imagined we would be fortunate enough to have the majority agree to write essays, nor could we have imagined that the essays would be as personal, powerful, and informative as they are. The contributors include people that we have known and worked with for years, and some whom we met more recently. Bettina Aptheker, David Duffield, Olive Garrison, Daniel Hurewitz, Lauren Jensen, Lil Miss Hot Mess, Justin Martinez, J.B. Mayo, Jr.,

Rick Oculto, John Palella, Don Romesburg, Wendy Rouse, Sandy Slater, and Jinnie Spigler: thank you for your time, your heart, and your candor. We are eternally grateful for the stories you told, the experiences you shared, the pedagogical ideas and resources you included in your writing, and your ceaseless efforts to make educational spaces safer and more representative. We hope this experience was as meaningful for you as it was for us and will be for the readers and their students. It is an honor to provide a platform to people who work tirelessly to make sure everyone's voices are heard.

We worked with the most supportive and patient editor, Emmie Shand, and editorial assistant, Jessica Sawin, as we completed this book. Emmie and Jessica answered all of our questions, indulged our new ideas, and gave us the flexibility we needed to manage all of the moving parts that make up this manuscript. Their enthusiasm for this project remained high throughout our time working together. We appreciate their trust in us and our process more than we can say.

This book focuses on and advocates for including LGBTQ+ history throughout the curriculum, in history and social studies classes and other academic spaces. We are so grateful to the teachers across the country and around the world who do this work, especially those who face significant obstacles in the service of providing their students with a complete, accurate, and representative version of history. We see and appreciate everything you do. To the organizations that support educators and students who identify as LGBTQ+ and equip teachers with the resources that they need to bring this information into their classrooms: thank you for the work that you do. It is meaningful, important, and lifesaving.

In addition to the individuals whose efforts, collaboration, and contributions made this book possible, people in our professional and personal lives played a role in supporting this work.

Stacie Brensilver Berman would like to thank:

I would not be where I am today without Robby Cohen, my co-author and co-editor on this project. As my doctoral advisor, Robby encouraged me to immerse myself in topics and ideas that I believed were important and to embrace my position as a researcher and a scholar. Robby champions my work, respects my ideas and contributions on topics from the Constitution to student protests, and has helped me seamlessly navigate my transition from student to colleague at NYU. I am forever indebted to him.

I have incredible colleagues at NYU who inspire me on a daily basis. Diana Turk introduces me to new ways of thinking about inclusivity, accessibility, and adolescent brain development. I hear her voice and her advice in all of the work I do and know that my ideas about pedagogy are better for it. It is a privilege to work and collaborate with her on the multiple projects we share. Jim Fraser remains a trusted sounding board and advisor even after his retirement. Jim sees the best in everyone and goes out of his way to let them know it. Working with Jim in the early stages of my career made me feel capable and confident in a way that I carry with me today. Terrasina Mitchell and Jamie Baldwin are patient, kind, knowledgeable, and resourceful. Terrie and Jamie made this entire process as smooth as possible and helped me navigate NYU offices outside of our own. I am forever grateful.

Over the past five years, I have had the privilege of working with faculty at the American Social History Project (ASHP) on their biannual summer institute on LGBTQ+ Histories of the United States. Through this work, I have learned more about LGBTQ+ history, met and interacted with some of the most prominent scholars in the field, and had the opportunity to mentor and engage with teachers from all over the country who are committed to integrating this history into their classes. My colleagues at ASHP – Anne Valk, Rachel Pitkin, Donna Thompson Ray, Danielle Bennett, and David Scheckel – are extraordinary; I am so lucky that they include me in this institute and that I have the opportunity to learn from and with them. The teachers who attended the institutes were one of the inspirations for this book.

I firmly believe that all of my achievements are the product of the people around me. My brother, Peter, took a profound interest in how people treat each other when we were teenagers, long before it was part of a wider, societal conversation. I learned from him then, and I continue to learn from him now. Some of the best, most laughter-filled times of my life are the moments that I share with him, my sister-in-law, Stephanie, and my niece and nephew, Scarlett and Miles. My parents, Vicki and Alvin Brensilver, provided us with a life full of possibilities. My mother wants her children to have the opportunities she did not and has worked her entire life to make that goal a reality. My father's greatest wish was that I be independent and accomplished in my own right; I carry his wish with me in everything I do. My aunt, Helen, modeled the ways that a teacher should be invested in her students throughout my childhood. I hope that, as a teacher, I make her proud.

Jeff Berman is the most incredible partner that any human being could have. He is generous, patient (with me), selfless, and supportive. Despite his busy schedule and day-to-day stresses, he never hesitates to do things to ease my load and make my day better. Jeff listens to countless rants, indulges the very deep rabbit holes I explore on a regular basis, and is genuinely happy as long as I am. Jeff finishes my sentences and thoughts, often with a movie quote, and laughs at my "dad jokes." He is my home, and because of that, I can thrive.

Mia, all of this is for you. Like my father's wish for me, I want you to see all of the ways that you can be strong, fearless, and independent, and that when you hustle and put in the work anything is possible. Watching you develop a love of books and learning has deepened my own; I am so happy we share that. Thank you for helping me with the pseudonyms in this book and, even more, for inspiring me and always keeping me on my toes. Love you forever. Best thing.

Robby Cohen would like to thank:

Bettina Aptheker, Blanche Wiesen Cook, and the late Jesse Lemisch for awakening him to the importance of LGBTQ+ history, and Stacie Brensilver Berman whose brilliant work has made NYU a center for teacher education in LGBTQ+ history.

This book was made possible by the generous support of Lucille Werlinich, and by the crucial support for teacher education provided by Teaching and Learning department chair Sarah Beck and dean of NYU Steinhardt Jack Knott, as well as his able staff.

Located as we are in Greenwich Village, all of us at NYU owe a debt to the LGBTQ+ activists from Stonewall '69 to the present who have battled so heroically for a world free of hatred and bigotry.

Abbreviations

AB	Assembly Bill
ADL	Anti-Defamation League
AHA	American Historical Association
AIDS	Acquired Immunodeficiency Syndrome
ASHP	American Social History Project
BANGLE	Bay Area Network of Gay and Lesbian Educators
DSH	Drag Story Hour
FAIR Education Act	Fair, Accurate, Inclusive, and Respectful
GLAAD	Gay and Lesbian Alliance Against Defamation
GLISTN	Gay and Lesbian Independent School Teachers Network
GLSEN	Gay, Lesbian, & Straight Education Network
GSA	Originally Gay Straight Alliance; now Genders and Sexualities Alliance
HIV	Human Immunodeficiency Virus
K-12	Inclusive of elementary, middle, and high school grades
LEA	Local Education Agency
LGBTQ+	Lesbian, Gay, Bisexual, Transgender, Queer and other gender identities and sexualities
LGHM	Lesbian and Gay History Month
NCSS	National Council for Social Studies
NYC DOE	New York City Department of Education
PBS	Public Broadcasting Systems
PD	Professional Development
PLGTF	Philadelphia Lesbian and Gay Task Force
SB	Senate Bill
UVA	University of Virginia

Introduction: The Imperative to Teach LGBTQ+ History in Challenging Times

Integrating LGBTQ+ historical content into history and social studies curriculum makes it more accurate, representative, and relevant to the world outside the classroom. In fact, individuals who, in twenty-first-century terminology,[1] identify as LGBTQ+ and events and trends relevant to the LGBTQ+ population play a role in every era in United States and world history, from the distant past to the present. With historical accuracy as an educational goal, therefore, it is imperative for teachers and schools to include the LGBTQ+ experience.

The absence of LGBTQ+ history, even and especially where it is most relevant, is a long-standing and glaring omission in students' historical learning in the United States that, despite efforts and advocacy over the past forty years, has not yet been properly addressed. For example, generations of middle and high school students studying the ancient world learned nothing about the Sacred Band of Thebes because homophobia within the educational system prevented the acknowledgement of and discussions about greater acceptance and the positive impact of same-sex relationships in ancient Greece. Though the Band of

DOI: 10.4324/9781032689678-1

Thebes, a legendary military force of gay soldiers, was discussed by the great ancient historian Plutarch and for years seemed invincible in battle, in American classrooms, invincible became invisible. Such omissions attest to how history is distorted by textbooks dedicated to heteronormativity. The same can be said for modern American history, where for decades Bayard Rustin went unmentioned in US history textbooks, though this openly gay civil rights activist was famed in the movement for organizing the March on Washington, where Martin Luther King, Jr. gave his historic "I Have a Dream" speech. These omissions, and therefore inaccuracies, persist when curricula gloss over references to homosexuality in Allen Ginsberg's epic poem "Howl" and exclude movements for LGBTQ+ rights in the United States, Latin America, Europe, and Africa in units on worldwide twentieth-century rights revolutions. In other words, an approach that ignores LGBTQ+ topics puts students on a path to historical illiteracy, yielding a marginalization of the LGBTQ+ experience that may increase the exclusion and othering of queer and transgender students, which can pave the way for homophobic and transphobic violence in schools.[2]

The path to inclusivity, though, has long been filled with challenges and obstacles, often caused by backlash to LGBTQ+ individuals' or the LGBTQ+ rights movement's accomplishments. In 1977, for example, in response to a Florida anti-discrimination law that included sexual orientation, Anita Bryant launched her bigoted "Save Our Children" campaign, warning Americans about gay teachers' immoral influence.[3] State legislators such as California's John Briggs sponsored restrictive bills that aimed to prohibit information on gender and sexuality and teachers who identify as LGBTQ+ from entering the classroom.[4] New York City's Children of the Rainbow Curriculum (1991) and California's Bias-Free Curriculum Act (2006) encountered opposition and backlash that stymied their implementation.[5] By 2019, however, the path seemed clearer, and a sense of optimism emerged among advocates for LGBTQ+-inclusive curriculum. In the wake of the passage of California's Fair, Accurate, Inclusive and Respectful (FAIR) Education Act in 2011, four additional states with Democratic majorities–New Jersey, Colorado,

Oregon, and Illinois–legislated curriculum mandates requiring teachers to include LGBTQ+ history in social studies classes.[6] States that formerly prohibited positive representations of the LGBTQ+ community in schools through No Promotion of Homosexuality laws (labeled "No Promo Homo" by LGBTQ+ rights advocates)—Utah (2017), Arizona (2019), South Carolina (2020), and Alabama (2021)—repealed or overturned those laws, paving the way for increased openness and acceptance in school buildings.[7] In 2021 Nevada passed its LGBTQ+ curricular mandate, becoming the sixth state to do so. Though the majority of these mandates were unfunded and organizations and activists that pushed for their passage acknowledged that legislation was the first of many steps in this process, there was a sense that decades of work promoting inclusive curricula, by groups and individuals across the country, were at last finding success.[8]

California's FAIR Education Act, the first law to mandate that K-12 social science courses include LGBTQ+ history, added LGBTQ+ Americans and persons with disabilities to the state's existing list of groups to be included in the curriculum. It establishes:

> Instruction in social sciences shall include the early history of California and a study of the role and contributions of both men and women, Native Americans, African Americans, Mexican Americans, Asian Americans, Pacific Islanders, European Americans, lesbian, gay, bisexual, and transgender Americans, persons with disabilities, and members of other ethnic and cultural groups, to the economic, political, and social development of California and the United States of America, with particular emphasis on portraying the role of these groups in contemporary society.[9]

The law was set to go into effect in 2012. In order for that to happen, though, the state Framework needed to be updated and new, more inclusive textbooks had to be reviewed and adopted. This arduous process, which continued for more than five years, delayed implementation and meant that teachers throughout

California were unaware of—or felt no obligation to integrate—this mandate.[10] In 2018, historians and teachers who worked to update the Framework and create curriculum materials in support of the law began hosting workshops throughout the state to educate teachers and assuage their concerns.

The laws enacted in 2019 in New Jersey, Colorado, Oregon, and Illinois similarly mandated that schools should include LGBTQ+ individuals in the curriculum, covering their contributions and perspectives. Colorado's law provided for coverage of "the intersectionality of significant social and cultural features within [marginalized] communities."[11] In New Jersey, Garden State Equality planned a pilot program through which twelve schools would integrate prepared lessons and resources.[12] Equality Illinois and the Legacy Project collaborated to publish a guide listing resources for teaching LGBTQ+ history in Illinois that included charts indicating the ways in which covering this history aligns with existing state standards.[13] Colorado, meanwhile, included modest funding provisions in its mandate with an allocation for "content specialists."[14] This implementation process, like other educational and curricular reforms, would be slow and not without its hurdles, but it was progressing.

The cycle of triumph and backlash persisted, however. Similar opposition that led to "No Promo Homo" laws and earlier attempts to pass "Don't Say Gay" legislation came roaring back into the mainstream as conservative pundits and politicians raised alerts about "woke" curriculum and liberal "indoctrination" in a nation ambivalent about reckoning with systemic oppression following the COVID-19 pandemic and national conversations about race and violence after George Floyd's murder by police. These attacks, which dominated headlines and became the rallying cry of right-wing "populist" groups, aimed to undermine the credibility of LGBTQ+ history as an academic field and individuals, including teachers, who believed it was important for students to learn this content. Across the country, bills were introduced in state legislatures restricting teachers' academic freedom and prohibiting discussions of "divisive concepts," an open-ended phrase intended to have a chilling effect on any instruction inclusive of ideas related to race, gender, class, ability, and ethnicity–all of which the FAIR Education Act and the laws passed subsequently sought to incorporate at a statewide level. This backlash was linked to right-wing opposition to what journalist Juan Williams calls the "second civil rights movement," which emerged in response to the "extrajudicial killing of Black people" and the disappointment that accompanied the lack of a post-racial society following the supposed advancements of the Obama administration.[15] As opposition to this movement mounted, illiberalism on race melded with gender illiberalism, creating an environment in which restricting rights and access to LGBTQ+ content in schools was promoted as an appropriate response throughout conservative America. This was further reinforced by the Trump campaign invoking transphobia to garner support in the 2024 election.[16]

These laws, and the book bans that followed in schools and libraries in red states and conservative regions in blue states, paved the way for the reintroduction of so-called "Don't Say Gay/Trans" laws explicitly prohibiting the inclusion of LGBTQ+ topics in the curriculum, preventing teachers from supporting students who identify as LGBTQ+ or question their gender and/ or sexuality. They also restrict students' access to school facilities aligned with their gender identity.[17] The first such law, officially titled the Parental Rights in Education Act, was passed in Florida in March 2022. Other states with Republican majorities, emboldened by Florida's legislation, passed similar laws in its wake.[18] Locally, conservative communities in blue and purple states enacted district level policies restricting or prohibiting LGBTQ+ topics; teachers in these communities censored themselves in response to community culture and norms. Conversely, intrepid teachers and those in more progressive pockets in red states continued to seek entry points to integrate LGBTQ+ content to support students and maintain their sense of academic integrity. As of 2024, then, in an increasingly divided country, the specific location in which a teacher worked and a student attended school was an essential factor in determining their daily experience, ability to learn LGBTQ+ history, and, for students who identify as LGBTQ+, their overall safety.

Advocating for LGBTQ+- Inclusive History

The FAIR Education Act and other laws passed in the twenty-first century were the culmination of decades of advocacy on the part of LGBTQ+ rights organizations, specifically those focused on education. Adolescents and their rights were not initially a significant focus in the post-Stonewall era gay rights movement,[19] which prioritized the battle against discrimination adults faced in public life, employment, housing, healthcare, and marriage. This began to change, however, as activists and the media discovered and revealed the harassment, bullying, and violence that LGBTQ+ students and teachers faced in schools.

In 1990, Kevin Jennings, then an independent school teacher at Concord Academy in Massachusetts, founded the Gay and Lesbian Independent School Teachers Network (GLISTN). Initially, Jennings stated, "The idea was to bring together people so that they can learn from one another and build from there. There was no vision at that point certainly of becoming this big national organization. It was more the idea that we would be stronger and more effective if we organized ourselves better and we're supporting each other and sharing ideas."[20] Jennings intended to create a space where teachers who identified as LGBTQ+ and felt isolated and targeted in their workplaces could come together and advocate for themselves. Within a decade, the organization grew from a New England-based support network for independent school teachers, to a nationwide network of public and private school teachers, to an organization advocating for safer schools and improved climates for students, teachers, and school personnel throughout the United States; GLISTN evolved into GLSEN, the Gay, Lesbian, & Straight Education Network. Jennings called GLSEN's growth "an opportunistic responding to people's expressed desire to get involved."[21]

In 1998, youth organizer Carolyn Laub began working with Gay Straight Alliances[22] (GSAs) in the San Francisco area to encourage and support students attempting to establish these clubs at their schools. GSA Network, the organization she founded, went statewide within three years and national by 2005.[23] Under Laub's leadership, the number of GSAs in California alone grew from 40 to 940.[24] GLSEN built a national organization that would conduct research, develop resources, and support schools aiming for a more inclusive and unbiased educational climate and culture. Laub and her network, meanwhile, took a more grassroots approach, training students hoping to start GSAs at their schools and working to strengthen students' leadership skills and build on the student-led organizations they established. GSA Network, then, aims to develop students' activism and sense of agency in school settings and beyond. In creating an interconnected network, Laub established a support system for all GSA members from which their activism could expand.[25]

GLSEN and GSA Network, leaders in advocating for safer schools and access to necessary resources and networks for LGBTQ+ students and teachers, have expanded their reach and goals over time to think more inclusively and meet individuals' evolving needs in changing circumstances. Both organizations promote integrating LGBTQ+ topics in the curriculum and offer materials for teachers to do so, but their main focus is on supporting individuals rather than developing academic content. Since the 1990s other individuals and organizations have emerged to meet that need. Advocacy organizations including Learning for Justice, Anti-Defamation League, ONE Archives, and OutHistory offer lesson plans and curricular materials that teachers can access online and use in their classrooms. Educational organizations such as University of California History/Social Science Project and the American Social History Project (ASHP) curate LGBTQ+ history resources for teachers to use in their classrooms. The National Archives and Library of Congress provide access to primary sources and activities to support their implementation through their DocsTeach and Teaching with Primary Sources programs. Historian Don Romesburg and his colleagues in California publish position papers detailing organic entry points for incorporating LGBTQ+ history in elementary, middle, and high school social studies classes; their impressive white paper, "Making the Framework

FAIR," demonstrated that LGBTQ+ history could be a through thread woven throughout California's statewide curriculum.[26] These organizations thus sustain a community of practice and provide educators and learners with resources to support academic inclusivity and historical accuracy.

In 2019, the National Council for Social Studies (NCSS) issued a policy statement entitled, "Contextualizing LGBT+ History within the Social Studies Curriculum." It states:

> NCSS fully recognizes and supports the civic, ethical, and moral imperatives to advance a more historically accurate, complete, and empowering social studies curriculum that contextualizes LGBT+ history—and the histories of other marginalized cultural groups. The social, cultural, and political implications of sidelining, omitting and/or misrepresenting certain cultural groups are damaging and antithetical to a true democratic education rooted in our collective code of ethics to "do no harm."[27]

NCSS is the nation's largest organization representing and supporting social studies teachers. This position statement, therefore, establishes integrating LGBTQ+ history as a necessity within the discipline. Since 2019, NCSS has issued additional statements reiterating its support for LGBTQ+-inclusive history curricula in response to attempts to remove it from classrooms and restrict teachers' academic freedom, including signing onto the American Historical Association's (AHA) 2023 statement opposing a Florida ban on instruction focused on gender identity and sexual orientation in grades 4-12. The AHA demanded that Florida's Department of Education, "reconsider its vague and destructive policy of censorship, and instead encourage the teaching of accurate and inclusive histories of the United States and the world."[28] The United States' most prominent historical organizations, then, understand the need for all students to learn LGBTQ+ history, acknowledging the benefits that advocates have long fought to entrench in educational spheres.

Benefits of Teaching LGBTQ+ History

The benefits of including LGBTQ+ history–and LGBTQ+ topics in general–are well documented. Studies and anecdotal evidence confirm that inclusive curriculum has the power to increase LGBTQ+ students' connection to what they learn and feel valued and represented in their classes. For students who do not identify as LGBTQ+, interacting with this material can increase understanding of experiences different from their own. All of this helps to create welcoming school climates, which is also crucial for students who identify as LGBTQ+ to feel safe in the spaces they inhabit. It is therefore a matter of both academic accuracy and students' well-being.

Some of the strongest evidence of the factors essential to LGBTQ+ students' sense of belonging comes from GLSEN. Since 1999, in its effort to foster safe school environments for students and teachers who identify as LGBTQ+,[29] GLSEN has conducted a biannual school climate survey that assesses "experiences of LGBTQ+ youth in schools, including the extent of the challenges that they face at school and the school-based resources that support LGBTQ students' well-being."[30] The survey, which is conducted online, asks students between the ages of 13-21 years old about school safety, harassment, discriminatory practices, availability of support systems, and inclusive curriculum, among other topics. Though inclusive curriculum is only a small part of the survey, responses related to it prove how significant it can be.

The most recently published report (2022), based on the 2021 survey, revealed that although a minority of students reported that their classes included LGBTQ+ topics (28.4%), inclusive curricula had an overall positive effect on the school environment and students' experiences in general. Based on the survey results, LGBTQ+ students whose schools implemented LGBTQ+-inclusive curriculum were less likely to: hear homophobic remarks or negative comments about transgender individuals; feel unsafe at school as a result of their gender or sexuality; or miss school because they felt unsafe or uncomfortable. Moreover, GLSEN reported that these students "felt greater belonging to their school community, performed better academically in school, and were more likely to plan on pursuing postsecondary education" and 66.9% said that "their classmates were somewhat or very accepting of LGBTQ+ people."[31] Incorporating LGBTQ+ topics into the curriculum, then, can significantly improve students' daily experience at school, set them up for future success, and create the welcoming environments for which school climate workshops strive.

Other leading scholars and educational and advocacy organizations have documented that LGBTQ+-inclusive curriculum is important for students, schools, and the health of our democracy. In 2013, GSA Network declared, in *Implementing Lessons That Matter*, "LGBTQ-inclusive curriculum was identified by students as one strategy that could substantially improve safety, engagement, learning, academic achievement, self-esteem, and success in school and beyond." Incorporating LGBTQ+ topics, the study found, contributed to "an increase of support for LGBTQ people and issues in various school contexts."[32] A 2015 study conducted by researchers from the University of Arizona, the University of Minnesota, and Texas A&M University who examined the correlation between inclusive curricula and school safety, found, "the presence and supportiveness of LGBTQ-inclusive curricula reduce students' reports of bullying and have positive implications for safety, which suggests that the overall school climate improves when inclusive curriculum is taught and is supportive."[33] In 2022, Learning for Justice shared an article from Melanie Willingham-Jaggers and the GLSEN team that stated, "Accurate and inclusive lessons not only affirm LGBTQ+ students, but also give non-LGBTQ+ students clear information about the diverse world around them and help prepare all young people to navigate and contribute to a multicultural society."[34] New York City's Department of Education posited, in its *Hidden Voices: LGBTQ+ Stories in United States History* curriculum guide, "Without a doubt, [teaching LGBTQ+ history] not only changes the way students think about the gendered and sexual identities of individuals in the past, but it demonstrates the fact that LGBTQ+ lives are currently—and have always been—a vital part of the American story."[35] Twenty-first-century students have endless access to information, which they often consume without the necessary context. As these organizations attest, teaching LGBTQ+ history provides that context and better enables students to process and make sense of what they see in the present.

According to GLSEN, "Inclusive curriculum supports a student's ability to empathize, connect, and collaborate with a diverse group of peers, and encourages respect for all."[36] Teaching LGBTQ+ history, therefore, is important for all students, not only those who identify as such or question their gender or sexuality. Omitting an entire group from a history class conveys an inaccurate and unrealistic version of events of the past; integrating that group allows students to more fully understand the scope of history and the ways in which LGBTQ+ individuals–including those who would not have been aware of and/or used those labels–contributed to America's democratic traditions and cultural heritage. Students are able to build the critical thinking and literacy skills that form the foundation of social studies education when groups that exist in the margins become the main characters. Integrating LGBTQ+ history is, therefore, essential.

Legal and Policy Challenges to Teaching LGBTQ+ History

Though the benefits of LGBTQ+-inclusive curriculum are well documented, opposition to its implementation persists and, since 2021, has found a stronger foothold in states and regions with conservative-dominated governments and education departments. Though laws and policies restricting discussions of LGBTQ+ topics are not new–in fact, Oklahoma passed the first such law in 1978–they were on the decline in 2020.[37] The increase in curriculum censorship laws, though, which were proposed and passed as the uproar around Critical Race Theory, the 1619 Project on slavery in America, and the focus on marginalized populations in classrooms across the United States swept the nation, renewed conservative pundits', parent groups', and lawmakers' attention on the role of LGBTQ+ topics in the curriculum. Laws and policies intended to limit students' access to this information soon followed.

Since 2021, forty-four states have proposed bills and/or policies aimed at restricting instruction on race, racism, and so-called "divisive concepts." According to *Education Week*, eighteen states "impos[ed] these bans and restrictions either through legislation or other avenues."[38] These laws originated from a Trump Executive Order banning diversity training in federal agencies as well as pushback against curricular changes in the wake of the emerging Black Lives Matter-led national reckoning with systemic racism and oppression. The repression soon expanded to include restrictions and prohibitions on teaching about any group, topic, or concept that might be considered "divisive" or "controversial."[39] The legislation, which stripped teachers of their academic freedom, endangered their jobs, and gave parents the power to target teachers whose lessons and resources they opposed, left educators in the precarious position of figuring out how to teach effectively and protect their careers and livelihoods. These policies also emboldened politicians and conservative organizations to advocate for legislation specifically aimed at removing LGBTQ+ topics from classrooms.

Before March 2022, when Governor Ron DeSantis signed Florida's Parental Rights in Education Act–dubbed the "Don't Say Gay/Trans" law by LGBTQ+ rights advocates and media outlets– previous statewide attempts to enact total prohibitions on LGBTQ+ topics in schools had failed. Ten years prior, the Tennessee and Missouri state legislatures debated such laws, which were ultimately vetoed or unable to garner sufficient support among conservatives because of the perceived homophobia attached to them.[40] Laws restricting what and how school faculty could discuss LGBTQ+ topics with students were enacted as nine states passed "No Promo Homo" laws by 2017, dictating that teachers could only discuss negative depictions of LGBTQ+ topics with students, and LGBTQ+ issues were glaringly omitted from several states' health education standards.[41] "Don't Say Gay/Trans" laws, though, were not able to gain the same traction in the early years of the twenty-first century. That changed as curriculum censorship laws were introduced and passed throughout the United States after conservative organizations, most predominantly Moms for Liberty, loudly voiced their opposition to the presence of topics related to gender and sexuality in school curricula.

As of 2025, nine states have "Don't Say Gay/Trans" laws on the books. The first was Florida's, which, in its initial iteration, explicitly applied to grades K-3. The law states, "A school district may not encourage classroom discussion about sexual orientation or gender identity in primary grade levels or in a manner that is not age-appropriate or developmentally appropriate for students." The Florida law justified this restriction as a means to "reinforce the fundamental right of parents to make decisions regarding the upbringing and control of their children by requiring school district personnel to encourage a student to discuss issues relating to his or her well-being with his or her parent or to seek permission to discuss or facilitate discussion of the issue with the parent."[42] A second Florida law, passed a year later in May 2023, stated, "Classroom instruction by school personnel or third parties on sexual orientation or gender identity may not occur in prekindergarten through grade 8… If such instruction is provided in grades 9 through 12, the instruction must be age-appropriate or developmentally appropriate for students in accordance with state standards."[43] This law mandated that school personnel define sex as "an immutable biological trait," expanded the reasons for which schools could ban books, and gave parents increased access to classroom resources and the power to file formal protests if they disagreed with the curricula schools implemented.[44]

Florida's repressive law led to outrage among LGBTQ+ advocates and students and teachers all over the country; several major news outlets amplified Florida students' protests. It also served as an indication to other conservative-dominated states, where the legislatures were similarly inclined, that it was possible to pass such laws in that moment's reactionary political climate. Within three years, eight additional states passed "Don't Say Gay/Trans" laws. Alabama, the second state to do so, prohibited "an individual or group of individuals providing classroom instruction to students in kindergarten through the fifth grade at a public K-12 school" from "engag[ing] in class-room discussion or provid[ing] classroom instruction regarding sexual orientation or gender identity in a manner that is not age appropriate or developmentally appropriate for students in accordance with state standards."[45] The Alabama law also mandates that students must use the bathroom that aligns with their biologically assigned sex. Laws passed in Indiana, Iowa, and North Carolina establish similar restrictions: they prohibit LGBTQ+-inclusive instruction at the elementary level; assert that such instruction at the secondary level must be "age appro-priate"; and grant parents significant latitude to intervene in pedagogical planning. North Carolina's law, in fact, includes in its "Parents' Bill of Rights" that one rationale for this legislation is to afford parents the power "to direct the upbringing and moral or religious training of his or her child."[46] Though the majority of these laws include prohibitions on LGBTQ+-inclusive educa-tion in elementary schools, they establish a stifling atmosphere in which information on sexuality and gender diversity is absent from classrooms at every level and teachers live with the looming threat of parental opposition and interference. Each of these laws forces LGBTQ+ students to submerge their authentic identities, exist in spaces where discrimination and bias have been tacitly condoned through legislation, and navigate environments that undermine and attack their health, morale, and safety.

Louisiana's law, enacted in 2024, prohibits discussions of sexual orientation or gender identity in "grades kindergarten through twelve." This bars "covering the topics of sexual orien-tation or gender identity in any classroom discussion or instruc-tion in a manner that deviates from state content standards or curricula developed or approved by public school governing authorities" and "during any extracurricular academic, ath-letic, or social activity under the jurisdiction of the school or public school governing authority."[47] Unlike previous laws that emphasized parental rights and focused on younger students, Louisiana's applies to all students and grade levels, prohibits teachers from discussing their sexual orientation or gender iden-tity, and restricts students' rights to engage in discussions rela-tive to their identity in and outside the classroom. Louisiana, one of four states that maintained a "No Promo Homo" law prior to the most recent wave of restrictive legislation, placed some of the harshest limitations on students' and teachers' access to resources and academic freedom.

With the passage of Ohio's law in early 2025, 20% of LGBTQ+ teens "live in states that explicitly censor discussions of LGBTQ people or issues throughout all school curricula."[48] Many of these laws were passed and imposed on schools without the same media attention or fanfare that Florida received when it was the first to do so, making them that much more insidious. The continued intent to pass laws that restrict instruction on LGBTQ+ content, which PEN America asserts is a primary focus of what it calls "educational gag orders," is reinvigorated each time a new law is passed, to the detriment of students and teachers.[49] These laws, in addition to those prohibiting transgender students from participating in interscholastic sports (on the books in twenty five states) and using school facilities that align with their gender identity (fourteen states) and mandating parental notification of LGBTQ+-inclusive curricula (eight states) make attending school fraught for students and teachers who identify as LGBTQ+ and deny all students the benefits of inclusive education.[50]

The "Don't Say Gay/Trans" laws proposed and passed beginning in 2022 prioritized one group's rights above teachers and students: parents. Florida's law allows parents to opt children out of counseling services and requires schools to inform parents if children seek such services.[51] Iowa's law grants parents broad latitude to request that books be removed from libraries and to review instructional materials prior to classroom implementation.[52] Arkansas's law requires that students under the age of 18 provide written parental permission for school faculty to use their proper names and pronouns.[53] Beyond creating unsafe situations in school buildings, these laws place students in precarious positions at home. As Anna Marks asserted in her response to Ohio's "Don't' Say Gay/Trans" bill (now signed into law) in the *New York Times*, "Should their parents be at all queerphobic, the consequences of state-mandated outing will be dangerous, if not deadly."[54] A University of Connecticut study "found that about one-third of youths who were outed without their consent were more likely to experience major symptoms of depression and lower family support than those who were not."[55] These laws, then, do more than restrict academic content; they remove support services and expectations of privacy on which students depend.

The impact of these homophobic and transphobic laws, and the extent to which they trample students' freedom to learn and teachers' freedom to teach, cannot be overstated. Five of the nine states that passed "Don't Say Gay/Trans" laws as of 2025—Alabama, Arkansas, Florida, Kentucky, and Louisiana—also enacted more expansive curriculum censorship laws restricting the ways teachers can approach race, ethnicity, ability, and other identities in classrooms,[56] contributing to more significant limitations on the ways in which students can interact with accurate historical narratives. States that do not explicitly prohibit topics related to gender and sexuality but do maintain wide-ranging curriculum censorship laws create similarly unsafe environments for teachers and students who identify as LGBTQ+ and/or seek instruction on this content. These laws, and the states where they exist, underscore the reality that in terms of education and academic freedom—in addition to myriad other criteria—the United States is deeply divided in ways that will irrevocably separate students and teachers into two groups: those with opportunities to learn, engage, and draw conclusions for themselves and those who, because of lack of access, remain ignorant of LGBTQ+ history unless they find ways to independently explore it. Teachers in conservative states and regions are restricted from participating in and interacting with new research that might benefit their students. Students who are not exposed to this information enter college unaware of information that their professors, who have more freedom to discuss LGBTQ+ history, want them to know.[57] Maps illustrating the presence of curriculum censorship across the United States offer visual evidence of this: the South, from the Atlantic Ocean westward to Texas, is solidly united in censoring what and how students learn.[58] As the country turns towards right-wing "populism" and entrenched conservatism following the 2024 presidential election it is clear, then, that the central question of whether teachers have academic freedom

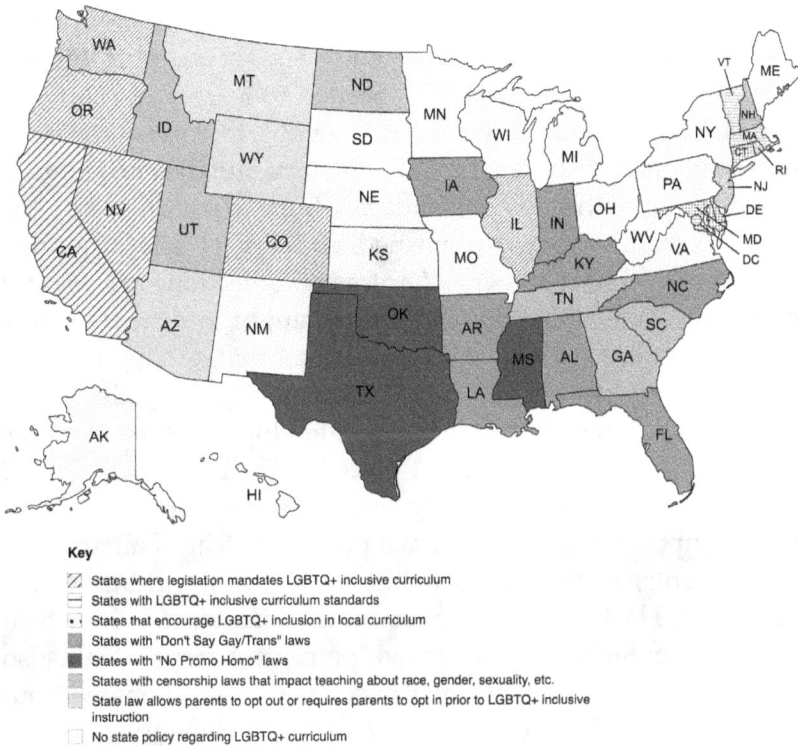

Key

⧄ States where legislation mandates LGBTQ+ inclusive curriculum
═ States with LGBTQ+ inclusive curriculum standards
• States that encourage LGBTQ+ inclusion in local curriculum
▨ States with "Don't Say Gay/Trans" laws
■ States with "No Promo Homo" laws
▒ States with censorship laws that impact teaching about race, gender, sexuality, etc.
▫ State law allows parents to opt out or requires parents to opt in prior to LGBTQ+ inclusive instruction
▫ No state policy regarding LGBTQ+ curriculum

FIGURE I.1
Map indicating LGBTQ+ curriculum policies and censorship laws in the United States.[78]

and the option to include LGBTQ+ history in their classes comes down to one key factor: location, location, location.

A Critical Moment

Advocates of LGBTQ+-inclusive curriculum face an uphill–but not impossible–battle. This is true even in red states with conservative-dominated legislatures and governments, where there are pockets of blue and individual teachers determined to incorporate LGBTQ+ history. The optimism of 2019 has been replaced by an atmosphere of uncertainty and fear but, as history demonstrates, this is not unexplored territory. Curriculum censorship laws have a chilling effect on teachers' academic freedom, but the greater attention paid to the presence of LGBTQ+ content in schools alerted many teachers who were not aware of this history or its significance that they needed to learn more about it. Amid these censorship laws and restrictions, then, it is even more imperative to incorporate LGBTQ+ history into the curriculum.

The State of the American Teacher Survey, conducted by the RAND Corporation and published in February 2024, revealed key findings about teachers' concerns and reactions to state and local restrictions, whether or not they taught in districts where such restrictions existed. RAND reported that, among teachers surveyed, 55% decided to "limit instruction about political and social issues," including LGBTQ+-related topics, "even in places where restrictions were not in place."[59] Teachers cited several reasons for this self-censorship, including feeling uncertain of district support in case of parental pushback, fear of altercations with parents, insufficient guidance on how to address these topics, and a lack of confidence about teaching topics with which they were unfamiliar. Twenty five percent of respondents also expressed a fear of losing their jobs, even in locations without legislation or policies restricting instruction.[60] This survey reveals the widespread negative impact of censorship laws, the chilled atmosphere they have created nationwide, and an alarming trend. But, it also establishes concrete conditions for supporting teachers who hope to incorporate LGBTQ+ history: districts need to be clear on how they plan to support educators and provide guidance on how to incorporate political and social issues into the classroom and teachers need increased opportunities to familiarize themselves with these concepts.

This insight into what teachers need is even more important in light of the persistent divisions and discriminatory actions against LGBTQ+ individuals in the United States. According to Pew Research Center's "Race and LGBTQ Issues in K-12 Schools" study, published in February 2024, US teenagers' comfort level and opinions on whether or not schools should incorporate discussions on gender identity and sexual orientation aligned with their stated political affiliation. Similarly, 79% of Republican respondents asserted that parents should be able to opt students out of lessons on LGBTQ+ content compared to 32% of Democrats.[61] These statistics are especially resonant considering that 39% of teachers in the RAND study claimed that they self-censor out of fear of parental opposition.[62] Also sobering is a study conducted by Anti-Defamation League and GLAAD that "recorded a total of 356 anti-LGBTQ+ incidents between June 2022 and April 2023, including 305 acts of harassment, 40 acts of vandalism and 11 incidents of assault" with "at least 191 anti-LGBTQ+ incidents of harassment, vandalism and assault making explicit references to 'grooming' or 'pedophilia'."[63] For several reasons, then, teachers must contend with challenging and potentially unsafe circumstances as a result of these "Don't Say Gay/Trans" and other censorship laws and their impact. This includes, but is not limited to, the tacit acknowledgement by government and school boards that support these policies that it is acceptable and, in some cases, encouraged, to question teachers' practices and lifestyles. Under these circumstances, it makes sense that teachers feel the need to censor themselves, yet their reasons for doing so serve as an indication of why it is so vital that LGBTQ+ topics are present in academic courses in K-12 settings.

Project 2025, the conservative policy agenda report published by the Heritage Foundation prior to the 2024 presidential election, deepened teachers' and students' concerns in the wake of Trump's victory. This anti-intellectual report recommends censoring instruction on LGBTQ+ topics; banning books on LGBTQ+ topics or themes, and criminalizing librarians who recommend them; forcing schools and teachers to misgender students who identify as transgender or non-binary; and rolling back Biden-era revisions to Title IX that protect LGBTQ+ students.[64] Months into the second Trump administration, amid an onslaught of Executive Orders targeting transgender individuals and "radical indoctrination" in education, fears are rising that the Project 2025 agenda will multiply homophobic and transphobic school policies and laws that threaten LGBTQ+ students and teachers. This clearly poses a threat to LGBTQ+ individuals whose safety will be at risk in school settings and to the academic freedom of teachers who have been seeking to teach inclusive and accurate history that explores the LGBTQ+ experience, who now must worry, especially in conservative-dominated states and communities, about censorship and even the risk of firing.

Resistance

Vocal and inspiring advocates, however, refuse to be silenced by legislation and policies that promote discrimination and attack individuals' identities. Florida high school students, followed by students in other conservative states that passed laws restricting LGBTQ+ content, raised their voices and exercised their power as they protested their state's "Don't Say Gay/Trans" law, staging walkouts when the law was passed in 2022 and airing their opposition to the law in public forums.[65] In Jacksonville, Mandarin High School students organized as the bill made its way through the state legislature. Gracie Warner, a student at the time, told the *Florida Times-Union*, "It showed unity… Not just in our school, but around the entire state. [There will be] people who don't approve of us … but that makes us stronger as one voice. When we do something peacefully and together as one, we can get change."[66]

Even in the face of political repression, students found ingenious ways of demonstrating opposition to restrictive policies. Zander Moricz, the 2022 valedictorian at Pine View School in Osprey, Florida defied prohibitions on discussing his sexuality or the state's "Don't Say Gay/Trans" law in his speech, metaphorically talking about the difficulties of having curly hair:

> I used to hate my curls. I spent mornings and nights embarrassed of them trying desperately to straighten this part of who I am. But the daily damage of trying to fix myself became too much to do. So while having curly hair in Florida is difficult, due to the humidity, I decided to be proud of who I was and started coming to school as my authentic self… Now I'm happy. Now I'm happy, and that is what is at stake. There are going to be so many kids with curly hair, who need a community like Pine View and they won't have one. Instead, they'll try to

fix themselves so that they can exist in Florida's humid climate. I've been preparing for this speech since I was elected my freshman year. Do you think that I want it to be about this? It needs to be about this for the thousands of curly haired kids who are going to need to speak like this for their entire lives as students....[67]

Students were not alone in challenging restrictions on LGBTQ+ -inclusive education. Nineteen plaintiffs, including "students, parents, educators, and LGBTQ advocacy organizations" challenged Florida's "Don't Say Gay/Trans" law. The plaintiffs claimed victory when an appellate court ruled that students and teachers could discuss LGBTQ+ topics, students could write about these topics in academic assignments, LGBTQ+ student organizations and library books not used for instruction were outside the scope of the law, and "instruction must be neutral on issues of sexual orientation or gender identity, meaning that teachers cannot, for example, teach that heterosexuality is superior to homosexuality or bisexuality."[68]

Dissenting state legislators defended students' right to learn and teachers' academic freedom. One of the most striking defenses of students' right to learn came from Mallory McMorrow, a Democratic state senator in Michigan. McMorrow's speech came in response to Republican Lana Theis accusing her of "grooming and sexualizing children" after she walked out of Theis's invocation defending her party's efforts to "block teachings that address LGBTQ issues as well as America's history of racism."[69] McMorrow declared:

> ...each and every single one of us bears responsibility for writing the next chapter of history. Each and every single one of us decides what happens next and how we respond to history and the world around us. We are not responsible for the past. We also cannot change the past. We can't pretend that it didn't happen or deny people their very right to exist. I am a straight, white, Christian, married suburban mom. I want my daughter to know that she is loved, supported, and seen for whoever she

becomes…. I want every child in this state to feel seen, heard, and supported, not marginalized and targeted because they are not straight, white, and Christian. We cannot let hateful people tell you otherwise to scapegoat and deflect from the fact that they are not doing anything to fix the real issues that impact people's lives. And I know that hate will only win if people like me stand by and let it happen. So I want to be very clear right now. Call me whatever you want…. I know who I am. I know what faith and service means and what it calls for in this moment. We will not let hate win.[70]

Teachers across the country have sought information on how to include LGBTQ+ history in their lessons in ways that do not threaten their jobs or directly violate state or local restrictions. A government teacher in Indiana, for example, teaches students about their state's "Don't Say Gay/Trans" law, asking them to evaluate its validity and constitutionality based on their understanding of students' rights. There are teachers throughout the country who live and/or work in regions with state or local restrictions who oppose these laws and courageously seek ways to integrate LGBTQ+ history, despite those efforts placing them in precarious positions. Teaching LGBTQ+ history has always been a grassroots movement led by intrepid teachers who, for myriad reasons, decide that they must teach, and their students deserve, an inclusive, representative historical experience.[71] Despite restrictions that aim to stifle this spirit, and evidence that this repression has a chilling effect on teaching and learning about LGBTQ+ history, that grassroots movement and its commitment to supporting and protecting LGBTQ+ students continue to grow.

As of 2023, 28% of Generation Z–individuals born between 1997 and 2012, including current high school students–identified as LGBTQ+.[72] Politicians, pundits, and parent organizations whip up support for curricular restrictions, but LGBTQ+ figures and themes are a regular part of young people's lives in the media they consume, the news they hear/read, and the public figures with whom they engage. More than twenty years ago, in his article "Does Everybody Count as Human?" Stephen Thornton wrote, "Lesbian/gay material is more than an issue to be debated; it is a clearly visible thread in the American social fabric."[73] Two decades later this thread is even more visible, placing a greater demand on schools to support inclusive curriculum to align with changes in society. In the twenty-first century schools are no longer the primary places where students are introduced to information for the first time. They have endless access to content and a plethora of options for how to consume it. Teachers' and schools' job, then, is to provide students with the tools they need to contextualize, process, and apply information so that they are able to engage with the wider world. When schools fail to accurately align with society, they are unable to fulfill this civic mission.

One cannot ignore the pervasiveness of "Don't Say Gay/Trans" laws, curriculum censorship, book bans, attacks on libraries and drag queen story hours, or any other attempt to silence the LGBTQ+ community and its allies. It is imperative, though, that teachers understand how important LGBTQ+-inclusive curriculum is and have the support they need to implement it. Statistics on mental health and suicide risk among LGBTQ+ youth make clear the extent to which this is, without exaggeration, lifesaving work. The Trevor Project, a suicide and crisis prevention organization supporting LGBTQ+ youth, concluded that "there is a significant association between anti-LGBTQ+ victimization and disproportionately high rates of suicide risk" based on their 2024 survey results indicating that 12% of LGBTQ+ youth attempted suicide, 39% considered suicide, and a majority of LGBTQ+ youth reported feeling symptoms of anxiety (66%) and depression (53%). The report also revealed a correlation between gender-affirming schools and lower suicide attempt rates.[74] GLSEN's 2021 survey similarly found that LGBTQ+ students who encountered supportive educators "[r]eported better psychological wellbeing: higher levels of self-esteem, lower levels of depression, and lower likelihood of having seriously considered suicide in the past year."[75] Politicians and pundits on the right intent on portraying efforts to include LGBTQ+ topics in the curriculum as evidence of a "woke" agenda, then, completely miss the mark as they willfully ignore students' needs and disparage teachers' efforts for their own personal and political gain.

While conservative forces remain intent on finding new ways to attack schools and curricula, targeting the most vulnerable groups in society, educators and historians are equally as committed to resisting these intolerant forces. Jeremy Young, the Director of State and Higher Education Policy at PEN America, asserted that polling indicated that sweeping restrictions on academic freedom were not popular among the public, but that attacks on transgender identity were most likely to resonate with people. This, he posited, led to a shift in politicians' and think tanks' priorities.[76] Similar to discriminatory efforts to gain political footholds in the past, these assaults are actually a sign of weakness as people in positions of power target marginalized communities as a means of retaining their status and ensuring that their voices are the most prominent. History demonstrates that these attempts to stifle individual rights and academic freedoms are not successful in the long term. While Republican politicians and so-called "parents' rights" groups persist in proposing, supporting, and enacting policies that create unsafe environments for LGBTQ+ students and teachers who advocate for them, local districts develop resources and curriculum guides to support this instruction and Washington, D.C. changed its social studies standards in 2023 to include LGBTQ+ history beginning in elementary school. Historians, teachers, and scholars gather at conferences to devise ways for those with power—university professors, major historical associations, and allies who do not personally identify as LGBTQ+—to support teachers and students most at risk of attack. Cultural institutions such as the Stonewall National Museum Archives & Library in Fort Lauderdale, FL, offer programming to supplement what students are not learning in schools. And, significantly, historians in red states like Florida, Texas, and Oklahoma persist in their efforts to teach queer history and weave it into all of their relevant courses to ensure that students who did not feel valued or represented earlier in their education have that experience on college campuses.

As historian Julio Capo, Jr. stated, the right's strategy focuses on exhausting those who advocate for and teach LGBTQ+ history.[77] But this strategy seems doomed to fail. Advocates for teaching and learning LGBTQ+ history are part of a principled grassroots movement determined to make schools more inclusive and humane. That commitment—which prioritizes adolescents' learning and well-being— has not, and will not, waver, no matter the challenges along the way.

Goals of This Book

Integrating LGBTQ+ history into the curriculum is not a decision that most teachers make lightly. For those who live in states with curriculum mandates, doing so requires a significant time investment, as teachers learn about people and events that were not a part of their K-12 or college educations or teacher preparation programs as well as revising plans and searching for new resources. Developing and implementing LGBTQ+-inclusive lessons opens teachers to parental pushback and student resistance, especially in conservative-dominated environments; though these circumstances are not a certainty, educators must be prepared for them nonetheless. Where state and/or local restrictions exist, the risks are more profound. Teachers need to be prepared to defend their choices and, in worst case scenarios, their jobs. This book, which is divided into two parts–why and how–offers support, inspiration, community, and classroom resources to all of the teachers incorporating LGBTQ+ history, considering doing so, and curious about what it might entail.

The book's goals, therefore, are multi-pronged. First, we hope to create a community of practice facilitating the teaching of LGBTQ+ history in schools. Often the pioneers of this grassroots movement take on such teaching individually. Ample evidence exists, though, that teachers benefit from identifying and collaborating with similarly minded colleagues with whom they can share ideas, methods, and strategies as they seek to forge a new path. We saw this in the working group that we assembled for this book, and we see it in professional development sessions and workshops that bring together teachers committed to integrating LGBTQ+ history. We are also mindful of the fact that for teachers working in isolation, hearing from others with shared questions and experiences can be affirming and instructive; this book provides readers with the opportunity to learn from those who have been teaching LGBTQ+ history to build on their experience and learn from each other's insights and challenges. Second, this book provides teachers with methods, resources, and lesson plans that translate directly from the page to the classroom. Several of the essays discuss pedagogical strategies, activity ideas, and primary and secondary sources; the last chapter includes fully developed lesson plans. Third, we aim to equip teachers with the confidence and commitment necessary to teach LGBTQ+ history in the face of homophobic/transphobic bigotry. The following chapters demonstrate that teaching this history is both an intellectual necessity and a humane endeavor needed to battle anti-queer/trans bullying and violence. Teaching LGBTQ+ history is not a matter of "woke" or "anti-woke" curriculum. It is a way to teach history accurately and create a sense of belonging and representation in the face of despair, depression, and alarming suicide rates among teens who identify as LGBTQ+.

In the following chapters, historians, teachers, teacher educators, and activists share stories about the impact and challenges of doing this work. In Chapter 1, university-based historians share personal recollections of discovering their own identities and the way that those journeys influence their teaching and, in some cases, work with teachers. In Chapter 2, four teachers in different parts of the country and stages of their careers discuss why including LGBTQ+ history is important for students who identify as LGBTQ+ and students who do not, the impact of this history on individual students and classroom communities, the potential for students to develop ideas and identities and recognize the power of their voices, and educators' paths to incorporating LGBTQ+ figures, themes, and topics in their classes. In Chapter 3, meanwhile, teacher educators discuss their coming-of-age experiences, the ways that they encourage their students to explore LGBTQ+ themes, working with teachers to address the challenges of the moment, and the need to focus on LGBTQ+ joy. Among the teachers and teacher educators, all of whom are deeply invested in what and how K-12 students learn, there are underlying themes of the benefits of inclusive education, the dangers of curricular omission, and the importance of supportive educational spaces for all students. The activists in Chapter 4, including organizationally based educators and a founder of Drag Queen Story Hour, implore readers to recognize the necessity of incorporating LGBTQ+ history and offer concrete strategies and curriculum resources to support teachers' efforts. Across all four chapters, the essays are deeply personal, insightful, thought provoking, and candid. Each of the authors understands and embraces the power of their story and shares it in an effort to remind readers that teaching LGBTQ+ history is meaningful and that they are not alone in their efforts.

Chapter 5, which focuses on the "how," discusses four teachers' work to develop LGBTQ+-inclusive lesson plans, the process of implementing them in middle and high school classes, and reflections on students' experiences and the teacher-perceived impact of teaching LGBTQ+ history. Each teacher explains their rationale for designing these lessons, the activities in which their students participated, the conclusions students reached and questions they asked, and how they might continue and expand on this work in the future. Teachers who want to teach this material need resources to do so; Chapter 5 includes fully developed lesson plans and links to text, visual, and media sources that any reader can immediately use with middle and high school students.

Every teacher's experience is distinct, but ultimately all dedicated teachers seek to educate and support students and provide them with the tools and skills they need to navigate the world. Both sections of this book aim to meet those goals. The essays in Part I demonstrate the vast possibilities that exist for educators who incorporate LGBTQ+ history and the students in their orbit, including concrete pedagogical resources and strategies and a sense of community within the pages of this book. Part II embodies the collaborative nature of teaching; four teachers who came together to bring LGBTQ+ history to their students share their plans and resources so that other teachers might do the same. Both sections of the book represent seeds that this grassroots movement needs. As teachers, it is important to remember–and sometimes be reminded of–the "why." The "how" makes the "why" a reality, and, as the following pages share, has the power to change education and even save students' lives.

Notes

1 The acronym LGBTQ+ has evolved over time and was not used, or known, by many of the individuals whom we might label as such in our own era. Throughout this book you will notice several iterations of this acronym, including LGBT, LGBTQ, LGBTQ+, LGBTQIA+, etc. This acronym, which came into common usage in the late twentieth century, has expanded over time to include all gender identities and sexual orientations.

2 This omission exemplifies the idea of curriculum violence, defined by Stephanie P. Jones as pedagogical practices and omissions that cause harm to students. (Stephanie P. Jones, "The Language of Curriculum Violence," *English Journal* 111, no. 5 (May 2022).)

3 Jay Clarke, "Gay Rights Fight Shaping Up in Miami," *Washington Post*, March 27, 1977, www.washingtonpost.com/archive/politics/1977/03/27/gay-rights-fight-shaping-up-in-miami/e4f596c1-f8e0-4785-b528-599077a478ba/.

4 Clifford Rosky, "Anti Gay Curriculum Laws," *Columbia Law Review* 117, no. 6 (October 2017).

5 Lori Arnold, "Gov. Schwarzenegger Vows to Veto Gay-Friendly Curriculum Bill," *The Christian Examiner,* June 9, 2006, www.christianexaminer.com/article/gov.schwarzenegger.vows.to.veto.gay.friendly.curriculum.bill/43205.htm; "Governor Says He Will Veto Bill Protecting Students and Fostering Tolerance in Schools," Equality California, May 25, 2006, www.eqca.org/site/apps/nlnet/content2.aspx?c=kuLRJ9MRKrH&b=4025925&ct=5195357; Steven Lee Myers, "Ideas & Trends; How a 'Rainbow Curriculum' Turned Into Fighting Words," *The New York Times*, December 13, 1992, accessed April 24, 2018, www.nytimes.com/1992/12/13/weekinreview/ideas-trends-how-a-rainbow-curriculum-turned-into-fighting-words.html.

6   Stacie Brensilver Berman, *LGBTQ+ History in High School Classes in the United States since 1990* (London: Bloomsbury, 2021).

7   Berman, *LGBTQ+ History in High School.*

8   This success happened at the state level in blue states with Democratic majorities in the state legislature and Democratic governors. Success at local and grassroots levels was more widespread and occurred in liberal pockets of conservative states in addition to more progressive areas of the country as teachers began integrating LGBTQ+ history in ways that worked in their communities.

9   "SB-48 Pupil instruction: prohibition of discriminatory content," California Legislative Information, July 14, 2011, https://leginfo.legi slature.ca.gov/faces/billNavClient.xhtml?bill_id=201120120SB48.

10   For additional information on this see Brensilver Berman, *LGBTQ+ History in High School Classes in the United States since 1990* and Don Romesburg, *Contested Curriculum: LGBTQ History Goes to School* (Newark, NJ: Rutgers University Press, 2025).

11   101st General Assembly, State of Illinois, "HB0246," Springfield, IL, August 9, 2019, www.ilga.gov/legislation/fulltext.asp?DocName= 10100HB0246&GA=101&SessionId=108&DocTypeId=HB&LegID= 114183&DocNum=0246&GAID=15&Session=; General Assembly of the State of Colorado, "House Bill 19-1192," Denver, Colorado, May 28, 2019, https://leg.colorado.gov/sites/default/files/2019a_1192 _signed.pdf, 5; New Jersey State Legislature, "An Act concerning instruction and instructional materials in public schools and supplementing chapter 35 of Title 18A of the New Jersey Statutes," Trenton, NJ, January 31, 2019, www.njleg.state.nj.us/2018/Bills/ PL19/6_.HTM; Oregon Legislative Assembly, "House Bill 2023," Salem, Oregon, May 23, 2019, https://olis.leg.state.or.us/liz/201 9R1/Downloads/MeasureDocument/HB2023/Enrolled.

12   Ashley Chiappiano, interview with the Stacie Brensilver Berman, January 15, 2020, Brooklyn, NY.

13   Equality Illinois, Illinois Safe Schools Alliance, a program of Public Health Institute of Metropolitan Chicago, & The Legacy Project, "Inclusive Curriculum Implementation Guidance, Condensed Edition," Illinois Inclusive Curriculum Advisory Council, accessed October 17, 2020, www.isbe.net/Documents/Support-Students-Implementation-Guidance.pdf.

14 General Assembly of the State of Colorado, "House Bill 19-1192," Denver, Colorado, May 28, 2019, https://leg.colorado.gov/sites/default/files/2019a_1192_signed.pdf, 7.

15 Juan Williams, "Pay attention: There's a second civil rights movement," *Washington Post*, January 2, 2025, www.washingtonpost.com/opinions/2025/01/02/juan-williams-book-second-civil-rights/.

16 Bill Barrow, "Trump and Vance make anti-transgender attacks central to their campaign's closing argument," Associated Press, November 1, 2024, https://apnews.com/article/trump-harris-transgender-politics-61cff97a64fac581ffc5f762be4c57d3; Aja Romano, "The cruel truth behind Trump's new attacks on trans people," Vox, October 30, 2024, www.vox.com/2024-elections/380861/trump-transphobic-anti-trans-ads-scapegoating.

17 Florida Education Association, American Federation of Teachers, and National Education Association, "What You Need to Know about Florida's "Don't Say Gay" and "Don't Say They" Laws, Book Bans, and Other Curricula Restrictions," National Education Association, accessed October 30, 2024, www.nea.org/sites/default/files/2023-06/30424-know-your-rights_web_v4.pdf

18 Dustin Jones and Jonathan Franklin, "Not just Florida. More than a dozen states propose so-called 'Don't Say Gay' bills," NPR, April 10, 2022, www.npr.org/2022/04/10/1091543359/15-states-dont-say-gay-anti-transgender-bills.

19 Kevin Jennings, interview with the Stacie Brensilver Berman, January 3, 2018, Brooklyn, NY; Kevin Jennings, *Mama's Boy, Preacher's Son: A Memoir* (Boston: Beacon, 2006).

20 Ibid.

21 Ibid.

22 In an effort to be more inclusive of all gender and sexual identities Gay Straight Alliances have been renamed Genders and Sexualities Alliances. There are also student led organizations founded to support and provide a safe space for LGBTQ+ students operating under different names across the country.

23 "Mission, Vision, and History," GSA Network, accessed December 26, 2024, https://gsanetwork.org/mission-vision-history/.

24 "Carolyn Laub," Public Equity Group, accessed January 3, 2025, www.publicequitygroup.org/carolyn-laub.

25 "Carolyn Laub," Public Equity Group, accessed January 3, 2025, www.publicequitygroup.org/carolyn-laub.

26 Don Romesburg, Leila J Rupp, and D M Donahue, *Making the Framework FAIR: California History-Social Science Framework Proposed LGBT Revisions Related to the FAIR Education Act* (San Francisco, CA: Committee on Lesbian, Gay, Bisexual, and Transgender History, 2014),

27 Debra Fowler and Steven LaBounty-McNair, "Contextualizing LGBT+ History within the Social Studies Curriculum," National Council for the Social Studies, September 2019, www.socialstudies.org/position-statements/contextualizing-lgbt-history-within-social-studies-curriculum#:~:text=NCSS%20fully%20recognizes%20and%20supports,of%20other%20marginalized%20cultural%20groups.

28 "NCSS Supports the American Historical Association's Statement Opposing Exclusion of LGBTQ+ History in Florida," NCSS, May 2023, www.socialstudies.org/news/ncss-supports-aha-statement-opposing-exclusion-lgbtq-history.

29 "About Us," GLSEN, accessed October 30, 2024, www.glsen.org/about-us#snt--1.

30 "The 2021 National School Climate Survey," GLSEN, accessed October 30, 2024, www.glsen.org/research/2021-national-school-climate-survey

31 GLSEN, *The 2021 National School Climate Survey Executive Summary: The Experience of LGBTQ+ Youth in our Nation's Schools* (New York: GLSEN, 2022), 13-14, www.glsen.org/sites/default/files/2022-10/NSCS-2021-Executive_Summary-EN.pdf

32 Hilary Burdge, Shannon Snapp, Carolyn Laub, Stephen T. Russell, & Raymond Moody, *Implementing Lessons That Matter: The Impact of LGBTQ-Inclusive Curriculum on Student Safety, Well-Being, and Achievement* (San Franciso, CA: GSA Network, 2013), 31, https://gsanetwork.org/wp-content/uploads/2018/08/Implementing_Lessons.pdf.

33 Shannon D. Snapp, Jenifer K. McGuire, Katarina O. Sinclair, Karlee Gabrion, & Stephen T. Russell, "LGBTQ-inclusive curricula: why supportive curricula matter," *Sex Education* 15, no. 6 (2015): 592. The findings of this study are based on a survey conducted with 1232 middle and high school students from 154 schools in California.

34   Melanie Willingham-Jaggers and the GLSEN Team, "Inclusive Education Benefits All Children," Learning for Justice, Fall 2022, www.learningforjustice.org/magazine/fall-2022/inclusive-educat ion-benefits-all-children.

35   New York City Department of Education, *Hidden Voices: LGBTQ+ Stories in United States History* (New York, NYCDOE, 2021), 8. This *Hidden Voices* guide and its accompanying lesson plans are part of the New York City Department of Education's larger Hidden Voices program, which seeks to provide teachers with information and primary sources on marginalized individuals and communities to promote including them in the social studies curriculum.

36   "Developing LGBTQ-Inclusive Classroom Resources," GLSEN, accessed October 30, 2024, www.glsen.org/activity/inclusive-cur riculum-guide#:~:text=Inclusive%20curriculum%20supports%20 a%20student's,come%20from%20LGBTQ%2Dheaded%20families.

37   Rosky, "Anti Gay Curriculum Laws"; Brensilver Berman, *LGBTQ+ History in High School Classes in the United States since 1990.*

38   Sarah Schwartz, "Map: Where Critical Race Theory Is Under Attack," *Education Week*, updated August 28, 2024, www.edweek.org/policy-politics/map-where-critical-race-theory-is-under-attack/2021/06.

39   Schwartz, "Map, updated August 28, 2024, www.edweek.org/policy-politics/map-where-critical-race-theory-is-under-attack/2021/06.

40   Paige Hamby Barbeauld, ""Don't Say Gay" Bills and the Movement to Keep Discussion of LGBT Issues out of Schools," *Journal of Law and Education* 43, no. 1 (Winter 2014): 137–146.

41   Rosky, "Anti Gay Curriculum Laws."

42   HB 1557, Florida House of Representatives, 2022, 3–4, www.flsen ate.gov/Session/Bill/2022/1557/BillText/Filed/PDF.

43   CS/CS/HB 1069, Florida House of Representatives, 2023, 7, www. flsenate.gov/Session/Bill/2023/1069/BillText/er/PDF. This is the law that the AHA statement referenced earlier in this chapter opposed.

44   Paul O. Burns, "Memorandum: House Bill 1069, K-12 Education, School District Responsibilities," Florida Department of Education, October 13, 2023, https://info.fldoe.org/docushare/dsweb/Get/Document-10014/DPS-2023-90.pdf.

45   "Bill Text: AL HB322," Alabama House Bill 322, Legiscan, 2022, 2 https://legiscan.com/AL/text/HB322/2022.

46 House Enrolled Act No. 1608, General Assembly of the State of Indiana, 2023, https://iga.in.gov/pdf-documents/123/2023/house/bills/HB1608/HB1608.05.ENRS.pdf; Senate Bill 49, General Assembly of North Carolina, 2023, 1 www.ncleg.gov/Sessions/2023/Bills/Senate/PDF/S49v5.pdf; Senate File 496, State of Iowa General Assembly, 2023, www.legis.iowa.gov/legislation/BillBook?ga=90&ba=SF496.

47 House Bill 122, Louisiana State Legislature, 2024, 1, www.legis.la.gov/legis/ViewDocument.aspx?d=1382702

48 "LGBTQ Curricular Laws," Movement Advancement Project, accessed March 15, 2025, www.lgbtmap.org/equality_maps/curricular_laws.

49 "America's Censored Classrooms 2023," PEN America, November 9, 2023, https://pen.org/report/americas-censored-classrooms-2023/#heading-4. This report contends and presents evidence indicating that though curriculum censorship efforts initially targeted content related to race and racism, by 2023 there was a clear shift towards gag orders focused on LGBTQ+ topics and identities.

50 "Bans on Transgender Youth Participation in Sports," Movement Advancement Project, accessed October 30, 2024, www.lgbtmap.org/equality-maps/youth/sports_participation_bans; "Bans on Transgender People Using Public Bathrooms and Facilities According to their Gender Identity," Movement Advancement Project, accessed March 15, 2025, www.lgbtmap.org/equality-maps/youth/school_bathroom_bans; "LGBTQ Curricular Laws," Movement Advancement Project.

51 Dana Goldstein, "Opponents Call It the 'Don't Say Gay' Bill. Here's What It Says," New York Times, March 18, 2022, www.nytimes.com/2022/03/18/us/dont-say-gay-bill-florida.html.

52 Senate File 496, State of Iowa General Assembly, 2023, www.legis.iowa.gov/legislation/BillBook?ga=90&ba=SF496.

53 "Know Your Rights: Use of Names, Pronouns, And Restrooms In Public Schools," ACLU Arkansas, accessed January 5, 2025, www.acluarkansas.org/en/know-your-rights/know-your-rights-use-names-pronouns-and-restrooms-public-schools.

54 Anna Marks, "Ohio Is About to Make Queer Kids Miserable," New York Times, December 31, 2024, / www.nytimes.com/live/2024/12/17/opinion/thepoint#ohio-queer-kids-legislation.

55 Vincent Gabrielle, "UConn study: Why being outed as LGBTQ is bad for youth mental health," *CT Insider*, April 21, 2024, www.ctinsider.com/news/article/ct-lgbtq-outed-youth-mental-health-uconn-study-19398381.php.

56 "PEN America Index of Educational Gag Orders," PEN America, accessed December 26, 2024, https://airtable.com/appg59iDuPhlLPPFp/shrtwubfBUo2tuHyO/tbl49yod7l01o0TCk/viw6VOxb6SUYd5nXM?blocks=hide.

57 John D'Emilio; email interview with the Stacie Brensilver Berman, July 13, 2016, Brooklyn, NY. Originally published in *LGBTQ+ History in High School Classes in the United States since 1990*.

58 "America's Censored Classrooms 2024," PEN America, October 8, 2024, https://pen.org/report/americas-censored-classrooms-2024/; GLSEN, "Inclusive Curricular Standards Policies," GLSEN Navigator, accessed December 26, 2024, https://maps.glsen.org/inclusive-curricular-standards-policies/.

59 Ashley Woo, Melissa Kay Diliberti, & Elizabeth D. Steiner, *Policies Restricting Teaching About Race and Gender Spill Over into Other States and Localities: Findings from the 2023 State of the American Teacher Survey* (Santa Monica, CA: RAND, 2024), 2. This report can be accessed via www.rand.org/pubs/research_reports/RRA1108-10.html.

60 Woo, Diliberti, & Steiner, *Policies Restricting Teaching About Race and Gender Spill Over into Other States and Localities: Findings from the 2023 State of the American Teacher Survey*, 12.

61 Luona Lin, Juliana Menasce Horowitz, Kiley Hurst, & Dana Braga, "Race and LGBTQ Issues in K-12 Schools: What teachers, teens and the US public say about current curriculum debates," Pew Research Center, February 22, 2024, www.pewresearch.org/social-trends/2024/02/22/public-views-on-parents-opting-their-children-out-of-learning-about-race-and-lgbtq-issues/.

62 Woo, Diliberti, & Steiner, *Policies Restricting Teaching About Race and Gender Spill Over into Other States and Localities: Findings from the 2023 State of the American Teacher Survey*, 12.

63 "ADL and GLAAD Report: More than 350 Anti-LGBTQ+ Hate and Extremism Incidents Recorded as Anti-LGBTQ+ Rhetoric Soared," Anti-Defamation League, June 22, 2023, www.adl.org/resources/press-release/adl-and-glaad-report-more-350-anti-lgbtq-hate-and-extremism-incidents. ADL acknowledges in this report that

many of these incidents go unreported and the actual numbers are likely much higher.

64 "Project 2025 Policies Would Make Schools Less Safe for All Students," Center for American Progress, September 9, 2024, www. americanprogress.org/article/project-2025-policies-would-make-schools-less-safe-for-all-students/.

65 Kiara Alfonseca, "Students challenge 'Don't Say Gay' laws amid wave of anti-LGBTQ legislation," ABC News, June 10, 2022, https:// abcnews.go.com/US/students-challenge-dont-gay-laws-amid-wave-anti/story?id=85256706.

66 Emily Bloch, "'History is LGBTQ+ History': Jacksonville Students Speak Out Against 'Don't Say Gay' Bill," *Florida Times-Union*, updated March 10, 2022, www.jacksonville.com/story/news/education/2022/03/08/jacksonville-students-decry-dont-say-gay-bill-becoming-law/9424133002/.

67 Zander Moricz, "Graduation Speech," May 22, 2022, Pine View High School, Osprey, FL, YouTube, 7:00, www.youtube.com/watch?v=qpTVyozS7M0&t=318s.

68 Patricia Mazzei, "Legal Settlement Clarifies Reach of Florida's 'Don't Say Gay' Law," New York Times, March 11, 2024, www.nytimes.com/2024/03/11/us/florida-dont-say-gay-law-settlement.html#:~:text=Cecile%20Houry%2C%20one%20of%20the,say%20gay%2C%E2%80%9D%20said%20Dr; Dhanika Pineda & Davi Merchan, "Settlement in challenge to Florida's 'Don't Say Gay' law clarifies scope of LGBTQ+ restrictions," ABC News, March 12, 2024, https://abcnews.go.com/US/settlement-challenge-floridas-dont-gay-law-clarifies-scope/story?id=108042198.

69 Curtis M. Wong, "Michigan State Senator Delivers Fiery Rebuke After Colleague Accuses Her Of 'Grooming' Kids," HuffPost, April 19, 2022, www.huffpost.com/entry/michigan-state-senate-mallory-mcmorrow-viral-speech_n_625f088ce4b0e97a3523ae6d.

70 Mallory McMorrow, "WATCH: Michigan lawmaker says, 'We will not let hate win,'" April 19, 2022, Michigan State Senate, PBS Newshour, YouTube, 4:44, www.youtube.com/watch?v=iLWo8B1R0MY.

71 Brensilver Berman, *LGBTQ+ History in Classes in the United States since 1990*.

72 PRRI, *A Political and Cultural Glimpse Into America's Future: Generation Z's Views on Generational Change and the Challenges and*

Opportunities Ahead (Washington D.C.: Public Religion Research Institute, 2023), 7, www.prri.org/wp-content/uploads/2024/01/PRRI-Jan-2024-Gen-Z-Draft.pdf.

73   Stephen J. Thornton, "Does Everybody Count as Human?" *Theory and Research in Social Education* 30, no. 2 (2002): 184.

74   R. Nath, D.D. Matthews, J.P. DeChants, S. Hobaica, C.M. Clark, A.B. Taylor, & G. Muñoz, *2024 US National Survey on the Mental Health of LGBTQ+ Young People* (West Hollywood, California: The Trevor Project, 2024), pp. 1-2 & 6, www.thetrevorproject.org/survey-2024.

75   GLSEN, *The 2021 National School Climate Survey Executive Summary: The Experience of LGBTQ+ Youth in our Nation's Schools*, 14.

76   Jeremy Young, "Listening Session: LGBTQ+ Challenges and Strategies in an Era of 'Anti-Woke' Legislation" (conference roundtable, American Historical Society Annual Meeting, New York, NY, January 5, 2025).

77   Julio Capo, Jr., "Listening Session: LGBTQ+ Challenges and Strategies in an Era of 'Anti-Woke' Legislation" (conference roundtable, American Historical Society Annual Meeting, New York, NY, January 5, 2025).

78   Several states on this map are sites of overlapping curriculum laws. The coding on this map indicates the highest level of inclusion or censorship relevant to LGBTQ+ inclusive curriculum present in the state. Map information from "LGBTQ Curricular Laws," Movement Advancement Project and GLSEN, "Inclusive Curricular Standards Policies," GLSEN Navigator.

References

ACLU Arkansas. "Know Your Rights: Use of Names, Pronouns, and Restrooms in Public Schools." Accessed January 5, 2025. www.acluarkansas.org/en/know-your-rights/know-your-rights-use-names-pronouns-and-restrooms-public-schools.

Alfonseca, Kiara. "Students Challenge 'Don't Say Gay' Laws Amid Wave of Anti-LGBTQ Legislation." ABC News. June 10, 2022. https://abcnews.go.com/US/students-challenge-dont-gay-laws-amid-wave-anti/story?id=85256706.

Anti-Defamation League. "ADL and GLAAD Report: More than 350 Anti-LGBTQ+ Hate and Extremism Incidents Recorded as Anti-LGBTQ+

Rhetoric Soared." June 22, 2023. www.adl.org/resources/press-rele ase/adl-and-glaad-report-more-350-anti-lgbtq-hate-and-extrem ism-incidents.

Arnold, Lori. "Gov. Schwarzenegger Vows to Veto Gay-Friendly Curriculum Bill." *The Christian Examiner.* June 9, 2006. www.christianexaminer. com/article/gov.schwarzenegger.vows.to.veto.gay.friendly.curricu lum.bill/43205.htm.

Barbeauld, Paige Hamby. ""Don't Say Gay" Bills and the Movement to Keep Discussion of LGBT Issues out of Schools." *Journal of Law and Education* 43, no. 1 (Winter 2014): 137–146.

Barrow, Bill. "Trump and Vance make anti-transgender attacks central to their campaign's closing argument." Associated Press. November 1, 2024. https://apnews.com/article/trump-harris-transgender-polit ics-61cff97a64fac581ffc5f762be4c57d3

Berman, Stacie Brensilver. *LGBTQ+ History in High School Classes in the United States since 1990.* London: Bloomsbury, 2021.

"Bill Text: AL HB322." Alabama House Bill 322. Legiscan. 2022. https://legis can.com/AL/text/HB322/2022.

Bloch, Emily. "'History is LGBTQ+ History': Jacksonville Students Speak Out Against 'Don't Say Gay' Bill." Florida Times-Union. Updated March 10, 2022. www.jacksonville.com/story/news/education/ 2022/03/08/jacksonville-students-decry-dont-say-gay-bill-becom ing-law/9424133002/.

Burdge, Hilary, Snapp, Shannon, Laub, Carolyn, Russell, Stephen T., & Moody, Raymond. *Implementing Lessons That Matter: The Impact of LGBTQ-Inclusive Curriculum on Student Safety, Well-Being, and Achievement.* San Francisco, CA: GSA Network, 2013. https://gsanetw ork.org/wp-content/uploads/2018/08/Implementing_Lessons.pdf.

Burns, Paul O. "Memorandum: House Bill 1069, K-12 Education, School District Responsibilities." Florida Department of Education. October 13, 2023. https://info.fldoe.org/docushare/dsweb/Get/Document- 10014/DPS-2023-90.pdf.

California Legislative Information. "SB-48 Pupil Instruction: Prohibition of Discriminatory Content." Last modified July 14, 2011. http://legi nfo.legislature.ca.gov/faces/billNavClient.xhtml?bill_id=201120 120SB48.

Capo, Jr., Julio. "Listening Session: LGBTQ+ Challenges and Strategies in an Era of 'Anti-Woke' Legislation." Conference roundtable at the

American Historical Society Annual Meeting, New York, NY, January 5, 2025.

"Carolyn Laub." Public Equity Group. Accessed January 3, 2025. www.publicequitygroup.org/carolyn-laub.

Center for American Progress. "Project 2025 Policies Would Make Schools Less Safe for All Students." September 9, 2024. www.americanprogress.org/article/project-2025-policies-would-make-schools-less-safe-for-all-students/.

Clarke, Jay. "Gay Rights Fight Shaping Up in Miami." *Washington Post*. March 27, 1977. www.washingtonpost.com/archive/politics/1977/03/27/gay-rights-fight-shaping-up-in-miami/e4f596c1-f8e0-4785-b528-599077a478ba/.

Equality California. "Governor Says He Will Veto Bill Protecting Students and Fostering Tolerance in Schools." Last modified May 25, 2006. www.eqca.org/site/apps/nlnet/content2.aspx?c=kuLRJ9MRKrH&b=4025925&ct=5195357.

Equality Illinois, Illinois Safe Schools Alliance, a program of Public Health Institute of Metropolitan Chicago, & The Legacy Project. "Inclusive Curriculum Implementation Guidance, Condensed Edition." Illinois Inclusive Curriculum Advisory Council. Accessed October 17, 2020. www.isbe.net/Documents/Support-Students-Implementation-Guidance.pdf.

Florida Education Association, American Federation of Teachers, and National Education Association. "What You Need to Know about Florida's 'Don't Say Gay' and 'Don't Say They' Laws, Book Bans, and Other Curricula Restrictions." National Education Association. Accessed October 30, 2024. www.nea.org/sites/default/files/2023-06/30424-know-your-rights_web_v4.pdf

Florida House of Representatives. CS/CS/HB 1069. 2023. www.flsenate.gov/Session/Bill/2023/1069/BillText/er/PDF.

Florida House of Representatives. HB 1557. 2022. www.flsenate.gov/Session/Bill/2022/1557/BillText/Filed/PDF.

Fowler, Debra and LaBounty-McNair, Steven. "Contextualizing LGBT+ History within the Social Studies Curriculum." National Council for the Social Studies. September 2019. www.socialstudies.org/position-statements/contextualizing-lgbt-history-within-social-studies-curriculum#:~:text=NCSS%20fully%20recognizes%20and%20supports,of%20other%20marginalized%20cultural%20groups.

Gabrielle, Vincent. "UConn sSudy: Why Being Outed as LGBTQ is Bad for Youth Mental Health." *CT Insider*. April 21, 2024. www.ctinsider. com/news/article/ct-lgbtq-outed-youth-mental-health-uconn-study-19398381.php.

General Assembly of the State of Colorado. "House Bill 19-1192." May 28, 2019. https://leg.colorado.gov/sites/default/files/2019a_1192_sig ned.pdf

General Assembly of the State of Indiana. House Enrolled Act No. 1608. 2023. https://iga.in.gov/pdf-documents/123/2023/house/bills/ HB1608/HB1608.05.ENRS.pdf;

General Assembly of North Carolina. Senate Bill 49. 2023. www.ncleg. gov/Sessions/2023/Bills/Senate/PDF/S49v5.pdf.

GLSEN. "The 2021 National School Climate Survey." Accessed October 30, 2024. www.glsen.org/research/2021-national-school-climate-survey

GLSEN. The 2021 National School Climate Survey Executive Summary: The Experience of LGBTQ+ Youth in our Nation's Schools. New York: GLSEN, 2022. www.glsen.org/sites/default/files/2022-10/NSCS-2021-Executive_Summary-EN.pdf.

GLSEN. "About Us." Accessed October 30, 2024. www.glsen.org/ about-us#snt--1.

GLSEN. "Developing LGBTQ-Inclusive Classroom Resources." Accessed October 30, 2024. www.glsen.org/activity/inclusive-curriculum-guide#:~:text=Inclusive%20curriculum%20supports%20a%20 student's,come%20from%20LGBTQ%2Dheaded%20families.

GLSEN. "Inclusive Curricular Standards Policies." GLSEN Navigator. Accessed December 26, 2024. https://maps.glsen.org/inclusive-curricular-standards-policies/.

Goldstein, Dana. "Opponents Call it the 'Don't Say Gay' Bill. Here's What it Says." *New York Times*. March 18, 2022. www.nytimes.com/2022/03/ 18/us/dont-say-gay-bill-florida.html.

GSA Network. "Mission, Vision, and History." Accessed December 26, 2024. https://gsanetwork.org/mission-vision-history/.

Jennings, Kevin. *Mama's Boy, Preacher's Son: A Memoir*. Boston: Beacon, 2006.

Jones, Dustin & Franklin, Jonathan. "Not just Florida. More than a dozen states propose so-called 'Don't Say Gay' bills." NPR. April 10, 2022. www.npr.org/2022/04/10/1091543359/15-states-dont-say-gay-anti-transgender-bills.

Jones, Stephanie P. "The Language of Curriculum Violence." *English Journal* 111, no. 5 (May 2022): 15–17.

Lin, Luona, Horowitz, Juliana Menasce, Hurst, Kiley, & Braga, Dana. "Race and LGBTQ Issues in K-12 Schools: What teachers, teens and the US public say about current curriculum debates." Pew Research Center. February 22, 2024. www.pewresearch.org/social-trends/2024/02/22/public-views-on-parents-opting-their-children-out-of-learning-about-race-and-lgbtq-issues/.

Louisiana State Legislature. House Bill 122. 2024. www.legis.la.gov/legis/ViewDocument.aspx?d=1382702.

Marks, Anna. "Ohio is About to Make Queer Kids Miserable." *New York Times.* December 31, 2024. www.nytimes.com/live/2024/12/17/opinion/thepoint#ohio-queer-kids-legislation.

Mazzei, Patricia. "Legal Settlement Clarifies Reach of Florida's 'Don't Say Gay' Law." *New York Times.* March 11, 2024. www.nytimes.com/2024/03/11/us/florida-dont-say-gay-law-settlement.html#:~:text=Cecile%20Houry%2C%20one%20of%20the,say%20gay%2C%E2%80%9D%20said%20Dr.

McMorrow, Mallory. "WATCH: Michigan lawmaker says, 'We will not let hate win.'" April 19, 2022. Michigan State Senate. PBS Newshour, YouTube, 4:44. www.youtube.com/watch?v=iLWo8B1R0MY.

Moricz, Zander. "Graduation Speech." May 22, 2022. Pine View High School, Osprey, FL. YouTube, 7:00. www.youtube.com/watch?v=qpTVyozS7M0&t=318s.

Movement Advancement Project. "Bans on Transgender People Using Public Bathrooms and Facilities According to their Gender Identity." Accessed October 30, 2024. www.lgbtmap.org/equality-maps/youth/school_bathroom_bans.

Movement Advancement Project. "Bans on Transgender Youth Participation in Sports." Accessed October 30, 2024. www.lgbtmap.org/equality-maps/youth/sports_participation_bans.

Movement Advancement Project. "LGBTQ Curricular Laws." Accessed October 30, 2024. www.lgbtmap.org/equality_maps/curricular_laws.

Myers, Steven Lee. "Ideas & Trends; How a 'Rainbow Curriculum' Turned Into Fighting Words." *The New York Times.* December 13, 1992. www.nytimes.com/1992/12/13/weekinreview/ideas-trends-how-a-rainbow-curriculum-turned-into-fighting-words.html.

Nath, R., Matthews, D.D., DeChants, J.P., Hobaica, S., Clark, C.M., Taylor, A.B., and Muñoz, G. *2024 US National Survey on the Mental Health of LGBTQ+ Young People.* West Hollywood, California: The Trevor Project, 2024, www.thetrevorproject.org/survey-2024.

National Council for the Social Studies. "NCSS Supports the American Historical Association's Statement Opposing Exclusion of LGBTQ+ History in Florida." May 2023. www.socialstudies.org/news/ncss-supports-aha-statement-opposing-exclusion-lgbtq-history.

New Jersey State Legislature. "An Act Concerning Instruction and Instructional Materials in Public Schools and Supplementing Chapter 35 of Title 18A of the New Jersey Statutes." January 31, 2019. www.njleg.state.nj.us/2018/Bills/PL19/6_.HTM.

New York City Department of Education. *Hidden Voices: LGBTQ+ Stories in United States History.* New York: NYCDOE, 2021.

Oregon Legislative Assembly. "House Bill 2023." May 23, 2019. https://olis.leg.state.or.us/liz/2019R1/Downloads/MeasureDocument/HB2023/Enrolled.

PEN America. "America's Censored Classrooms 2023." November 9, 2023. https://pen.org/report/americas-censored-classrooms-2023/#heading-4.

PEN America. "America's Censored Classrooms 2024." October 8, 2024. https://pen.org/report/americas-censored-classrooms-2024/.

PEN America. "PEN America Index of Educational Gag Orders." Accessed December 26, 2024. https://airtable.com/appg59iDuPhILPPFp/shrtwubfBUo2tuHyO/tbl49yod7I01o0TCk/viw6VOxb6SUYd5nXM?blocks=hide.

Pineda, Dhanika & Merchan, Davi. "Settlement in challenge to Florida's 'Don't Say Gay' law clarifies scope of LGBTQ+ restrictions." ABC News. March 12, 2024. https://abcnews.go.com/US/settlement-challenge-floridas-dont-gay-law-clarifies-scope/story?id=108042198.

PRRI. *A Political and Cultural Glimpse into America's Future: Generation Z's Views on Generational Change and the Challenges and Opportunities Ahead.* Washington D.C.: Public Religion Research Institute, 2023. www.prri.org/wp-content/uploads/2024/01/PRRI-Jan-2024-Gen-Z-Draft.pdf.

Romano, Aja. "The cruel truth behind Trump's new attacks on trans people." Vox. October 30, 2024. www.vox.com/2024-elections/380 861/trump-transphobic-anti-trans-ads-scapegoating.

Romesburg, Don. *Contested Curriculum: LGBTQ History Goes to School.* Newark, NJ: Rutgers University Press, 2025.

Romesburg, Don, Rupp, Leila J., and Donahue, D M. *Making the Framework FAIR: California History-Social Science Framework Proposed LGBT Revisions Related to the FAIR Education Act.* San Francisco, CA: Committee on Lesbian, Gay, Bisexual, and Transgender History, 2014.

Rosky, Clifford. "Anti Gay Curriculum Laws." *Columbia Law Review* 117, no. 6 (October 2017): 1461–1541.

Schwartz, Sarah. "Map: Where Critical Race Theory is Under Attack." *Education Week*. Updated August 28, 2024. www.edweek.org/ policy-politics/map-where-critical-race-theory-is-under-attack/ 2021/06.

Snapp, Shannon D., McGuire, Jenifer K., Sinclair, Katarina O., Gabrion, Karlee, & Russell, Stephen T. "LGBTQ-inclusive curricula: why supportive curricula matter." *Sex Education* 15, no. 6 (2015): 580–596.

State of Illinois. "HB0246." 101st General Assembly. August 9, 2019. www. ilga.gov/legislation/fulltext.asp?DocName=10100HB0246&GA= 101&SessionId=108&DocTypeId=HB&LegID=114183&DocNum= 0246&GAID=15&Session=.

State of Iowa General Assembly. Senate File 496. 2023. www.legis.iowa. gov/legislation/BillBook?ga=90&ba=SF496.

Thornton, Stephen J. "Does Everybody Count as Human?" *Theory and Research in Social Education* 30, no. 2 (2002): 178–189.

Willingham-Jaggers, Melanie & the GLSEN Team. "Inclusive Education Benefits All Children." *Learning for Justice*. Fall 2022. www.learnin gforjustice.org/magazine/fall-2022/inclusive-education-benefits-all-children.

Wong, Curtis M. "Michigan State Senator Delivers Fiery Rebuke After Colleague Accuses Her Of 'Grooming' Kids." *HuffPost*. April 19, 2022. www.huffpost.com/entry/michigan-state-senate-mallory-mcmor row-viral-speech_n_625f088ce4b0e97a3523ae6d.

Woo, Ashley, Diliberti, Melissa Kay, & Steiner, Elizabeth D. *Policies Restricting Teaching About Race and Gender Spill Over into Other*

States and Localities: Findings from the 2023 State of the American Teacher Survey. Santa Monica, CA: RAND, 2024.

Young, Jeremy. "Listening Session: LGBTQ+ Challenges and Strategies in an Era of 'Anti-Woke' Legislation." Conference roundtable at the American Historical Society Annual Meeting, New York, NY, January 5, 2025.

Part I

Why We Need to Teach LGBTQ+ History: Voices of Experience

1

Voices from the Academy: Historians Advocate for Including LGBTQ+ History

College and university professors, as mentioned in the introduction, have greater academic freedom in most areas of the US and more opportunities to engage in and teach LGBTQ+ history. They are not beholden to the state standards that teachers must follow and, in most states, are not as deeply impacted by censorship laws and policies and fears of family pushback. The historians whose essays are included in this chapter, who live and work in New York, California, and South Carolina, echo scholars' and research studies' findings on the significance and necessity of integrating LGBTQ+ history and teaching courses devoted to this content. In doing so, they advocate for personal, political, and pedagogical change. They recognize the power and importance of including LGBTQ+ history in their courses, and, where possible, supporting K-12 educators who hope to do this work in their schools. Each essay highlights common themes: education and educational spaces have the power to open the closet and transform—and possibly save—students' lives; this history is not new and deserves its place in the curriculum; learning LGBTQ+ history inspires historical empathy; and the more we teach this history the more awareness we build.

DOI: 10.4324/9781032689678-3

These scholar-activists discuss their profound interest in and involvement with high school teachers and LGBTQ+ curriculum development and the ways in which they go beyond conventional norms in caring about and mentoring students. In deeply personal essays, many of which trace the authors' personal trajectory to self-awareness/acceptance and discuss the impact of those journeys on their teaching and scholarship, the historians in this chapter focus on what is possible in their classrooms, what they believe and hope can happen in K-12 education, and the power of LGBTQ+ history to bring humanity into educational spaces. Through their descriptions of moments with their students, colleagues, teachers, and, in one essay, their own children, the essays demonstrate what inclusive curriculum and honest depictions of history can mean for all students and the ways in which these historians' work may inspire others to follow in their footsteps.

Past and Presence in Making FAIR History Education

Don Romesburg

As of 2024, California's FAIR (Fair, Accurate, Inclusive, and Respectful) Education Act has been in effect for a dozen years. A law requiring the state's K-12 educators to include the "roles and contributions" of "lesbian, gay, bisexual, and transgender Americans" in history and social studies was an important step toward implementation. It was not the first, though, and certainly not the last. As early as the 1980s, efforts toward LGBTQ-inclusive history education emerged across the country. The passage of the FAIR Education Act, and its subsequent implementation in policy, training, and educational materials, accelerated those efforts. Today, despite censorious "Don't Say Gay or Trans" laws, more possibilities exist than ever before for educators, administrators, advocates, and policymakers. My book, *Contested Curriculum: LGBTQ History Goes to School*, details this long history and its current implications. Here I just want to highlight a couple of the key points.

First, there is nothing new about creating LGBTQ-inclusive K-12 history. Across the 1980s, identifying lesbian, gay, and bisexual youth as an at-risk population compelled institutional and supplemental curricular interventions. In 1984, for example, Philadelphia School Superintendent Dr. Constance Clayton invited the Philadelphia Lesbian and Gay Task Force (PLGTF) to make suggestions on how to make schools safer for gay students. Among other requests, PLGTF Executive Director Risa Addessa urged "mandates" for "the fair and representative treatment of gay and lesbian people ... as part of the ongoing process of curricular revision, particularly in the areas of history [and] social studies."[1]

A small number of educators in Massachusetts and elsewhere also began tentatively adding content in their classrooms. Most notable in this regard was history teacher Kevin Jennings, who went on to found what became the Gay, Lesbian, and Straight Teachers Network (GLSTN, now GLSEN) across the 1990s. In

FIGURE 1.1
Gay and Lesbian Community Action Council poster highlighting historical figures who identified as LGBTQ+.

addition to informal and institutional strategies, educators and others crafted curricular supplements. In 1988, to commemorate the first National Coming Out Day, the Gay and Lesbian Community Action Council of Minneapolis printed a widely distributed poster of ten famous historical figures, including James Baldwin, Willa Cather, Eleanor Roosevelt, Bessie Smith, and Walt Whitman, with the headline, "UNFORTUNATELY, HISTORY HAS SET THE RECORD A LITTLE TOO STRAIGHT." More substantial was the *Struggle for Equality: Lesbian and Gay Community*, an optional supplement that the New York City Mayor's Office for the Gay and Lesbian Community developed for seventh and eighth-grade social studies in the Fall of 1989.[2]

Across the 1990s, the curricular resources available to history teachers wanting to include LGBTQ content only expanded. Opponents of inclusive education may frame it as something new. LGBTQ-inclusive history education, however, has long been well thought out, researched, and age-appropriate.

Second, for decades, advocates have been pushing for LGBTQ-inclusive history education policy at local and state levels. Over the late 1980s and early 1990s, while cities such as Philadelphia and New York initiated supplemental lesbian and gay history curricula for K-12 classrooms, activists in California and Massachusetts took the effort statewide. Mobilizing state-level change for inclusive history education did not succeed. It became collateral damage in wider battles over multiculturalism and the religious right's antigay culture war.

As early as 1986, Bay Area Network of Gay and Lesbian Educators (BANGLE) pushed the California Department of Education to include lesbian and gay content in the state's 1987 History-Social Science Framework. Instead, token inclusion related to the Holocaust appeared in its related supplemental *Model Curriculum Guide for Human Rights*. In 1990, lesbian, gay, and bisexual advocates pushed for the state to require inclusion in approved history textbooks. This was also unsuccessful. Nonetheless, the advocacy—and the state's refusal to make framework or textbook changes to address it—led San Francisco Unified School District to create lesbian and gay history education supplements. Piloted lesson plans for high school social studies teachers included "In the Life: Lesbians, Gay Men, and Bisexuals in the Harlem Renaissance," homosexuals targeted during the Holocaust, and lesbian and gay organizing in the context of 1960s and 1970s social movements. In 1995, the lessons became a published series distributed to educators. For its efforts, San Francisco Unified was held up as a model of how local districts could launch LGBTQ history education initiatives.[3]

Massachusetts led the early Safe Schools movement, which promoted nondiscrimination policies, Gay-Straight Alliances, and culturally competent staff. Curriculum was generally not in the mix. During the 1992 hearings to establish the Governor's Commission on Gay and Lesbian Youth, GLSTN lobbied for curricular recommendations, especially in history. Unfortunately, Massachusetts' otherwise supportive Governor William Weld ordered them dropped from the final report. This had lasting consequences. In 1995, the state's Social Studies Framework committee recommended that students should analyze "individual and cultural components of identity," including sexual orientation. Because the Governor's Commission had excluded curriculum, though, the Board of Education eliminated sexual orientation in the final Framework. Still, Kevin Jennings and his colleague Arthur Lipkin would go on to produce books, other educational materials, and related teacher training on lesbian and gay history across the 1990s. In 1997, the Massachusetts Department of Education contracted the two men to create sample lesson plans and bibliographies.[4]

In addition, Lesbian and Gay History Month (LGHM) launched in October 1994, the brainchild of Rodney Wilson, a history teacher at Mehlville High School in suburban St. Louis. LGHM's High School Outreach Team consisted of Wilson, Jennings, San Francisco advocates, and Chicago area teacher Torey Wilson.[5] Still, over the next few years, what quickly became "Lesbian, Gay, and Bisexual History Month" lost steam for its K-12 efforts. Mid-1990s culture war struggles over inclusive vs. abstinence-based sex education, "special rights" framing of LGBTQ political and social recognition, and history wars that sought to marginalize "multiculturalism" in favor of teaching a "common story" took their toll. As such, History Month organizing shifted toward public history and higher education. Even so, by the turn of the century, quality K-12 curricular supplements and workshops were available on both coasts and in the Midwest.

This is all to say that while the FAIR Education Act may only be a dozen years old, it rests on a foundation built much earlier. Momentum has built since then. California has aligned its History-Social Science Framework and related textbooks, including content in elementary, middle, and high school grades. In 2018, Massachusetts added LGBTQ content to its History-Social Science Framework. Since 2019, New Jersey, Colorado, Illinois, Oregon, Connecticut, Nevada, and Washington have passed inclusive curriculum legislation. That year, the National Council for Social Studies issued a position statement affirming LGBTQ history education.[6] These have all generated even more high-quality materials, trainings, and calls for policy change.

It is easy to get discouraged by the raft of "Don't Say Gay or Trans" bills and laws our nation is currently enduring. The danger of them is real. At the same time, it is important to understand them as what they are—desperate acts of backlash. Honest history education will continue to advance. The American Historical Association's annual conference in 2024 held a roundtable about teaching in the context of "divisive concepts" legislation. Of the many excellent observations made by panelists and the teachers, professors, and administrators in the audience, one from Jacqueline Allain, coordinator of PEN America's Freedom to Learn program, stood out: "Don't do the censors' work for them." Relatedly, she said, "Wait until you're stopped."[7] Require the censors to act and justify their actions. Push back when they do.

This does not just have to fall on the shoulders of individual teachers or districts. In 2023, California passed AB1078, authored by Assemblymember Dr. Corey Jackson, a former member of the Riverside County Board of Education and the state's first Black openly LGBTQ state lawmaker. It authorizes the State Superintendent to provide textbooks at school districts' expense if a local board withholds them. It also specifies that school districts cannot ban any "appropriately adopted textbook, instructional material, or curriculum on the basis that it contains inclusive and diverse perspectives." This circumvents renegade local politicians who seek to censor LGBTQ-inclusive textbooks. Finally, it updates Education Code language shaped by the FAIR Education Act to recognize gender beyond the binary with more contemporary and expansive categories. By 2025, the California Department of Education must provide districts with guidance on related curriculum and materials.[8] We should all demand that our policymakers and legislators commit to implementing concrete and comprehensive inclusion.

For more than three decades, educators and advocates have demonstrated that LGBTQ-inclusive K-12 history education can be rigorous, age-appropriate, pedagogically powerful, and culturally important. We have to keep doing it until it wins out over ignorance and intolerance. Sometimes we get to do this in states, districts, schools, and communities that clearly support the work. Sometimes we have to consider what this can look like in places with explicit bans. Most teachers, however, are not in states with either LGBTQ-inclusive mandates or prohibitions. Showing through example can take courage but it speaks volumes against those who seek to silence inclusive history education. Research suggests that educators tend to fear parental complaint far more than it occurs. When it does happen, LGBTQ+ teachers and teachers of color are more likely to actually face it than their straight, white counterparts.[9] The latter therefore have a distinct obligation to make history education a brave space.

History is on your side. What are you waiting for?

The Mountains We Climb: Perspectives on Teaching Queer History from a Coal Miner's Daughter

Sandra Slater

It was my second semester of graduate school at the University of Kentucky, and I signed up for a class on the History of American Sexualities. I saw myself in the historical narrative and it changed my life. The idea was titillating, especially for an Appalachian girl raised in a conservative Baptist home. My mother was outraged, horrified that I would learn about "sex." In college, I had decided that I wanted to pursue graduate school in American women's history after my undergraduate advisor, a traditional Civil War historian, told me that I could not study African American history because I was white, and that as a white woman, women's history was more appropriate. In hindsight, I recognize the fallacy of his position, but it placed me on the pathway to what would become my life's work. My first graduate course was an introductory methodology class led by Ellen Furlough, a student of Joan Wallach Scott, the mother of historical gender theory. When I read *Gender and the Politics of History*, I was fascinated by the intersections gender scholarship provided. Women did not exist in isolation, but instead operate within a complicated intersectional framework of class, race, gender, and sexuality.[10] It was a complex web, an endlessly fascinating puzzle of power dynamics.[11] Joan Wallach Scott and Judith Butler's theories of performing identity spoke to me, to the very core of my own identity struggles.[12] I found myself in scholarly literature and the classroom. Queer people had a rich history, and it was also *my* history. The classroom became a place of self-discovery and acceptance and creating that for my students is one of my core professional objectives.

I knew I was queer in kindergarten. A red-haired classmate with a sprinkling of freckles became my heart's desire. Each day when the girls in my class passed love notes to the little boys, I wrote to her. It never occurred to me that this was anything abnormal, until her mother complained to mine. No longer could I write affectionate notes, and I received the message early on that something was "wrong" with me. It was the 1980s and people whispered about HIV/AIDS, family members gossiped derisively about my lesbian cousin who left eastern Kentucky, became a successful attorney, and never came back. They erroneously blamed her queerness for her father's suicide. On Sundays, we listened to fear-mongering sermons on the evils of deviant lifestyles as if sexual identity was a choice. The messages blazed with a fury in my childhood. Despite the admonitions to not send love notes to the red-haired girl, my crush persisted through elementary school. In third grade, I filled an antique locket from my grandmother with our pictures and wore it around my neck, a decision that greatly concerned my mother. In fourth grade, my only birthday wish was to have her visit and eat cake. It was slightly awkward and later my mom told me that the way I looked at the other girl made her "stomach turn." It was then that I embraced the silence of myself, a bit older and keenly aware of revealing too much. I was attracted to boys and girls, so I decided to internalize and hide the queerness and resolved to eventually date men or no one at all. I was strange. Disgusting. The sexual fluidity was destabilizing, scary, and difficult to comprehend. Sexuality was a binary in my upbringing, good heteronormativity, bad homosexuality. I did not date anyone in high school or college, focusing instead on books and education, something within my control and a process through which I received love, acclaim, and support. I squirreled away knowledge and watched the world, always keen on power dynamics and politics, the black sheep liberal in a family of conservatives.

In graduate school, I met my future wife. She was a gold star lesbian, out loud and proud. We were together for twelve years, and though the marriage eventually ended, she encouraged me to embrace myself. My sister, angry at some slight, outed me to the family behind my back and as one can imagine, all hell broke loose. Over the next decade my parents struggled to accept me, providing beautiful moments of support followed closely by hurtful denunciations. Always the concern for my soul and a reminder that I was doomed to burn for all eternity in hell. No one from my family came to our wedding and their absence was deeply wounding. It took a very long time and some difficult conversations to reach a place of growth and healing. My mom and I grew together and, although she still worries for my soul, she and I are extremely close.

I tell my story to my students and am very open about my struggle to claim identity and navigate family dynamics. As a professor of early American sexuality and gender, I recognize that our scholarship is deeply personal to us as academics but also as human beings. When I offer undergraduate and graduate courses on American Sexualities, Queer America, or History of American Women and Gender, I recognize that many students take these courses as part of their own journey to discover and affirm themselves. To offer documentation and narratives that confirm the presence of queerness in history grounds them in a discourse and reality that they are not alone. Their sexuality and gender performance are not anomalous. In this way, history can be a form of finding "home." It was for me, and I rest comfortably in the awareness that discovering my historical predecessors reassured me on a deeply personal level and helped pull me from the abyss of self-loathing. Students have incredibly powerful responses to the knowledge of queer history. Several students have openly wept when discussing queer persecution. One semester a young woman cried in every single class, both in grief and joy, as she came to terms with her own queer identity. Early in the semester, we discuss the classroom as a safe space of love and compassion, not just education. As a professor, I am responsible for my students, and as a queer professor, a source of inspiration and support. Sharing my story provides an opportunity for them to share theirs. We are together on this journey.

One of the greatest privileges of my life is the number of students who come out for the first time to me in the quiet safety of my office. Their sense of elation and freedom is beautiful. I teach in a deeply southern city, the "holy city" of Charleston, SC. Many of my students grew up in similarly conservative households and, like me, suppressed their identities for fear of family disownment and shame. I understand them, and they me. When they ask me for advice on how to talk to their families or friends, I always emphasize patience. Though likely some already suspect their children of being queer, parents need time to process and acclimate themselves to a new reality. Just as students struggled for years to reconcile themselves, sometimes parents need time and grace, too. Often, students report that their parents embrace them with love and support, an increasing phenomenon in the twenty-first century. Queer visibility in culture paved the way for a more accepting time in which queerness, gender fluidity, and sexuality are better understood. The closets are fewer and smaller.

My approach to teaching is profoundly personal to provide accessibility and warmth to young people learning to traverse a complicated world. I tell all my classes on the first day and reiterate throughout the semester that the study of history teaches empathy, life's most important lesson. We learn about people's lives and cultures, placing ourselves in their shoes, viewing the world through different lenses. People are the product of their lived experiences and social systems, good and bad. Our job as historians is to understand them on their terms, to wonder about historical perspectives and actions, and to recognize the intricate tapestry of a lived experience. We ask the questions because we want to know their stories, and each of those narratives is valuable. Every person matters in the historical record *and* in the classroom. Students leave my classes with an understanding and appreciation for diversity. Those who do not identify as queer embrace the material just as keenly because I emphasize that we are part of a larger process of existence, and we can effect good in the world through our daily interactions and social activism. Compassion and empathy for others increase acceptance and self-love.

Early in my career, elder queer colleagues imparted to me the responsibility of being a role model to my students, but also to the queer community at large. Dan Savage's "It Gets Better Project" was relatively new when I began my teaching career, an important campaign to reduce suicide amongst queer teens.[13] It coincided with my own awareness that for me, it did get better. Queer people could be successful and well-adjusted, even happy. It was not easy, but I made it and so could they. It was my job to convey this to my students, to be visibly and unapologetically queer. My first queer role model was my piano teacher in college, Candace Armstrong. Deep in my closet, her ability to live her truth inspired me. I felt less alone. We have been close for twenty years and she was one of the first people I came out to because I knew it was safe, and she would be a source of support and love. She gave me hope in a way I endeavor to provide my students. Good teachers spend time getting to know their students as people. The process is symbiotic. In sharing myself with my classroom, I invite them to do the same without judgement. Together we share our histories, learn the histories of others, and heal with the promise of a better and more inclusive world.

Why I Teach LGBTQ+ History

Daniel Hurewitz

I remember learning of Tyler Clementi's death. He was a student at Rutgers, a college across the river from the one I work at and full of students like ours. I felt not only saddened to hear about his suicide, but implicated, as well.

It was 2010, and by that time, I had already spent 15 years of my life reading and writing and thinking about LGBTQ history. In truth, my dive into the queer past had probably begun earlier – when I was just in college, reading gay novels in the school library as a way to come out. I was too afraid to actually check out the books, certain that someone at the circulation desk would mock me for my new literary exploration. So, I stayed in the basement, reading about gay men's fictionalized experiences and beginning to imagine who I might be through their stories. Writers like Felice Picano, James Baldwin, and Edmund White began to reveal to me a world that I was not yet brave enough to actually enter. It seemed exciting.

When I got to New York, in the 1990s, and began exploring that gay world in real time, I carried their stories with me. They gave me a way of understanding myself and the world around me, as well as piqued my curiosity about the differences between the world they had portrayed and the one I was discovering. Thinking about their stories raised questions for me about history and the past and how things change over time – questions that felt more powerful and compelling than history classes ever had before. That curiosity launched me into the world of queer history. I read what I could find, learning about queer lovers and performers, and leaders who impressed and inspired me. Their lives made me more excited about being queer in the present and made me want to become a historian and unearth more.

Certainly, in the fall of 2010, when Tyler Clementi started as a first-year student at Rutgers, his trajectory looked so different from mine. Of course, he was excited about his future, like so many beginning college students. But unlike me, he was not hiding his sexuality in the library. He had already come out to his parents; he arranged a date with another man; and he told his roommate that he wanted to use their room privately. All of that seemed so brave new world.

But then the familiar undertow of homophobia pulled him under. First, his roommate, deducing that Clementi was gay, set up a webcam to broadcast his date and invited other students to watch and make fun of him. And the same homophobia that drove him then crashed over Clementi. Feeling himself to have become a subject of ridicule in his new community, he took himself to the George Washington Bridge that connects New York and New Jersey and plunged to his death. The power of homophobia, societal and internalized, remained strong.

Clementi's tragic death provoked a broad national reaction from TV stars to President Obama. For me, personally, it pointed toward all the ways the world had not changed from the one I had known as a young man in the 1980s and 90s. Despite *Will & Grace* and Ellen DeGeneres, it seemed, here was yet another college student humiliated for being queer. But now I was an adult, a queer professional even. Who could I be in the face of the intransigence of homophobia?

To be fair, I had not dived into LGBTQ history as a way to make a difference in the world. In many ways, I had done it as a way to understand myself. But suddenly, I had to ask, how could I be just a bystander if this was where the world led young people like Tyler Clementi to such tragic ends? If he was not so different from the kid I had been, and the world was not actually so different from the one I had grown up in, how could I not do something? But I was a college history professor: what exactly could I do?

But then I spoke with a friend who was the director of GLSEN, and she turned on a lightbulb for me. GLSEN is a national organization focused on supporting queer youth, particularly high school students, and she described a powerful piece of GLSEN's research. When they parsed the data, she explained, their research demonstrated that if a single teacher spoke about queer life – queer individuals – in a positive or even non-negative way, that teacher had the capacity to shift the culture of the entire school. That teacher – let alone a handful of teachers – could sway the

climate in the school away from dominant homophobia to something more tolerant, even welcoming. Perhaps such a teacher
could not stop the suffering or loneliness of a specific young
person, but they could begin to turn the wider tide.

For me, this was eye-opening research. It impressed me both
because of what it said about the impact of individual teachers,
and because it pointed towards a way that I could make a difference. I started to learn about high school teachers who were
bringing LGBTQ content into their classes – mostly into their
history classes, my own area of expertise. And I started to think
about how to help teachers who wanted to teach that material –
but did not have the training or background – to find the knowledge and confidence to begin.

The teachers I spoke to were remarkable and moving. They
taught in schools in Brooklyn, Tucson, Northern California, and
Massachusetts. They were incredibly brave, stepping into visibility as one of the only out or pro-gay teachers in their school.
They taught, at times, in the face of students' reflexive homophobia, or their communities'. They were vulnerable. And yet,
they helped their students discover a new viewpoint. Repeatedly,
their students told them, "This is so interesting! Why have I never
learned this before?" They recognized the need to take small steps
and move slowly. But excitingly, they were not just teaching about
Stonewall or the LGBTQ rights movement: they were talking
about lesbians who drove the woman suffrage movement, or
the queer poets who lifted the Harlem Renaissance. They could
see the change in their students, and I could hear the emotion in
their voices as they felt the impact of what they were doing.

They told me that they wished they had more source
materials, more content that was pitched to high school students,
and more visual material, as well. And each time, I thought to
myself, "I know some of that content," or "I know people who
have worked on that subject." My colleagues and predecessors
in the larger world of queer history had been mining the archives
for the kinds of stories these teachers craved. But they had not,
mostly, presented what they had been finding in the kind of
format and media that made it accessible to school teachers. I did

not know, myself, what that format would be, but I thought it was time to start trying nonetheless.

Eventually, I started working in three different ways. First, I woke up to the fact that I was teaching in a Master's program that was, mostly, designed to help certify New York City public school teachers. Rather than bemoaning the fact that they were not headed off to PhD programs, as some of my colleagues did, I started recognizing our students for the change agents that they were. I began assigning more queer history books in my graduate classes, and I asked them to consider how they could incorporate the material into their US history surveys. I did not always do a good job: I consistently assigned more than they could tackle, and I did not know what a good high school lesson plan looked like. But I kept at it, and they latched onto some of the material. Chauncey's *Gay New York* captivated them; they were compelled by the stories of queer soldiers in World War Two; and they saw quick connections between the Lavender Scare and their own understandings of the Red Scare.

I also started investigating how to work with current teachers. I was invited into a few different high school classrooms around the city and started to dialogue with teachers about what they knew, and what they wanted to know. Sometimes what they wanted was content, and I tried to distill the material from my graduate classes into mini-seminars – even a seminar series, at one point. But sometimes they wanted to understand how: How could I bring this material into my classroom and feel safe? How could I talk about queer history and not have students spout homophobic comments? How could I navigate pushback from administrators? When those questions came up, I often listened to how the other teachers in the room answered. More often than not, if they did not have the answer, they had an idea about it. They thought about parallels to their work teaching Black history or women's history, and how they navigated the different responses. It was clear that these teachers wanted to do the work but were not without worries. But it was also clear that, with enough support, they would find a way to do so.

Eventually, I joined forces with a friend – Stacie Brensilver Berman – and we developed Professional Development workshops for teachers, figuring out how we could launch a group of teachers into this material in a concrete and hands-on way in the space of an hour or two. Here is a concept or a topic; here are some juicy primary sources; and here is a sketch of a lesson plan: now you fill out the details.

Those PD workshops were exciting. Often one or two teachers voiced a doubt, but others reassured them. More often, when left to their own devices to dream up how to work with their students and the documents, the teachers came up with promising do-able ideas.

By happenstance, soon after, I also got invited to work with the City's Department of Education to help them develop a curriculum guide specifically focused on teaching LGBTQ+ US History. We discussed various ways to structure it and agreed that our goal was not to ask teachers to develop a separate unit on LGBTQ history, isolated from the other material they were teaching and burdening them with finding the time to squeeze such a unit into their schedules. Rather, we agreed, we wanted them to be able to weave LGBTQ content into their existing classes, supplementing the stories they were already telling with ones about a lesbian suffragist or a trans soldier. We landed on a proposal with 20 biographical studies, profiling individuals across US history, as well as five pieces about a particularly significant moment or era in queer history.

The curriculum guide is titled *Hidden Voices*, and although it was released during the height of the COVID shutdowns, it has been met with steady success. WNET, the local New York PBS station, decided to develop a series of classroom-ready videos to complement the *Hidden Voices* biographies. And the Department of Education put together a supplementary volume, with detailed lesson plans to simplify the work of teachers adopting the material.

It is hard to measure the impact of all of this work. So much of the feedback we receive is anecdotal. The GLSEN research makes clear that the impact we are having is happening in the most local of ways – teacher by teacher, school by school – so anecdotal evidence makes sense. We know that *Hidden Voices* is available across the New York City school system – which is educating roughly one million students each year. We know that teachers continue to come to our professional development workshops, often hosted by WNET, to explore the material and how to use it. I have had teachers I have met in other contexts tell me how useful they have found the guide to be. Former students, who are working now as teachers, have written me to say how excited they were to encounter *Hidden Voices* and start using it with their students. At the same time, we know that LGBTQ students and content have been the focus of dog-whistle attacks recently, particularly trans students, and that has definitely had a powerful impact on school climates.

Nonetheless, I was deeply moved when my own son came home from school last year, to tell me about the discussion they were having in his fourth-grade classroom. His experiences are already a constant reminder to me of how different his world is from the one where I grew up. Across elementary school, he has had multiple classmates with same-sex parents, as well as various friends who have explored modifying their pronouns. His cultural context feels so new.

On this day, as with many others, he started describing some of the material that had intrigued him in class. "Daddy, did you know..." And then he launched into a discussion of the gender ideals of some of the native peoples who had lived in the New York area. He talked about how women were highly regarded, but then began describing the way that some individuals, assigned to one gender at birth, were welcomed to live out their lives in another. Indeed, sometimes such individuals were treated with high esteem. I blinked and leaned in and asked him to repeat himself: my son was teaching me a unit from early American LGBTQ history.

As he repeated himself to me, I realized that his teacher, it turned out, had attended one of the PD workshops that Stacie and I had led at his school, a few years earlier. The content he described to me, though, was not a simple recitation of our material: the teacher had refashioned it, shaped it, and made it her own. We had planted a seed, but she had nurtured it, weaving it into her curriculum in her own way. And here was my

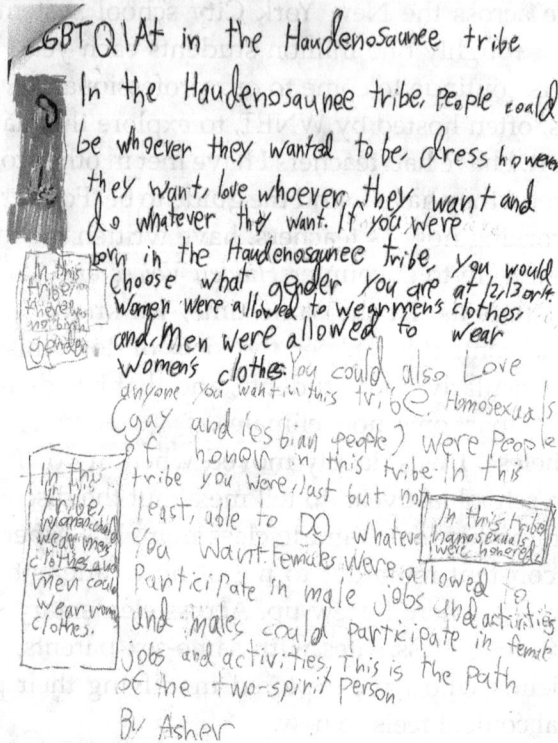

LGBTQIA+ in the Haudenosaunee tribe

In the Haudenosaunee tribe, people could be whoever they wanted to be, dress however they want, love whoever they want and do whatever they want. If you were born in the Haudenosaunee tribe, you would choose what gender you are at 12,13 or 14. Women were allowed to wear men's clothes, and Men were allowed to wear women's clothes. You could also Love anyone you want in this tribe. Homosexuals (gay and lesbian people) were People of honor in this tribe. In this tribe you were, last but not least, able to DO whatever you want. Females were allowed to Participate in male jobs and activities and males could participate in female jobs and activities. This is the Path of the two-spirit person

By Asher

In this tribe, there is no birth gender.

In this tribe, women could wear men's clothes and Men could wear women clothes.

In this tribe, homosexuals were honored.

FIGURE 1.2
Fourth-grade project on early American LGBTQ+ history.
Source: Photo by author

son, coming home from school, bearing the fruit of those efforts. I blinked again, this time with tears in my eyes.

What will it take to create a world where the homophobia that crushed Tyler Clementi is no longer part of the culture? I am sure that I do not know exactly. But I do know that every day, across the country, there are teachers who are, bit by bit, step by step, making that change happen. They are bravely and thoughtfully talking about LGBTQ lives as part of the broad sweep of American history and culture. In so doing, they are shifting the ways young people see the world around them. And I am terribly proud to play a role in that effort.

Reflections on Lesbian Pedagogy[14]

Bettina Aptheker

I began teaching at San Jose State University in the mid-1970s. I had a joint appointment as a lecturer in Women's Studies and Afro-American Studies. I was married, with two small children, a member of the US Communist Party and a deeply closeted lesbian. Mainly I taught an introductory course in Women's Studies, and another in Black Women's History. The Women's Studies class had a section on lesbian and gay people that I approached with the utmost trepidation. I focused mainly on the issue of civil rights for lesbian and gay people. This was, after all, only a few years after Stonewall. My trepidation came about, at least in part, because the Communist Party condemned homosexuality as a "degeneracy" and banned lesbian and gay people from membership. It had done so since 1938. (The ban was not lifted until 1991!). And I was a very closeted lesbian. In the course on Black women the issue did not (yet) arise. My courses emphasized radical and revolutionary movements propelling struggles for social justice. That was my comfort zone. I was a veteran of the Berkeley Free Speech Movement, the movement against the war in Vietnam, and the transnational movement to free Angela Davis.

Personally, I was a mess, riddled with contradictions, and with a yearning I was too terrified to realize.

This was *not* lesbian pedagogy.

The turning point for me came when I attended the Berkshire Conference on the History of Women in August 1978. A panel was scheduled with the title Lesbians & Power. The conference Program Committee, composed of university scholars, took the word "Lesbian" out of the title. The organizer of that panel was Audre Lorde. Audre Lorde described herself as a Black, Lesbian, Feminist, Mother, Warrior, Poet. She learned of the misnaming of the panel. And demanded that the word Lesbian be re-inserted. She printed a flyer with the correct title and the names of the three participants. Word spread like wildfire through the conference.

When the appointed time came almost 2,000 attended the panel in the largest auditorium on the Mt Holyoke College campus. Audre read her paper. It was called "The Erotic as Power." For me and many others, the idea of the erotic as a source of power was very new. She began:

> "There are many kinds of power, used and unused, acknowledged or otherwise. The erotic is a source within each of us that lies in a deeply female and spiritual plane, firmly rooted in the power of our unexpressed or unrecognized feeling."[15]

Lorde went on to explain that "every oppression {including the oppression of women} must corrupt or distort these various sources of power ..." because they "can provide energy for change."[16]

And then she described the erotic as both sexual and emotional, and as a source of knowing within each of us, and how writing, or teaching, or gardening, or dancing, or singing, or imagining can tap into that erotic knowledge of ourselves, of our deepest sources of joy and satisfaction.

I was mesmerized, dazzled, heart pounding.

The Q & A: Someone stood up and recounted the story I just told you, about the Program Committee changing the name and so on. And when she finished, she asked if all the lesbians in the room would please stand up. Almost the entire audience rose. I was glued to my seat, frozen and frightened. And I looked around me. I knew that many of the women who were standing were not lesbians. That was impossible. I was still sitting and everyone else had started to sit down again, and it occurred to me that the few of us who had not stood were the real lesbians, too afraid to show ourselves. And, in those moments, there was a dawning in my consciousness. Audre Lorde spoke the words: "The first thing a minority must do is make itself visible to itself." I knew about solidarity. I knew about how important allies were in social justice movements. I knew that all those women were standing in solidarity. In those moments I understood, in a visceral way, that visibility mattered, and that the way out of my fear was solidarity. Lorde's lesbian-rooted anti-racist pedagogy became a model for me. It would take me several more years before I could claim it and make it my own. In those intervening years I discovered Adrienne Rich's *Twenty-One Love Poems*, and her *Dream of a Common Language*, and myriad other works by her and by other lesbian feminist poets, artists, novelists, photographers, musicians, playwrights. All around me, there was a great flowering of radical feminist and lesbian culture, a new world awakening. And it awakened in me a new kind of pedagogy: from the personal to the political became a way of thinking, and a way of teaching. Delving into my experiences, and those of countless other women, drawing out their stories and the lessons to be learned. This was a kind of experiential teaching proposed by the Brazilian Marxist educator, Paolo Freire, but turned to an explicitly feminist purpose.[17] My assignments asked students to think about readings in relation to their own experience, and to analyze and interpret through that lens. This was a new way of thinking for a great majority of them. And sometimes it was very hard for them to do.

I began teaching as a lecturer at UC Santa Cruz in the winter of 1981. I had entered the History of Consciousness graduate program in fall 1979 with the grandiosity of youthful arrogance proposing to synthesize and reconcile Marxism and feminism! Of course, that's not what happened. Between San Jose State in 1975 and Santa Cruz in 1979 I divorced my husband, won physical custody of my children (in a joint custody arrangement), fell in love with a woman, left the Communist Party, published three books, and began teaching a course called Introduction to Feminism. I remained closeted. That is, I had a wide circle of friends who knew I was a lesbian, but I was not "out"/"out." I was developing a radical feminist pedagogy in which we explored gender, race, class, and sexuality as intersecting systems of domination always drawing upon women's experiences and putting "women at the center of our thinking," as I liked to say. I was still so nervous about sexuality and the lesbian experience that I always put that material towards the end of the class, almost like an epilogue!

I was not yet fully engaging a lesbian pedagogy, but I was getting closer to it.

Then near the end of the fall quarter in 1984, in my presentation on sexuality, a student asked a question which, if I had responded honestly, would have made clear my lesbian identity. I knew the student was gay, and I knew it really mattered to him. Nevertheless, I flubbed the question, deliberately answering it with a non-answer. I felt terrible about it. I wrestled with myself. And the next class, two days later, I told the students what I had done, why I had done it, and then threw out my lecture notes and talked about my experience as a closeted lesbian: my fears, brutalization by police and FBI, and why it mattered that I publicly claim a lesbian identity. There were some 400 students in that class, and they responded with unparalleled support and solidarity. It was a moment of great healing for me, and it ushered in a more fully articulated, more deliberate lesbian pedagogy. From then on, the lecture on sexuality came early in the quarter as I set up the theoretical/political framework for the course: women's oppression, racial oppression, class exploitation, and sexuality as a core identity. Then we could explore why a heteronormative, patriarchal, racist system of domination needed to control and suppress lesbian and gay identities, not as an afterthought, or as a phobia, or as a mere religious convention, but as an integral part of a structural apparatus of patriarchal domination and cultural imperative. This was an intersectional analysis begun almost a decade before Kimberley Crenshaw's ground-breaking law review essay, and the emergence of critical race theory. It grew out of the politics I had learned in the Communist Party, its homophobic insults, and antifeminist biases notwithstanding.

Teaching the introductory course, I was expected to use some kind of standard women's studies textbook, and for years I used varying editions of the text by Amy Kesselman, Lily D. McNair, and Nancy Schniedewind, Eds. *Women: Images and Realities, a MultiCultural Anthology*. I supplemented this with a long list of recommended books that often drew from those recently published focused on a variety of key issues. Publication of *This Bridge Called My Back*, edited by Gloria Anzaldúa and Cherríe Moraga in 1981, was a pivotal, paradigm-shifting intervention.

In fall 2008, the last year I taught the introductory course, I recommended, for example, Estelle B. Freedman, *No Turning Back: The History of Feminism* (2002), Angela Y. Davis, *Abolition Democracy: Beyond Empire, Prisons & Torture* (2005), Judith Herman, *Trauma and Recovery: The aftermath of violence – from domestic abuse to political terror* (1992 and 1997), Alison Bechdel, *Fun Home: A Family Tragicomic* (2006), among others. And then annually I put together my own reader, with essays, poems, stories, and/or oral histories. The reader was required. Over the almost thirty years that I taught this class, I variously included writings by Audre Lorde, Adrienne Rich, Gloria Anzaldúa, Paula Gunn Allen, Cherríe Moraga, Winona LaDuke, Mitsuye Yamada, bell hooks, Clarissa Pinkola Estés, Gail Nomura, Kitty Tsui, Alice Walker, Angela Davis, June Jordan, Irena Klepfisz, Judy Grahn, among others. Lectures expanded and varied as new issues emerged. Violence against women in its myriad forms and reproductive justice were always part of the core curriculum, but I included lectures in various years on Jewish women and the legacy of antisemitism, and/or prison abolition, and/or immigration, and so on. In every instance, I consciously sought to integrate anti-racist perspectives, and Black, Chicana, Native American, and Asian American women's voices, infused with what I thought of as a lesbian sensibility: women at the center, visible, with historical agency, and explicitly lesbian as often as possible. I showed films, played music, read poetry, using these mediums to keep the inter-locking systems of domination in a constant, dynamic play. This was how I developed a lesbian, pedagogical strategy that I intended to be inclusionary of everyone, including men. Likewise, I told students from the beginning that they didn't have to agree with me or write papers that were in accord with my views. I said the main thing was for them to think for themselves, using their own experience as they interpreted it, as long as they seriously engaged with the course materials.

Women were always at the course's interpretive center, and a woman-loving motif was at its emotional core. Alice Walker had once remarked that loving women "sexually and non-sexually" in a misogynist culture was a revolutionary act. I think this is at the center of lesbian pedagogy.

One of the most important things I learned about teaching is that regardless of the content of any particular curriculum, it is the energy we bring into the classroom that matters the most: inclusionary means open-hearted, and loving towards everyone, no exceptions. I also learned not to present material, especially if it was drawn from my own life experience, unless I was emotionally and intellectually comfortable with it. That is, I was no longer processing it, or integrating it, or synthesizing it. This meant that no matter how difficult the material – and women's suffering in all its multilayered, multicultural, multi-racial dimensions is often very great -- I could be relaxed, and non-defensive. This relaxation makes possible the energy of kindness, humor, and love.

I did not always succeed. Not by any means. Sometimes I kicked myself hard when a class didn't feel right to me, or didn't go the way I wanted it to. Insofar as I could, though, I would seek to "fix it" the next time we came together. And sometimes, you just can't do anything about the "chemistry" of a class, in which case, I learned that whatever I couldn't fix or change, I had to let go. That was often very hard.

Over the forty years that I worked at UCSC, I taught several undergraduate courses that included Feminism & Social Justice, Feminist Oral History & Memoir (a senior seminar), Feminist Cultural Productions, African American Feminist History. And I taught several graduate seminars including Feminist Pedagogy, and Black Feminist Reconstruction. I sought to maintain the same woman-centered and woman-loving strategies in all of those classes, even when there was little directly lesbian content. Later, at the invitation of the staff running the mass online learning program at UCSC, I produced a 4-lecture course on Feminism & Social Justice. It was launched on the Couresera Platform March 8, 2019. As of this writing (December 2023), more than 113,500 students have enrolled across every continent, forming a remark-able feminist global community. I have corresponded personally with scores of women.

In 2016 I developed a new senior seminar called Feminist/Queer Historiography. It was very much coming out of my experiences in archives while researching my book on lesbian and gay people in the Communist Party. Frustration abounded because Left or Communist archives almost never had a category for lesbian, gay, or even homosexual. And lesbian and gay archives almost never had a category for left, or socialist, or communist. By 2016, in the university, at least, the word "queer" had mostly supplanted "lesbian" or "gay" as being more inclusive of different sexualities, and transgender, inter-sex, and non-binary people. However, I was old enough to remember when "queer" was hurled at us as an insult in the 1940s and 1950s! Be that as it may, I was thrilled to teach this class and sought to employ the same elements of a lesbian pedagogy I had developed over the years. The purpose of the class, I wrote in the syllabus, was "to provide for a critical examination of canonical formations of history, and archives, and propose new ways of thinking about history from the point of view of those who have been marginalized and/or excluded by race, class, gender and/or sexuality. Issues will include the metaphysics of memory and the politics of memorializing, the significance of the personal as political, and the private as public; the politics of affect; queering historical agency; settler colonialism and the politics of elimination, epistemic violence, and professional accountability."[18]

I was especially keen on students thinking about archival sources that were not necessarily organized in libraries: "Our collective project will be to learn how to think about historical projects in creative, non-canonical, queer and imaginative ways and to re-vision what counts as archive, what counts as artifact, and what counts as history."

I was experimenting with ways of teaching about the "intersectional" and its exclusions at the very moments in which it was being institutionally constructed. I wanted to encourage students to think about history and archives outside of the conventional boxes. However, what was lost in the imaginative space of the "queer," was the singularity of the "lesbian." I was still a completely out lesbian, I was still woman-loving, the interpretive lens was still personal, and experiential. And yet …

Between my first teaching experiences in the early 1980s at Santa Cruz and my last in 2020, paradigms had shifted from "Women's Studies," to "Women & Gender Studies," or just

"Gender Studies," or in our case at UCSC to "Feminist Studies." Many of my colleagues insisted that the field of Feminist Studies was not exclusively or even primarily about "women," a designation increasingly made problematic by post-modern imperatives of categoric instability. This also included broad critiques of "identity politics" and racial and sexual identities. Did the "lesbian" actually exist?! I think in developing this class on "Feminist/Queer Historiography" I also was experimenting with these issues in my own mind, although it was not explicit in the curriculum.

Yes, I thought. We lesbians are alive and sometimes maybe even thriving. And I thought once again of Audre Lorde and a paragraph she wrote many years ago:

> Those of us who stand outside the circle of this society's definition acceptable women; those of us who have been forged in the crucibles of difference – those of us who are poor, who are lesbians, who are black, who are older – know that survival is not an academic skill...For the master's tools will not dismantle the master's house. They will never allow us to bring about genuine change.[19]

This is, perhaps, at the core of what we must think about as we continue to engage a lesbian/feminist pedagogy: what are the "master's tools"? How do we explore the paradox of teaching in universities in which we are departmentally successful and therefore increasingly institutionalized? Can the "master's tools" be strategically used without losing the more radical implications of a "women-centered," "woman-loving," inclusionary pedagogy?

In fact, these questions in one or another way, have informed the debates about Women's Studies from its inception, regardless of its post-modern nomenclature. This is because the field itself was born out of the Women's Liberation Movement, and for at least a dozen years it was animated by that political momentum. Theory was born out of practice, and practice informed theory. Likewise, debates in the 1980s reflected the strong influence of Marxist and socialist feminist ideas. Lorde's injunction against using the "Master's Tools" led some to question the position of

Marxism within that frame. For example, consider the debates in the 1980s and Heidi Hartmann's essay, "The Unhappy Marriage of Marxism and Feminism," or Catherine MacKinnon's essay around the same time, "Feminism, Marxism, Method, and the State." In addition, also in 1980, Gloria Bowles and Renate Duelli Klein edited their anthology, *Theories of Women's Studies,* that challenged the social sciences, especially on its insistence on "objectivity," privileging quantitative methods. The anthology by Gloria Anzaludúa and Cheríe Moraga, *This Bridge Called My Back,* made its heralded appearance in 1981. All of these works were much in tandem with what was happening in Afro-American Studies, Ethnic Studies, and Third World Studies more generally precisely because the experiential demonstrated the inadequacies of conventional, mainstream history and social science.[20]

It would seem to me that questions in the field of Women's and Gender Studies now, e.g., accessibility, inclusivity, and personal and political relevance, have circled back around insisting upon paradigm shifts that once again bring the potential for a woman-loving, woman-centered, racially inclusive, and transnational pedagogy to the fore.[21]

Notes

1   Rita Addessa, "Philadelphia Lesbian and Gay Task Force Education Equity Project Policy and Program Recommendations Report Excerpt," Carnegie Mellon University Libraries Digital Collections, September 1989, http://digitalcollections.library.cmu.edu/awweb/awarchive?type=file&item=553958.

2   Kevin Jennings, *Mama's Boy, Preacher's Son: A Memoir* (Boston: Beacon, 2006), 131–183; Laurie Casa Grande, "UNFORTUNATELY, HISTORY HAS SET THE RECORD A LITTLE TOO STRAIGHT" poster (Minneapolis: Gay and Lesbian Community Action Council, 1988); New York City Mayor's Office for the Gay and Lesbian Community, *Struggle for Equality: Lesbian and Gay Community,* New York City Board of Education Multicultural Education Curriculum (New York: Office of the Mayor, 1989).

3   California Department of Education, *Model Curriculum for Human Rights and Genocide: 1988 Edition with a New Forward and Preface* (Sacramento: California Department of Education, 2000 [1988]; Barbara Blinick, *Lesbian, Gay, and Bisexual Social Studies Lessons* (San Francisco: Support Services for Sexual Minority Youth, 1995).

4   Arthur Lipkin, "The Case for a Gay and Lesbian Curriculum," in *The Gay Teen: Educational Practice and Theory for Lesbian, Gay, and Bisexual Adolescents*, ed. Gerald Unks (New York: Routledge, 1995), 38; Commonwealth of Massachusetts Commission on Gay, Lesbian, Bisexual, and Transgender Youth, *Annual Report* (Boston: Commonwealth of Massachusetts Commission on Gay, Lesbian, Bisexual, and Transgender Youth, 2009), 32; Kevin Jennings, *Becoming Visible: A Reader in Gay and Lesbian History for High School and College Students* (Boston: Alyson, 1994); Arthur Lipkin, *The Stonewall Riots and the History of Gay and Lesbians in the United States* (Cambridge: Harvard Graduate School of Education, 1992); Arthur Lipkin, *Understanding Homosexuality, Changing Schools* (Boulder: Westview Press, 1999).

5   National Coordinating Council for Lesbian and Gay History Month, "Secondary Schools Packet for Lesbian and Gay History Month," August 1994, Jessea Greenman P.E.R.S.O.N. Project Records (GLC 104), Gay and Lesbian Center, San Francisco Public Library, Special Collections, Box 5, 1994.

6   Movement Advancement Project, "Equality Maps: LGBTQ Curricular Laws," www.lgbtmap.org/equality_maps/curricul ar_laws, accessed 10/04/2023; Massachusetts Department of Elementary and Secondary Education, *2018 History and Social Science Framework, Grades Pre-Kindergarten to 12* (Malden, MA: Massachusetts Department of Elementary and Secondary Education, 2018); Debra Fowler and Dr. Steven LaBounty-McNair, "Contextualizing LGBT History within the Social Studies Curriculum," National Council for the Social Studies, 2019, www.socialstudies.org/position-statements/contextualizing-lgbt-history-within-social-studies-curriculum.

7   "Historians and the 'Culture Wars' in Higher Education" roundtable, American Historical Association Annual Conference, San Francisco, January 5, 2024.

8   Instructional Materials and Curriculum: Diversity, AB1078, California Legislature (2023), https://leginfo.legislature.ca.gov/faces/billS tatusClient.xhtml?bill_id=202320240AB1078; Andre Scheeler and Lindsey Holden, "California Lawmakers Pass Bill Barring School Boards from Banning Inclusive Books, Curricula," *Sacramento Bee*, September 8, 2023, www.sacbee.com/news/politics-government/ capitol-alert/article279074994.html.

9   Elizabeth Meyers et al., "Elementary Teachers' Experiences with LGBTQ-Inclusive Education: Addressing Fears with Knowledge to Improve Confidence and Practices." *Theory into Practice* 58, no. 1 (2019): 6–17; Wendy Rouse and Don Romesburg, "Tips on Teaching K-12 LGBTQ+ History," *The American Historian* (Spring 2023), www. oah.org/tah/sports-and-leisure/tips-on-teaching-k-12-lgbtq-history/.

10 Joan Wallach Scott, *Gender and the Politics of History* (New York: Columbia University Press, 1999).

11 This idea is prominent in Michel Foucault's *The History of Sexuality*.

12 Judith Butler, *Undoing Gender* (New York: Routledge, 2004); *Gender Trouble: Feminism and the Subversion of Identity* (New York: Routledge Press, 2006).

13 "About Us," It Gets Better, accessed October 10, 2024, https://itget sbetter.org/about/.

14 This essay was originally published as Bettina Aptheker, "Reflections on Lesbian Pedagogy," *Journal of Lesbian Studies* (February 9, 2024): 1-9. Published online by Taylor and Francis Online, DOI: 10.1080/10894160.2024.2313260. Reprinted by permission of the publisher (Taylor & Francis Ltd, www.tandfonline.com).

15 Audre Lorde, "Uses of the Erotic, The Erotic as Power," in Audre Lorde, *Sister Outsider*, Trumansberg, New York: The Crossing Press, 1984, p. 53. Lorde's works have been reprinted in more recent editions. See, for example, *The Selected Works of Audre Lorde*, edited by Roxanne Gay, New York: W.W. Norton, 2020.

16 Lorde, *Uses of the Erotic*, p. 53.

17 Paulo Freire, *Pedagogy of the Oppressed*, 1970; reprint ed. New York, Continuum Publishing, 1995. bell hooks took him on about his sexism although he remained unrepentant. See, bell hooks, *Teaching* to Transgress: Education as the Practice of Freedom, New York and London: Routledge, 1994. See especially, "Paulo

Freire," pp. 45–58. bell hook's books were excellent resources that I used for mentoring both graduate and undergraduate students in teaching. However dated the sources given its date of publication, the book holds up in its insistence upon race conscious, feminist pedagogies.

18　The syllabus for this class, and syllabi for all of my courses, are available in my archive, Bettina Aptheker Papers, Special Collections, McHenry Library, University of California, Santa Cruz.

19　Audre Lorde, "The Master's Tools," in Audre Lorde, *Sister Outsider*, p. 112.

20　Heidi Hartmann, "The Unhappy Marriage of Marxism and Feminism," in Zillah Eisenstein, ed. *Capitlaist Patriarchy and the Case for Socialist Feminism*, New York: Monthly Review Press, 1979; Catharine Mackinnon, "Feminism, Marxism, Method and the State: An Agenda for Theory," *Signs, Journal of Women, Culture and Society,* Vol. 7, No. 2, 1982; Gloria Bowles and Renate Duelli Klein, eds., *Theories of Women's Studies*, Berkeley: University of California Press, 1980; Gloria Anzaldúa and Cheríe Moraga, eds. *This Bridge Called My Back: Writings By Radical Women of Color*, New York: Persephone Press, 1981. It is interesting also to consider the "Editor's Note" preceding the essay by Catharine Mackinnon in *Signs:* "Central to feminist theory and feminist method, as Catharine Mackinnon shows is consciousness-raising of women's conditions by examining their experience and by taking this analysis as the starting point for individual and social change. By its nature, this method of inquiry challenges traditional notions of authority and objectivity and opens a dialectical questioning of existing power structures, of our own experience, and of theory itself."

21　See, for example, Abigail Boggs and Nick Mitchell, "Critical University Studies and the Crisis of Consensus," *Feminist Studies*, Vol. 44, No. 2, 2018, pp. 432–463.

References

"About Us." *It Gets Better*. Accessed October 10, 2024. https://itgetsbetter.org/about/.

Addessa, Rita. "Philadelphia Lesbian and Gay Task Force Education Equity Project Policy and Program Recommendations Report Excerpt."

Carnegie Mellon University Libraries Digital Collections. September 1989. http://digitalcollections.library.cmu.edu/awweb/awarchive?type=file&item=553958.

Anzaldúa, Gloria and Moraga, Cheríe, eds. *This Bridge Called My Back: Writings By Radical Women of Color*. New York: Persephone Press, 1981.

Blinick, Barbara. *Lesbian, Gay, and Bisexual Social Studies Lessons*. San Francisco: Support Services for Sexual Minority Youth, 1995.

Boggs, Abigail and Mitchell, Nick. "Critical University Studies and the Crisis of Consensus." *Feminist Studies* 44, no. 2 (2018): 432–463.

Bowles, Gloria and Klein, Renate Duelli, eds. *Theories of Women's Studies*. Berkeley: University of California Press, 1980.

Butler, Judith. *Undoing Gender*. New York: Routledge, 2004.

Butler, Judith. *Gender Trouble: Feminism and the Subversion of Identity*. New York: Routledge Press, 2006.

California Department of Education. *Model Curriculum for Human Rights and Genocide: 1988 Edition with a New Forward and Preface*. Sacramento: California Department of Education, 2000 [1988].

Casa Grande, Laurie. "Unfortunately, History has set the Record a Little too Straight" Poster. Minneapolis: Gay and Lesbian Community Action Council, 1988.

Commonwealth of Massachusetts Commission on Gay, Lesbian, Bisexual, and Transgender Youth. *Annual Report*. Boston: Commonwealth of Massachusetts Commission on Gay, Lesbian, Bisexual, and Transgender Youth, 2009.

"Equality Maps: LGBTQ Curricular Laws." Movement Advancement Project. Accessed October 4, 2023. www.lgbtmap.org/equality_maps/curricular_laws.

Foucault, Michel. *The History of Sexuality*. New York: Pantheon Books, 1978.

Fowler, Debra and LaBounty-McNair, Steven. "Contextualizing LGBT History within the Social Studies Curriculum." National Council for the Social Studies. 2019. www.socialstudies.org/position-statements/contextualizing-lgbt-history-within-social-studies-curriculum.

Freire, Paulo. *Pedagogy of the Oppressed*. New York: Continuum Publishing, 1995 [1970].

Hartmann, Heidi. "The Unhappy Marriage of Marxism and Feminism." In *Capitlaist Patriarchy and the Case for Socialist Feminism*, edited by Zillah Eisenstein. New York: Monthly Review Press, 1979.

"Historians and the 'Culture Wars' in Higher Education" roundtable. American Historical Association Annual Conference. San Francisco, January 5, 2024.

hooks, bell. *Teaching to Transgress: Education as the Practice of Freedom*. New York and London: Routledge, 1994.

Instructional Materials and Curriculum: Diversity, AB1078. California Legislature. 2023. https://leginfo.legislature.ca.gov/faces/billStatu sClient.xhtml?bill_id=202320240AB1078

Jennings, Kevin. *Becoming Visible: A Reader in Gay and Lesbian History for High School and College Students*. Boston: Alyson, 1994.

Jennings, Kevin. *Mama's Boy, Preacher's Son: A Memoir*. Boston: Beacon, 2006.

Lipkin, Arthur. *The Stonewall Riots and the History of Gay and Lesbians in the United States* Cambridge: Harvard Graduate School of Education, 1992.

Lipkin, Arthur. "The Case for a Gay and Lesbian Curriculum." In *The Gay Teen: Educational Practice and Theory for Lesbian, Gay, and Bisexual Adolescents*, edited by Gerald Unks. New York: Routledge, 1995.

Lipkin, Arthur. *Understanding Homosexuality, Changing Schools*. Boulder: Westview Press, 1999.

Lorde, Audre. "The Master's Tools." In *Sister Outsider*, 110–113. New York: The Crossing Press, 1984.

Lorde, Audre. "Uses of the Erotic, The Erotic as Power." In *Sister Outsider*, 53–59. New York: The Crossing Press, 1984.

Lorde, Audre. *The Selected Works of Audre Lorde*. Edited by Roxanne Gay. New York: W.W. Norton, 2020.

Mackinnon, Catharine. "Feminism, Marxism, Method and the State: An Agenda for Theory." *Signs, Journal of Women, Culture and Society* 7, no. 2 (1982): 515–544.

Massachusetts Department of Elementary and Secondary Education. *2018 History and Social Science Framework, Grades Pre-Kindergarten to 12*. Malden, MA: Massachusetts Department of Elementary and Secondary Education, 2018.

Meyers, Elizabeth, et al. "Elementary Teachers' Experiences with LGBTQ-Inclusive Education: Addressing Fears with Knowledge to Improve Confidence and Practices." *Theory into Practice* 58, no. 1 (2019): 6–17.

National Coordinating Council for Lesbian and Gay History Month. "Secondary Schools Packet for Lesbian and Gay History Month." August 1994. Jessea Greenman P.E.R.S.O.N. Project Records (GLC 104). Gay and Lesbian Center, San Francisco Public Library, Special Collections. Box 5, 1994.

New York City Mayor's Office for the Gay and Lesbian Community. *Struggle for Equality: Lesbian and Gay Community*. New York City Board of Education Multicultural Education Curriculum. New York: Office of the Mayor, 1989.

Rouse, Wendy and Romesburg, Don. "Tips on Teaching K-12 LGBTQ+ History." *The American Historian*. Spring 2023. www.oah.org/tah/sports-and-leisure/tips-on-teaching-k-12-lgbtq-history/.

Scheeler, Andre and Holden, Lindsey. "California Lawmakers Pass Bill Barring School Boards from Banning Inclusive Books, Curricula." *Sacramento Bee*. September 8, 2023. www.sacbee.com/news/politics-government/capitol-alert/article279074994.html.

Scott, Joan Wallach. *Gender and the Politics of History*. New York: Columbia University Press, 1999.

2

Voices from the Classroom: Teachers' Perspectives on the Importance of LGBTQ+ History

The essays in this chapter, authored by high school teachers working in different parts of the country, focus on why and how they incorporate LGBTQ+ topics into their classes. They discuss the transformative effects that LGBTQ+-inclusive academic settings can have for students individually and collectively, and the need to integrate information that is too often omitted from the resources from which students learn. In addition to sharing stories from their backgrounds and their classrooms, each of the teachers affirms that it is feasible, enlightening, and important to weave LGBTQ+ topics throughout the curriculum over the course of the school year.

The essays highlight the importance of reversing years of curricular omissions in the interest of developing lessons, activities, and resources that honor students' identities, represent all learners, and push back against the inaccurate notion that queer and transgender individuals did not exist until modern times. They emphasize the need for safe, inclusive learning spaces where students feel comfortable being and expressing themselves without fear of reprisal and the ways that integrating LGBTQ+ topics can help to create those spaces. The teachers

DOI: 10.4324/9781032689678-4

also acknowledge the need for grassroots efforts to make inclusive academic classes a more widespread reality. They discuss working collaboratively with colleagues at their schools and beyond to develop materials and teachers' responsibilities to serve as role models leading the charge to create meaningful changes in students' experiences.

Ultimately, each of the teachers makes a compelling argument for consistently reflecting on their practice, considering the ways in which they are and are not serving their students, and dedicating themselves to revising their goals and philosophies to ensure that students leave their classes feeling seen, respected, valued, and inspired. In an era when teachers are too often put in positions where they fear opposition and censorship, these essays demonstrate that doing this work is possible and necessary because, in the words of Justin Martinez, "we must teach our students a history that loves them back."

The Words We Teach Our Children Shape the World

David Duffield

All journeys begin with a question signified by the words we teach each other. As a social studies teacher who studies queer history, the question often begins "where are the stories of queer people like me?" It is a question that promises discovery, passion projects, and great inward change, yet can be marked with fear and exceptional challenges to one's worldview. The way through the fear is to tell stories.

History is firstly a conversation about the past to understand the present. Secondly, it is a process of discovery and rediscovery through interpretation and reinterpretation. Finally, it is a generational allegory to create and foster self-awareness in storytelling. Thus, the words we teach our children shape the world in a process of conversation, discovery, and storytelling which culminates in establishing our shared heritage. The classroom is a special space for this process beginning in questions.

In the fall semester of 2020, a colleague asked me to help her bring examples of LGBTQ history into her eighth-grade American History classroom. I had a great deal of experience as an LGBTQ historian in Colorado, and we settled on the story of General Friedrich Wilhelm Von Steuben. He was a gay, Prussian, Revolutionary War general who helped save the Continental Army at Valley Forge, which, in effect, helped save the United States. Von Stueben's story is often footnoted, but his sexuality is almost always hidden. This reveals a duality of oppression and potential for liberation. Knowing his story creates empathy for people like him, a sense of injustice, and questions about the suppression of his story. It also moves the soul to right a historical omission – particularly if one is also queer. This same sense sparked questions that fostered choices for me.

I wondered what incorporating more LGBTQ history into world studies would be like, so I began with a question: What did LGBTQ history look like in the ancient world? I looked for examples of queer history in the ancient world. We were teaching curriculum on ancient Egypt and Babylon, so I pored over books on weekends focusing on the history of gender and sexuality in those cultures. The process was simple but time-intensive; I was enraptured in modes of discovery I never knew. I found I was able to describe queer stories throughout those cultures and link them to existing cultures. People shared similar names and ways of life. There were *many* ancient queer historical continuities and similarities. I felt like I had rediscovered a lost queer heritage.

I discovered that in ancient Babylon gender diverse people were often accepted in the priestly class. In ancient Egypt, some dynasties were highly accepting of lesbian relationships. I advanced the study to LGBTQ history in the African Diaspora, Islamic Golden Age, and Pre-Columbian peoples like Nahua (Aztec) and Maya. The weight of personal discovery was elating, but lingered in the question: Why did this work seem like the first of its kind?

I made notes on as many secondary sources as I could and put my research notes together for my fellow teachers. Our social studies team wholeheartedly supported the idea of teaching more LGBTQ history. Once I finished the notes, I created a list of key research points, which became the basis of lesson plans with examples of primary sources. Once we finished, we taught the lessons in the second semester in our school network, got student feedback data, and set our review timeframe for six months. During this process, we entered a transition period of civil unrest and political riots.

The riots at the Capitol on January 6, 2021, occurred in the middle of a planning meeting the first week back from our winter break. We tried to emphasize to our students that they were safe and discussed how to process and reflect on what the events meant. We had great conversations about the meaning of democracy and perspectives of both sides. They were the kinds of discussions that make you proud to be a history teacher. I realized we were changing history by talking about it. It was as if I beheld a generational change in our hybrid classroom because this generation would grow up with both resilience and good historical understanding. Their world would be shaped differently.

Over the course of the semester, we taught the lessons, gathered feedback data, and spoke at length about it. The student feedback was overwhelmingly positive. For a semester, hundreds of students learned about LGBTQ people in cultures to which they often had direct connections. Many were surprised that there were LGBTQ people, third-gender, and gender non-conforming people in history. One of my GSA students later remarked how a grandparent in their life was ignorant to think transgender people were a recent immoral development, though we realized that her grandparent had never been taught about transgender people in school like everyone else. This was a "heritage robbery" faced by most groups.

We all learned about queer people before the Spanish conquests who were accepted and valued. They read the poetry of a Nahua women loving woman to her partner. They learned about gender diverse expressions in syncretic religions like Voodoo and Santeria, as well as re-reading narratives like Olaudah Equiano's for LGBTQ references and the widespread, sacred roles for third-gendered people in Africa. They learned about the gender non-conforming *Mukhannath* in Islamic history, the traditions of women loving women known as *Tharifa*, and how Western modernization in Egypt and Turkey rejected homosexuality as immoral. It was apparent that the contemporary, Western world had *radically oppressed global queer heritage*.

I often reflected on that oppression. I knew it had many names and forms such as globalization, colonialism, and slavery. Most of the research came from authors in history, anthropology, and sociology which was often twenty to forty years old. It became a further puzzle why that knowledge had not been applied in American education. I wondered if I was simply one of the first to write on the subject of global queer history. I moved schools at the end of the Spring semester in 2021, so in order to keep the work alive I created a website—globalqueerheritage.com—as a free resource for teachers with lesson plans, research notes, and primary sources, with plans to add lessons on India and China.

In the year that followed, I reflected more and more on why this work had never been done before. In American history, it was apparent that LGBTQ history had never made the leap to education because of taboos about LGBTQ people. Until the 1980s, teachers could be fired for even being out, and not until the 2000s were LGBTQ groups for teachers and students more widely tolerated in spaces like Gender and Sexualities Alliances (GSAs). Even as I wrote my lesson plans others were writing "Don't Say Gay" legislation in states like Florida, banning discussion of LGBTQ people, or rolling back reproductive healthcare laws. Stigmas, fears, and taboos continued simply because LGBTQ people were forbidden from questioning history.

One evening in June of 2022, as I worked on the website for lessons on China and India, it occurred to me to see what inclusive LGBTQ social studies education looked like around the world. I pored over the globe continent by continent, country by country, and found groups like those in the US in California and New Jersey who helped get LGBTQ history into classrooms. Scotland mandated LGBTQ inclusive education in 2021. There were *many* people around the world asking similar questions. I discovered education professors in Canada and Tasmania who created guidance for more LGBTQ inclusive education, and groups of teachers and citizens in New Zealand and Mexico who developed LGBTQ inclusive lesson plans.

There were whole countries which seemed rife with potential to create LGBTQ inclusive education. Yet, oddly, they were always in developed countries, and for successful change they needed a constituent group of people to fight for inclusive LGBTQ history. In effect, they needed space to ask questions as well as foment change. It was apparent there was a potential global movement.

I was heartened to find out about the work of others who created Committees on LGBTQ History Month around the world, referencing Rodney Wilson, the teacher who created LGBTQ History Month in 1994. Yet, greater work must be done within education, and sparking the conversation between educators *everywhere* is the first step to begin the world of work ahead.

The end of this story is not simply a discovery of ancient knowledge. It is a realization that you and I, dear reader, are bound to something larger than ourselves. We are moved to rise with each other, to ask questions, to know that the chorus of our voices and stories may liberate queer heritage from the void of oppressive silence. Every conversation and story we tell in the classroom or especially between teachers changes history. The end of this chapter leaves an impression of erasure of global queer stories, and the posing of a question: do you see LGBTQ history in your classroom or world?

The beginning of the next story is other teachers' choice to tell these stories and ask that question. Teaching global queer heritage forces us to continue asking important questions and fervently moves one towards making profound discoveries. It foments great change, for the words we teach our children shape the world.

Our Pedagogy is Our Movement

Justin Martinez

When we ask better questions, we are forced to become better answers. So, let's start with a question: How can we create an island of transgressive joy in what can often be a sea of hatred, violence, and erasure for our LGBTQ+ students?

<u>Answer:</u> **Reject colonial logic.**
Colonial logic refers to mindsets and practices associated with the perpetuation of colonialism and its legacies. Oppressive social constructs such as racism and homophobia are firmly rooted in such colonial logic; it is imperative that we reject it. Society has never existed without queerness. The queer experience has existed longer than white supremacy and heteronormativity; it will persist as long as love and life do. If only my younger self had heard this rejection of colonial logic from a teacher—if only he had seen himself and those like him in the history being taught—he might have loved himself a bit more. His forced ignorance regarding people who shared identities similar to him deprived him of historical role models while also fostering an internalization of this historical erasure. The curriculum being taught to him was vicious. It taught him that people who loved the way he loved were not deserving of love. It taught him that people like him have no place in society since they had no place in history.

This is not simply anecdotal: Leaving queer histories out of curricula is both "irresponsible and violent," according to Stephanie P. Jones in her work on curricular violence. She goes on to state that such practices harm how LGBTQ+ students see themselves in history and damage them emotionally and intellectually.[1] Our society has been led to perceive violent curricula as a social norm, especially as we witness a contemporary climate of censorship and oppression in education. Consequently, our queer students have consistently been exposed to a master narrative that rejects their existence. It is only through the rejection of colonial logic—the logic that creates homophobia—that we can ensure that our queer students feel seen and loved. Therefore, we must not only teach our students a history that they love but, most importantly, we must teach our students a history that loves them back. A history that loves a student looks like them, shares experiences similar to theirs, and addresses their existence not as the historical other but as a beautiful, central component of the historical narrative.

Love is not inherently romantic; we can show our students love and so can our curriculum. In her foundational work *All About Love: New Visions*, bell hooks suggests that in order to love, one must consistently show "care, affection, recognition, respect, commitment, and trust, as well as honest and open communication."[2] It is worth asking to whom our curricula show each aforementioned quality of love. Is it showing **care** to our queer students? Is it showing **affection** to the young gay boy who was rejected by his family? Is it **recognizing** the intersectionality of the queer students of color? Is it **respecting** the pronouns of the student who just began their transition? Is it **committing** to deliver content that celebrates each of their identities? Is it **trusting** in the young lesbian woman's ability to be her authentic self? When we ask ourselves these questions, we become better answers as we open an honest dialogue with ourselves and with our students about what education can and should be. However, even if we are hitting all the questions above, there is still the reality that is the world outside of our classroom.

When schools institutionalize diversity, equity, and inclusion, classrooms that are culturally responsive and anti-racist in their pedagogical approaches become more commonplace; however, despite both individual and collective efforts, our society remains undeniably oppressive. Even the institution of education itself is systematically flawed and historically structured in a manner that has been antithetical to the success of marginalized populations. This harsh reality sets the foundation for what is perhaps the most challenging facet of ensuring the safety of our LGBTQ+ students: We, as educators, can make our classrooms spaces that both empower and provide a platform for students who hold marginalized identities, but we must simultaneously reckon with the fact that their identities will continue to be oppressed outside the classroom setting. It is for this reason that we must always remember that teachers are not neutral participants in their classrooms. Pedagogy is a protest against the injustices that exist both within and outside of the walls of academia.

Ask yourself: Does your protest result in catharsis or movement?

Merriam Webster defines catharsis as a purgation that brings about a release from tension whereas movement is defined as an individual or collective mobilization designed to promote or attain an end. This dichotomy defined by catharsis and movement is best exemplified by Tracey A. Benson's scholarship concerning race-conscious education which certainly applies to our LGBTQ+ students. Benson contends that equity is an adaptive challenge to which we wrongfully attempt to apply technical solutions.[3] We know that it is vital to include LGBTQ+ voices in our classroom, but the matter of *how* becomes far more complex. When considering a diverse curriculum, Benson suggests that we ask ourselves two questions:

1. What is in it for the students? How will it benefit them?
2. How will we know we have succeeded? Do we have the infrastructure to measure the success of what we deem an equitable curriculum?[4]

Taking these questions into consideration when constructing curriculum for our LGBTQ+ students informs us that our solution cannot be technical. Accordingly, one unit on Stonewall will not suffice. Adaptive challenges are messy and multifaceted, thereby requiring more complex and creative solutions. The identities of our students should be interwoven into our instruction, and they are the experts on this matter. Therefore, the adaptive solution to the adaptive challenge of inclusive curriculum is the establishment of a democratic classroom where students co-construct content. The act of a negotiated space and content not only humanizes the space, but it also ensures that the values of students and their identities are mirrored in the space.[5] When we entrust students with the development of their learning, not only are they engaged in the teaching and learning process, but they are also allowed to actively question, deconstruct, and disrupt systems. **What's in it for the students?** They co-construct an environment and curriculum that is meaningful to them and their identities, ensuring their safety and providing them with a platform for their voice and the voices of their peers. **How do we know we have succeeded?** Quantitatively, we can deduce this through student engagement and success data points. However, it is arguable that the qualitative answer is far more fulfilling: Students leave our class thinking not that we are the best teacher, but that they are a phenomenal human and that they are loved. Students should leave the class with a deep knowledge concerning how they embody excellence and how they can continue to be agents of change. Through doing so, we can establish and maintain healthy student-to-world relationships that promote joy and have the ability to heal trauma.

Overall, in the history classroom, it is our priority as teachers for students to determine their definition of what it means to be a good citizen and a good person. Not only does this benefit our LGBTQ+ students, but it benefits all of our students. Often, we are bombarded with the perception that in order to be effective citizens and people, we must be the facilitators of change on a relatively large scale. However, our students ought to know that it is equally powerful even if the only person they save through change is themselves. Self-care for queer individuals is something that is inherently radical as it transgresses what are all too often portrayed as dark histories plagued by oppression. Contrary to common portrayals, queer history is defined by beauty and liberation which are the essence of self-care. Taking the time to care for oneself is the purest form of resistance in a society that continues to oppress queerness. However, students may not innately have the tools of self-care, instead opting for numbing activities such as Netflix or endless scrolling on TikTok. While numbing activity can be contextually beneficial, it is not self-care. As educators, we have the power to provide our students with a toolkit of self-advocacy and care. For our queer students, this can include ensuring that school counseling staff are an active part of the classroom community, that we provide alternatives to what can be triggering content, and that we are trauma informed educators. We are models for their excellence and for the tools necessary to care for oneself in the history classroom and beyond. Accordingly, student well-being can be a form of protest, and leaving our class understanding this through finding voice and agency in a manner that is empowering to them is key to sparking movement as opposed to catharsis.

Question: What is movement, again?

Answer: Our pedagogy is our movement.

Education has long been weaponized by the United States: Native American assimilation via education or the withholding of education from African Americans, for starters. Today, the American trend persists when considering the censorship of the LGBTQ+ lived experience. This censorship is often in pursuit of a "true" history. Obviously, the history (or lack thereof) being advocated for when considering censorship is truth's antithesis. So, how do we actually teach a *true* history to our LGBTQ+ students? Find the counter-narrative, and that is where you will find the true history. Counter-narratives are stories that detail the experiences and perspectives of those who are historically oppressed, excluded, or silenced, and they have the power to empathize with *all* of our students; counter-narratives reject colonial logic. The counter-narratives exist already, and it is our job as educators to simply make them *the* narrative. James Baldwin famously stated that "you think your pain and your heartbreak are unprecedented in the history of the world, but then you read."[6] We are the authors of the book that is history for our students, and we are here to tell them that they are not alone. We, the queer, have existed longer than white supremacy and heteronormativity. We will persist as long as love and life do.

"After a Hurricane, Comes a Rainbow"[7]: Why Our LGBTQ+ Students Need Our Classrooms

Lauren Jensen

The lights dimmed, and my classroom monitor lit up my classroom creating a halo of light around Tiana.[8] She would be presenting her "moment memoir" movie to the class. As a culmination to our memoir genre study, students were tasked with writing their own memoir, zooming in on a moment in time, and then transforming their writing to film through accompanying music and personal photos. As I sat in the dark amongst my students in our community circle, I could feel my heart rate increasing and my pupils widening. Tiana took a deep inhale and then let out an audible exhale as she hit return on the keyboard and her digital memoir commenced. She and I exchanged a brief glance, I winked at her, gave her a thumbs up, and immediately her shoulders relaxed, and she confidently grounded her feet to the floor, commanding the attention of her sophomore peers in our English 10 class.

This was going to be her moment.

Carefully selected lyrics from Katy Perry's song "Firework" cradled the bottom of each image that appeared on the screen, accompanied by Perry's raspy and airy vocals. As Perry crooned the words, "Do you know that there's still a chance for you? / 'Cause there's a spark in you" tears welled up in Tiana's eyes. Her breaths quickened as she shifted her gaze between her peers and the computer screen.

Tiana, known to her parents and her peers as her birth name, Timothy, was transgender. While she waffled between her birth identity and who she *knew* she *really* was, changing clothes when she arrived at school and retrieving her Chanel lipsticks, Gucci eyeshadows, and Dior blushes from my bottom file cabinet drawer, only to securely stow away her "Tiana stash" in my classroom each afternoon before returning home, she had only "officially" come out to herself and me after intense journaling in my sophomore English class. Her peers had an inkling, but she was fraught with fear over how the world would react. While we had established a community of trust, care, and acceptance, at the time (2010) the world was far from embracing the transgender identity. Despite her initial hesitation, Tiana felt cautiously confident about publicly coming out in the cocoon of our classroom community.

Just as the tension that only she and I could feel reached a crescendo, the words ' "Cause baby, you're a firework/Come on, show 'em what you're worth/Make 'em go, "Oh, oh, oh"/As you shoot across the sky" '[9] consumed the computer screen as Katy Perry simultaneously belted the lyrics. On the screen: Tiana's favorite image of herself: a photograph of purely authentic, gorgeously real, confidently cool Tiana, donning cutoff denim shorts, and a face full of fresh makeup.

This was her moment. Her time to tell her story.

The video ended, but the lyrics "After a hurricane, comes a rainbow" burst through my computer speakers and the class erupted in applause. Students cheering, clapping, some giving a standing ovation, others lining up to high five and hug Tiana. No better words could have bolstered Tiana's coming out moment than those. In a release of the weight she had been shouldering for years, she wept. For herself. For the members of the LGBTQ+ community who came before her, and for those who would come after her. The road to self-acceptance can be rocky, especially when it is paved with the fear of others' reactions. Tiana could not ignore the opportunity to use the safe space of our classroom community to embrace her reality.

On many occasions, long after school was dismissed, Tiana and I discussed the tensions of being transgender –the desire to free herself of her assigned identity – but also the fear of rejection. It was not only our relationship and my overt support of her identity that fostered the safety of our classroom. The foundation of my teaching philosophy is hinged upon open and honest communication, respectful disagreement, and empathetic engagement with perspectives that we do not understand. While it does not happen overnight, I introduce students to these non-negotiables the first day they enter my classroom. Students embrace this ideology and are each other's champions well beyond the ten months they sit in my classroom.

It would be naive to think that Tiana's coming out journey was all sunshine and rainbow Pride flags. But at that moment, Tiana felt safe. Secure. Proud. Worthy. And most importantly, accepted.

Tiana was not the only student to come out in my class. There was Cristian. Eduardo. Devon. Emily.

I remember a phone conversation with Tiana's mother shortly after she came out. She was not angry at me for giving space to coming out, but she truly could not understand what it meant to be transgender, nor how to engage with this new reality. Grounding her did not work. Neither did throwing out her makeup. In a hesitant attempt at acknowledgement, she called me.

"Miss Jensen, please explain to me *how to love* my son when he is dressing like a girl. He is not my child. When we have family over, I am embarrassed. I do not know how to explain why our son is wearing girls' clothes. Teach me how to accept him. To love him. To not want to hide him from the world."

At that moment, when she needed words most, I was speechless. As a 27-year-old teacher, I was not equipped to respond to her plea. I consider myself a gifted teacher, but this was the Rolls-Royce of requests. I do not remember how I responded at that moment, but eventually, Tiana would undergo a gender transition.

Tiana's story, and the coming out experiences of my other LGBTQ+ students, often bring me back to the same questions: *Why my class? What is it about my class, or classrooms like mine, that foster the confidence to come out? Is it me as a teacher? Is it the content I prioritize? Is it the sense of community that we, myself and my students, cultivate in our class?*

Despite civil rights gains for individuals who identify as LGBTQ+, schools are still places where many students feel the need to conceal this part of their identity. There is much to learn in my English class, but above all else, I want students to feel proud to be themselves, to feel seen as worthy and beautiful just as they are, and to experience a community of respect, cultural curiosity, and pride.

A few years after Tiana graduated, I interviewed her for a graduate degree study that was unrelated to her coming out in my class, but somehow, we found ourselves recounting her "coming out memoir moment." I asked her if she could articulate the impetus for coming out in my class, resurfacing the *"Why me? Why my class?"* questions.

In her words: "What I think most LGBTQ+ students love, particularly about English class, is the ability to imagine realities that we grow up thinking are impossible. Your class helped me create worlds and realities for myself that helped me develop actual ideas of love and self-awareness. Journaling, too. Journaling in your class changed my life. The hardest thing about being different is being unable to put those feelings into words, and it really moved me on the journey to self-awareness. Not only did it teach me to write to process my thoughts and make discoveries about myself, but it also gave me the skills to tell my story in a way that brings listeners or readers to tears."[10]

To feel safe and seen. To feel valued and capable of success. To craft an authentic voice and harness the power to use it. These are simple concepts– and ultimately, they are expressions of our students' achievement and the outcomes of effective pedagogy. When I entered the classroom as an educator in 2002, I naively believed these outcomes would be easily achievable. I did not realize the extent to which these pillars of education are inaccessible for so many students, most especially members of the LGBTQ+ community.

In a world where "fewer than 25 percent of those students see positive representations of [LGBTQ+] people in their classrooms"[11], our students need advocates. They need windows and mirrors of their experiences in our classrooms. The pedagogical moves I make in my classroom to provide these opportunities and demonstrate advocacy include (but are not limited to):

◆ Writer's notebooks and daily writing time for students to discover and honor their voices.

- ◆ Genre studies such as the memoir unit which gave Tiana a platform to come out.
- ◆ An inclusive classroom library that is the home to many voices– authors and characters alike–age, race, gender, ethnicity, religion, sexuality, etc.—inspired by my students' reading requests.

These instructional strategies create an inclusive environment for my students wherein the curriculum prioritizes valuing their identities. This is not enough. Through my relationships with students–which begin the first day of school with my own letter of introduction to them – I break open my heart and hand it over to them. I share some of my life's greatest tragedies – the loss of my mom and dad, as well as my most difficult personal and professional decisions –choosing to leave a doctorate to return to teaching. Through my own vulnerability and daily interactions with my students, I have been able to build trust, encourage empathy, provoke a drive for understanding, and perhaps most importantly, spark safety and respect. These are the qualities that our LGBTQ+ students need. Scratch that– that *all* students need.

LGBTQIA+ History and the Dignity of Students

Olivia "Olive" Garrison

It is challenging to watch the news and not notice the clash of cultures that seems to be happening in schools and school boards across the United States surrounding the inclusion of LGBTQ+ issues in public education. 86.6% of students are never taught about LGBTQ+ people, their histories, or important events.[12] As a student, I searched every textbook and every lesson for a chance to spot anyone of significance who was like me. Despite all my searching, the only place I found anyone like me was the dictionary. This communicated to me that, while other people like me must exist, they did not do anything worthy of historical attention. Queer theorist and poet Adrienne Rich articulated this experience when she said,

> When those who have the power to name and to socially construct reality choose not to see you or hear you...when someone with the authority of a teacher, say, describes the world and you are not in it, there is a moment of psychic disequilibrium, as if you looked in the mirror and saw nothing. It takes some strength of soul--and not just individual strength, but collective understanding--to resist this void, this non-being, into which you are thrust, and to stand up, demanding to be seen and heard.[13]

To be part of a world that does not acknowledge your existence is a painful reality for most students.

This painful reality mirrored my own experience in many ways. Educators in my life were either too scared, under prepared, or too uncomfortable to teach about LGBTQ+ people. The result was an impression that LGBTQ+ people were not allowed to be spoken about by respectable people. Instead, conversations about them or even with them were relegated to the shadowy and lonely places.

In fifth grade, a friend of mine showed me the book, *The Care and Keeping of You* by Valorie Schaefer. The book is an educational self-help book for girls about puberty and the growing body. Immediately, I felt as though this book belonged in the shadows. To me, this book felt exposed, raw, and unashamed. The next week, my family went to the local bookstore. I impatiently tapped my foot, waiting for a moment alone; a moment to find that book. When I finally was set free in the children's section, I slowed my pace and meticulously ran my fingers across the spines of each book until I found it. I sat on the steps of the children's section and read the entire book as quickly as I could, one eye over my shoulder to protect my privacy. Each time my family went to the bookstore, I found my copy and I felt safe knowing that my body existed, if only in a book. Upon reflection, this was a pivotal moment in my adolescence. *The Care and Keeping of You* opened my eyes to the possibilities of literature. Reading the pages and absorbing the illustrations, I realized that not everyone lived their lives in the shadows.

In high school, a group of my friends decided that we wanted to create the first Gay-Straight Alliance (now called the Gender and Sexuality Alliance). We found members, a faculty advisor, and created plans to elect our student representatives. The administration of the school quickly reminded us that our place was in the shadows. Someone suggested we change our name to reflect "friendship" rather than sexuality. As if our mere existence was too shameful to read over the announcements. How could we expect students to say the word "gay," let alone attend meetings? The message was clear: we do not belong in the sun, and we do not deserve dignity. Our group persisted despite this pushback. Imagine if our energies were used to serve our community rather than to fight for a right to exist.

It is our responsibility to teach students fair, accurate, and inclusive history because LGBTQ+ people have been active agents in history and our students deserve the truth. LGBTQ+ did not solely exist in the shadows. Teachers should include LGBTQ+ history in their curriculum because it promotes school safety, improves student well-being, and because it ensures an accurate and critical portrayal of historical events. Our students should not be looking all over the curriculum just to catch a glimpse of themselves or even to settle for nothing.

All students deserve to feel safe at school and the inclusion of LGBTQ+ curriculum in schools is a necessary component of safety for LGBTQ+ youth. Students want to learn about their own histories, and they want their peers to, as well. In my experience, students feel safe when their identities are treated with respect and not hidden away. Ignorance breeds fear, and fear is at the heart of homophobia. In every classroom, students come to school with preconceived notions about the world and other cultures. Our role as history educators is to provide students with a safe environment to explore their ignorance and foster understanding and inclusivity. Most students are filled with empathy when they learn about the struggle for civil rights or the oppression of marginalized people.

Incorporating LGBTQ+ history in education is crucial for enhancing student well-being. The National School Climate Survey emphasizes the connection between inclusive curriculum and students' mental and emotional well-being. Compared to students in schools without an LGBTQ+-inclusive curriculum, LGBTQ+ students in schools with an LGBTQ+-inclusive curriculum "had better educational outcomes, were more comfortable engaging in conversations about LGBTQ+ issues with their teachers, and had a greater connection to their school community."[14] This is vitally important in a community in which depression and suicide rates are much higher than the national average. As a Gender and Sexuality Alliance advisor for many years and a queer person, I have seen firsthand the psychological strain that homophobia and transphobia have on queer youth. If we want to save lives, the data makes it clear how to achieve this goal: teach students about their histories in a way that is both respectful and truthful. Respect builds dignity and self-worth.

In her TED Talk titled, "The Danger of A Single Story," Chimamanda Ngozi Adichie outlines the dangers of funneling many stories into a single narrative.[15] She states, "The single story creates stereotypes, and the problem with stereotypes is not that they are untrue, but that they are incomplete. They make one story become the only story... ."[16] Nowhere is this more relevant than in the history classroom. Traditional history curriculum has often brushed over or explicitly excluded the contributions and experiences of LGBTQ+ people. Textbooks, a foundational resource in social studies classes, rarely include significant information on LGBTQ+ related content. Following the practices that are often used in history classrooms, educators are teaching core historical concepts with missing and, often, inaccurate information. Erasure communicates to students that only certain peoples' stories are worthy of our attention, no matter how impactful they are. As educators, we act as both archivists and as world-builders in our classrooms.

When we pick and choose whose voices will be highlighted and whose voices will be silenced, these choices speak volumes to our students. The art of exclusion works to support the status quo and repress the rights of our students. If you choose to cover the civil rights movements of the 20th century and you leave out Gay Liberation, your silence speaks. This practice of erasing and excluding Queer people from our own stories robs us of respect, dignity, and complexity. Queer stories are American stories and there is nothing un-American about our stories. In my own classroom, Queer stories are presented at the same level as other American stories. Students appreciate this approach because it does not further alienate them. Following the approach of James A. Bank, I have sought to incorporate LGBTQ+ curriculum with the goal of social action through a paradigm shift.

At the beginning of my journey to transform my curriculum to include the voices of diverse LGBTQ+ people, I began with small inclusions that celebrated the contributions of members of the LGBTQ+ community. The lesson was on the contributions of Alan Turing to the defeat of the Axis powers. I prepared myself for what I believed would be the inevitable negative remarks and backlash I would receive from students. In contrast, most of my students simply went about their day as if I was teaching any other historical event. After the class ended, two students lingered behind their peers, dancing awkwardly on their Converse. One foot and then the other. When I approached them, the bravest of the two said, "You know, I have never heard a teacher talk about gay people before. Ever. Thank you for doing that." I was not shocked to hear this because, as I previously mentioned, I had also never learned about LGBTQ+ people in school. The first time I heard a teacher talk about LGBTQ+ people within the context of history was in college. However, the reality that few things had changed since my own primary education left me feeling empowered to give these students the education that they deserve. After all the fear and anticipation, the reaction I remember most from my students was gratitude.

This interaction pushed me to think about ways that I could include LGBTQ+ people in the major themes and concepts of my classes rather than adding single-day lessons. I began to work with a team of social studies teachers across the state of California to create lessons and curriculum that either could be added to current curriculum (like the Lavender Scare in the Red Scare or the Gay Liberation movement during Civil Rights) or events that would benefit from a queer analysis (HIV/AIDS pandemic, the Black Freedom Movement, etc.). We were able to successfully include LGBTQ+ history in each unit and develop a queer thematic perspective of the curriculum as a whole.

The result of this hard work was a well-developed queer curriculum that placed queer voices as one of the central experiences of American History. Students interact with inter-sectional queer people and themes throughout the entire course. This allows students to develop critical thinking around the development of queerness and their own identities. One of my favorite lessons examines Queer Suffragettes during the Women's Suffrage movement. Students are particularly drawn to Mary Walker, who fought for women to have equal rights with men on all social fronts. In one interview she said, "I don't wear men's clothing; I wear my clothing." One of my non-binary students pointed out that it was inspiring to learn about other gender transgressive people in history because it made them feel "seen." As if they looked in the eye of Mary Walker and saw themselves.

I recently collaborated with my college level students to create a project in which students examine marginalized voices in United States History. To do this, we ask students to consider

FIGURE 2.1
Portrait of Dr. Mary Edwards Walker. Photo courtesy of the Library of Congress.

what it means to be marginalized and how marginalized people have responded and rebelled against erasure. Students have the option to explore the intersectionality of these marginalized voices and write an argument for why our history classes should include the important contributions and voices of this specific marginalized person in the curriculum. In accordance with past experiences, students created essays and presentations that pulled these marginalized voices from the shadows into the light of the classroom. One of my favorite essays and presentations focused on the composer Julius Eastman, who once said, "To be what I am to the fullest: Black to the fullest, a musician to the fullest, and a homosexual to the fullest." The student argued that all music classes should examine his brilliance, especially since his work has been erased because of being unapologetically gay and Black. Another student argued that to learn about religion and abolition in America we must include the Public Universal Friend, an agender Quaker activist. Others focused on Marsha P. Johnson's contributions to transgender liberation and the gay rights movement. This project was important to my students because it allowed them to teach their peers about a person that deserves our attention.

In conclusion, the ongoing struggle over the inclusion of LGBTQ+ issues in public education reveals a divisive cultural clash in schools and school boards across the United States. It is evident that LGBTQ+ history is indispensable in public schools for the safety and well-being of all students and for the sake of historical accuracy. To address these shortcomings, it is essential for educators to recognize the responsibility they hold as both archivists and storytellers in the classroom. Our students deserve our respect. The impact that LGBTQ+ history education has had on my students, our campus climate, and my own dignity has been profound. When I began my teaching journey, I was deep in the closet. I let fear and shame lead my curricular choices. I chose to include LGBTQ+ history in my own classroom because I was determined to give my students a more meaningful experience than the one I had. Ignoring LGBTQ+ history perpetuates a void that causes psychic disequilibrium for students whose stories are neglected. Embracing inclusivity in education, on the other hand, empowers students to confront oppression, build dignity, and to acknowledge the rich diversity of American stories.

Notes

1   Stephanie P Jones, "Ending Curriculum Violence," Learning for Justice, Spring 2020, www.learningforjustice.org/magazine/spring-2020/ending-curriculum-violence.
2   bell hooks, All about Love: New Visions (New York, NY: William Morrow, an imprint of HarperCollins Publishers, 2022), 5.
3   Tracey A. Benson, "Education for Liberation: The Role of the Race-Conscious Educator in Combating Oppression." (People of Color Conference, St. Louis, 12/01/2023).
4   Benson, Education for Liberation.
5   Carla Marschall, "The Power of a Democratic Classroom," Edutopia, July 27, 2021, www.edutopia.org/article/power-democratic-classroom.
6   Jane Howard, "Doom and Glory of Knowing Who You Are," LIFE Magazine, May 1963, 81.
7   Katy Perry, "Firework," recorded August 2010, track 4 on Teenage Dream, Capital Records.
8   All student names are pseudonyms.
9   Katy Perry, "Firework," recorded August 2010, track 4 on Teenage Dream, Capital Records.
10 Conversation with Tiana, January 2012.
11 "Best Practices for Teaching LGBTQ Students: A Teaching Tolerance Guide," Learning for Justice, accessed October 10, 2024, www.learningforjustice.org/sites/default/files/2018-09/TT-LGBTQ-Best-Practices-Guide.pdf.
12 "Teaching Respect Finds Having an LGBT-Inclusive Curriculum..," GLSEN, accessed January 24, 2024, www.glsen.org/news/teaching-respect-finds-having-lgbt-inclusive-curriculum.
13 Adrienne Rich, Blood, Bread, and Poetry: Selected Prose, 1979–1985 (New York: W.W. Norton & Company, 1986), 199.
14 Joseph G. Kosciw, Caitlin M. Clark, & Leesh Menard, The 2021 National School Climate Survey: The experiences of LGBTQ+ youth in our nation's schools (New York: GLSEN, 2022), 131.

15   Chimamanda Ngozi Adichie, "The Danger of a Single Story," TED Talk, accessed January 24, 2024, www.ted.com/talks/chimamanda_ngozi_adichie_the_danger_of_a_single_story?language=en.
16   Adichie, The Danger of a Single Story.

References

Adichie, Chimamanda Ngozi. "The Danger of a Single Story." Chimamanda Ngozi Adichie: The danger of a single story | *TED Talk*. Accessed January 24, 2024. www.ted.com/talks/chimamanda_ngozi_adichie_the_danger_of_a_single_story?language=en.

Benson, Tracey A. "Education for Liberation: The Role of the Race-Conscious Educator in Combating Oppression." People of Color Conference, St. Louis, MO, January 12, 2023.

"Best Practices for Teaching LGBTQ Students: A Teaching Tolerance Guide." Learning for Justice. Accessed October 10, 2024. www.learningforjustice.org/sites/default/files/2018-09/TT-LGBTQ-Best-Practices-Guide.pdf.

hooks, bell. *All About Love: New Visions*. New York, NY: William Morrow, an imprint of HarperCollins Publishers, 2022.

Howard, Jane. "Doom and Glory of Knowing Who You are." *LIFE Magazine*. May 1963.

Jones, Stephanie P. "Ending Curriculum Violence." Learning for Justice. Spring 2020. www.learningforjustice.org/magazine/spring-2020/ending-curriculum-violence.

Kosciw, Joseph G., Clark, Caitlin M., & Menard, Leesh. *The 2021 National School Climate Survey: The Experiences of LGBTQ+ Youth in Our Nation's Schools*. New York: GLSEN, 2022.

Marschall, Carla. "The Power of a Democratic Classroom." *Edutopia*. July 27, 2021. www.edutopia.org/article/power-democratic-classroom.

Perry, Katy. "Firework." Recorded August 2010. Track 4 on Teenage Dream. Capitol Records.

Rich, Adrienne. *Blood, Bread, and Poetry: Selected Prose, 1979–1985*. New York: W.W. Norton & Company, 1986.

"Teaching Respect Finds Having an LGBT-Inclusive Curriculum..," GLSEN. Accessed January 24, 2024. www.glsen.org/news/teaching-respect-finds-having-lgbt-inclusive-curriculum.

3

Voices in Higher Education: Teacher Educators' Perspectives on LGBTQ+ Inclusive Curriculum

Teacher educators are in a unique position to contribute to efforts to integrate LGBTQ+ topics into K-12 classrooms. They are responsible for preparing emerging teachers and equipping them with the concrete and intangible skills they need to educate their students. Moreover, they have the power to impart knowledge and influence emerging teachers' pedagogical philosophies. Practicing teachers, including those who incorporate LGBTQ+ history, assert that one reason it is omitted from the curriculum is because it is largely absent from most teacher preparation programs.[1] Ultimately, the way that we prepare teachers has an impact on the ways that they teach their students. When teacher preparation programs provide strategies for teaching LGBTQ+ topics, including focusing on joy and resistance, the middle and high school students in those new teachers' classrooms reap the benefits.

The essays in this chapter, by teacher educators in California, New York, Minnesota, and Rhode Island, discuss building media literacy skills, working with diverse and engaging sources, emphasizing joy and resilience in learning, overcoming challenges, and instilling in teachers and students the knowledge

DOI: 10.4324/9781032689678-5

that they are agents of change. They focus on the benefits of learning and teaching LGBTQ+ history and share a variety of strategies for doing so. The essays also highlight the need for authentic learning experiences and the necessity of providing students with "windows and mirrors" so that they become more aware of themselves and the world around them. The authors understand the obstacles that exist and the challenges that teachers have to navigate to incorporate this information in the curriculum. But this does not diminish their resolve that LGBTQ+ history belongs in all history and social studies classes, can be made more accessible for all students, and that a teaching force prepared to do this work has the power to change lives.

"These Walls Aren't Straight and Neither Am I": Reflections of a Gay Black Professor

J.B. Mayo, Jr.

For over 20 years, I have been thinking and writing about the lives of queer people – primarily gay men – in educational settings. In an explicit move to take back a derogatory phrase referring to straight men who will do anything for money, I joke with my students saying that I have been "gay for pay" for a long time. In 2003 when I discovered that I could actually conduct a study centered on gay people and themes, I was simultaneously surprised and elated because I never before had imagined being able to study something so personally meaningful that would actually "count" as research. And so, I embarked upon this journey trying to figure out how gay male teachers were able to navigate their identities as gay men, while teaching young people and figuring out how to bring their authentic selves into the classroom. My dissertation project was, in fact, an attempt to make sense of my own lived experience as a closeted gay teacher who taught middle school in rural and suburban Virginia. To this day, I still seek ways to live and teach authentically, feeling quite fortunate having landed in a city and at a university as a professor of social studies education where I do not feel compelled to hide important aspects of my identity. Here, I am able to bring my whole self to the many spaces that I occupy.

In this essay, I respond to the important question, *Why is it essential to integrate LGBTQ+ history into the curriculum in the 21st century?*, and I take up this task by reflecting on a key moment in my younger adulthood when I more fully realized the strength of the queer community I had found after 30+ years of searching and hoping. I will then reflect back to memories and feelings from my younger self growing up in rural Virginia and how one historical site began to open doors for me even before I had the courage to walk through them. As I take you along this personal journey, I hope the rationale for integrating LGBTQ+ history into the curriculum will become evident.

The key moment to which I referred earlier took place in June 2001 at a gay alumni event at the University of Virginia. Known as the Serpentine Society, this group of LGBTQ+ alumni meets each year during class reunions located on UVA's grounds in Charlottesville. Because I was teaching middle school in the area, I attended this annual event even though it was not my reunion year. Besides, it always felt good to hang out with other gay alumni, many of whom had built successful, professional lives while I remained closeted in my middle school classroom. At some point during this weekend event, a speaker retold the story about why Thomas Jefferson had constructed the many curved, brick walls – known as the serpentine walls – found all over the site of the original UVA grounds. There was a shortage of bricks at the time, which only allowed for a single layer of bricks to be used during the construction of the walls, and Jefferson knew that the curved shape offered more strength and stability than the more-commonly used single-layered (and straight) construction. Upon hearing this retelling, someone yelled out, "Yes, the walls aren't straight, and neither are we!" There was a roar of laughter among the people at this outdoor event, and we were all reminded of the reason our gay alumni group was known as the Serpentine Society. Like the walls that were found all over our beloved university, we were not straight. In that moment of laughter, I felt like I was part of a larger community – not some idealized group plucked from a movie or work of fiction, but rather a community of fellow LGBTQ people who had the common experience of having gone to college at this particular university and in my home state of Virginia … so close to home.

That last part is particularly significant because "home" had never been a safe place for me to fully realize, embrace, and live out my gay identity. Home was never a place where I heard positive things said about gay people. Home was not the site of any LGBTQ knowledge at school. Home was a rural community, located in central Virginia where my family had lived for generations before me. I came of age during the 1980s at a time when the AIDS pandemic evolved from a blip on society's radar to dominating the headlines, a time when those who contracted HIV were shunned, ridiculed, and ultimately left to die – often alone – when their HIV status evolved into full-blown AIDS. In this rural area, the church was an important site of community, and it was particularly important to my grandmothers that I attend church regularly. And though I excelled there, teaching Bible School lessons to younger peers when I was a pre-teen and fully accepting the Biblical stories I heard as "truth," I also knew that my burgeoning gay spirit would not be accepted there. Though not openly spoken, I knew that members of the congregation wholeheartedly believed that HIV/AIDS was a punishment sent directly from God, handed down because of the immoral behaviors of gay people, and gay men in particular, similar to the Biblical story of Sodom and Gomorrah, two cities destroyed by God for their wickedness. Because I did not have any knowledge that would provide me a counter narrative, I accepted the idea that all gay people were a special brand of sinner, and that I was one of them. Further, if I allowed myself to act upon the feelings that were stirring inside, especially during those difficult years when puberty raged, I was doomed to eternal damnation. Therefore, I decided at a very young age that I would keep my feelings a secret, that I would bury them so deeply that they would, in fact, disappear and allow me to have a "normal" life, which included finding a girlfriend, asking her to be my wife, and then having children with her. I had made up my mind, and I was barely 11 years old at the time.

I remember this time period so vividly and can pinpoint the age of this vital life decision because though there was no knowledge being presented at school about gay people, gay history, or gay themes, there were fleeting moments when glimpses of LGBTQ+ themes appeared as I watched the television in the family room, a common pastime for me and my family. In fact, as the family sat down to watch *Dynasty* (1981–1989), a weekly nighttime drama depicting the lives and tensions between two rich, rival families – the Carringtons and the Colbys – I was completely intrigued by the younger son in the Carrington family, Steven, whose boyfriend was "accidently" killed after falling down a long, winding staircase in one of the earliest episodes of the show. I distinctly remember how Steven grieved the loss of his loved one and how his boyfriend's death forced Steven's dad, Blake Carrington, to acknowledge Steven's gay identity. In a very dramatic moment, Fallon, Steven's sister and confidante, demanded that their dad say the words out loud. *Steven. is. gay!* I remember thinking to myself, "I hope Daddy never has to say that about me." To my knowledge, he never did. Daddy passed away on April 27, 2020, without me ever "officially" coming out to him.

Part of the reason this moment was so compelling to me was because I had already become cognizant that I was different from my other male friends. Though I did not have the word "gay" as part of my vocabulary two years earlier in 1979 – at the tender age of 9 years – I knew that I had a serious crush on the main character, BJ McKay, in the television series *BJ and the Bear* (1979–1981). In this popular TV drama/comedy, BJ – played by Greg Evigan – traveled the countryside, driving his big rig alongside his pet chimpanzee, Bear, solving the problems of various damsels in distress along the way. Indeed, the lyrics sung using BJ's voice before each episode said in part:

> *Rollin' down to Dallas,*
> *Who's providin' my palace,*
> *Off to New Orleans or who knows where.*
> *Places new and ladies, too,*
> *I'm B.J. McKay and this is my best friend Bear.*[2]

So, while I endured believing that my ultimate fate was eternal damnation as evidenced by the plight of gay men acquiring HIV and eventually AIDS, I also experienced childhood crushes and all the joy and wonder that came along with them. While keeping my dark secret safely tucked away, I was enamored by various male characters on TV and eventually by a few of my childhood, male friends with whom I could safely wrestle, sit (too) close to during school choir practice, and join for sleepovers. Particularly fond memories place me at summer camp, coincidentally located at the University of Virginia, having intimate conversations with male roommates long after mandatory "lights out." There was something magical found in the darkness of those hot, non-air-conditioned dormitory rooms that allowed my roommates and me to share things in our inquisitive minds that would never come out during the light of day. I held on to those moments knowing that whatever had been shared had to be concealed the next morning.

This emotional back-and-forth and the charade that caused it continued throughout high school and my undergraduate years at the University of Virginia. While secretly admiring various male bodies from afar, I worked hard to cover my gay identity. I went through the expected motions of asking various female friends to high school dances, including Homecoming and two proms, and even had a "fraternity sweetheart" during the pledging period of my historically Black fraternity. Whenever I was questioned about not having any serious relationships with women, I shrugged it off saying that I was just too busy with my academic work and the many clubs to which I belonged in high school and college. I then engaged in serious exercise as a way to literally "run away" from having to acknowledge my gay identity and what that meant for me as a young person, now in his 20s, with an uncertain future in terms of family. During my years in the classroom, I fully engaged in extracurricular activities like sponsoring the Student Council Association, participating in the running club, and attending as many student soccer/football/basketball games as possible. I worked hard never to reveal any aspects of my gay identity. I monitored closely the clothes I wore, the way that I talked, and my body's movements while in front of the classroom. I never talked openly about my private life to fellow teachers, and I even allowed students to create false girlfriends for me. At one point in the minds of my curious middle schoolers, I was engaged in a torrid love affair with the English teacher on my team at school, and I let them run with it, as long as it did not take up too much time in class. In the meantime, making myself extra busy, running those many miles, and living in denial could not contain my desire to experience something more. I met someone, came out to myself, and normalized my dual identity. I was a straight, single teacher at school, the straight good son at home, and a young, fit gay man living in a small city, feeling guilt and shame after each encounter with a man.

And so this brings me back to that fateful meeting of the Serpentine Society in June 2001. At that moment, I realized there was a community for me. I realized that many people like me found happiness and enjoyed successful careers. I also realized that like those serpentine walls at UVA, I was actually stronger because I was *not* straight. I realized how resilient I had been over those many years of doubt, confusion, and denial. Even if living a dual existence was heartbreaking at times, as I often shed tears after openly lying to loved ones about where I had been and/ or who I was with, I had learned to cope and I drew strength from overcoming many of the stereotypes associated with gay men. I even rejoiced in the reframing of my "sexual deviance" into acts of defiance against the heteronormative world in which I lived. Despite owning these seemingly positive perspectives, however, many of the challenging lived experiences I endured could have – and perhaps should have – been avoided. I feel very fortunate having found academic success at school and having a strong network of friends and teachers who stood by me even when they did not fully understand the root cause of my down times. And even the family members who openly expressed homophobic views loved me. Because of these circumstances and the many people in my corner, I enjoyed enduring feelings of self-worth and confidence. I fully realize, however, that not all young people are so fortunate. For them and for me, given the homophobic community in which I was raised, the impact of a history curriculum that included LGBTQ+ people and themes would have been life changing. If I had been exposed to only a few of the courageous, intelligent, visionary (and even the villainous) LGBTQ+ people and groups that have always existed, I would have felt less isolated sitting in classrooms thinking that I was uniquely abnormal. I would have realized that I was by far not the only one having had these tension-filled feelings as I witnessed the relative ease with which my straight friends moved through the dating years. Importantly, a curriculum that included LGBTQ+ people and themes would have normalized the existence of gay people and offered me language and the counter narrative that I so deeply desired when I repeatedly heard gay people referred to as abnormal, sinful, shameful, and deserving of sickness and even death given the choices they had made.

And this gets to the fundamental reason why an LGBTQ+-inclusive curriculum must be offered in history classes: Kids like (late elementary-high school age) me are still sitting in classes yearning to see people like us appear in the class materials that teachers use. Kids like us are still waiting to be included in the historical accounts retold by our history teachers and for our experiences to be counted as part of the norm. Kids like us are bringing queerness into the classroom despite all the negativity that, to this day, plagues our society. If a kid like me found ways to experience moments of queer fascination and wonder in his rural classroom during the 1980s without the advantage of smartphones and the Internet, then surely modern-day queer kids are bringing more of their authentic selves into all the spaces they occupy. Therefore, these young people would greatly benefit from an LGBTQ+-inclusive curriculum and teachers who are equipped to teach it. Queer students deserve teachers who are aware of their various needs, regardless of the students' sexual orientation or gender identity. When teachers are able to offer students an LGBTQ+-inclusive curriculum, queer students feel safer at school, and their sense of well-being and achievement increases. Students remind us that when they feel unsafe at school because of their sexual or gender identity, it negatively impacts their school engagement and work ethic. Further, a lack of safety impacts the overall learning environment, causing academic success to be hindered. But when teachers offer an LGBTQ+-inclusive curriculum, "LGBTQ youth see themselves reflected [there], and they can feel hopeful about their own futures."[3] At the same time, all students – queer, straight, and everyone in between – experience nuanced learning opportunities and an increased ability to understand others when teachers offer a curriculum that is inclusive of LGBTQ+ materials.[4] So, despite this current (political) moment when conservatives are advocating for book bans and curriculum censorship, teachers must be brave and push back. At this moment when homophobia and transphobia appear to be on the rise, it is more important than ever for teachers to include LGBTQ+ themed materials in their history lessons so that students have the knowledge and language they need to verbalize and live a more inclusive truth. Teachers, kids like me are depending on you.

Queer Comics as Windows, Mirrors, and Magical Portals in LGBTQ+ History

John M. Palella, PhD

"Professor P, Professor P," my student Leo shouts from the doorway of my classroom one crisp September morning. I am intently preparing a "Queering US History" timeline on the board and reply, "Yes Leo, is everything ok?" He excitedly responds, "I read ahead on the syllabus and saw that we are reading comic books! I love comic books, but what do comic books have to do with LGBTQ+ history?" I look at Leo and laugh because of his enthusiasm but also at the uncomfortable familiarity of being asked how something Queer-related "has to do with history?" I know that comic books, not LGBTQ+ history itself, drive the question, and my "discomfort" proves fleeting. Students start filing in behind Leo, and I return to my incomplete timeline as I proclaim: "Ahh, Leo, comics are just one of the many windows, mirrors, and magical portals in LGBTQ+ history that we are exploring this semester, and in my opinion, the most important!"

Leo is one of 20 students in my "Teaching LGBTQIA History" course at Brown University. Students in this undergraduate seminar reimagine secondary US history curriculum through the experiences of LGBTQ+ folx from the Revolutionary War up through the current Culture Wars. We begin with the premise that LGBTQ+ histories belong in every social studies class because of the examples of resilience, resistance, and joy that the curricula provide to all students. After delving into chronologically structured Queer historiography and culturally sustaining pedagogies, my students then create a unit plan on American LGBTQ+ history that high school social studies teachers could actually teach. We align all of our units with the Rhode Island Social Studies Standards as well as the National Council for the Social Studies thematic strands. We ultimately "donate" the unit plans to Brown University's student and mentor teachers in our partner-schools. While my own students have carte-blanche in

terms of content for the unit, I do require each unit plan to provide all potential learners with windows, mirrors, and magical
portals through LGBTQ+ history.[5] Simply, a high school student
of any intersectional identity could learn about an individual
or a community whose experiences differ from their own; the
curriculum equips and empowers students to see themselves or
reflect on their own experiences; students take a creative journey
through the vast universe of LGBTQ+ history via a storytelling
apparatus such as comic books.

"Windows" into various communities and cultures com-
prise the foundations of secondary social studies education.
Moreover, the intersectional nature of LGBTQ+ historiography
provides all students with an infinite number of windows into
the lives of various individuals and communities. My students
slated Queer comics as the perfect teaching tool for exploring
these windows, and more specifically, as windows into histories
of HIV/AIDS activism of the 1980s and '90s. Students plunged
into robust discussions of Marvel Comics' first openly gay character, Northstar, who in one issue, "came out" as a Gay man,
living with HIV/AIDS, and raising an adopted HIV+ daughter.
The class decided that Northstar's story provided all potential
learners a "window" since no students would encompass all
of those identities. Highschoolers could use Northstar's story
to discuss the complex experiences of people living with HIV/
AIDS in different historical periods as they reflected on their own
understandings of HIV/AIDS today.

The windows into Northstar's experiences generate
discussions of LGBTQ+ resilience in the face of persecution
and discrimination. The comics reframe HIV/AIDS "victims"
as changemakers through their portrayal of activist groups like
ACT-UP and AIDS Vancouver. My own college students had
not all learned about ACT-UP and none had heard of AIDS
Vancouver. Thus, the comics sparked lively discussions of young
people also learning new content through comic books. Learners,
my students concluded, can leverage both the visual and textual
portrayals of the HIV/AIDS activism as counternarratives
to the typical texts that they encounter in their social studies
classrooms. Moreover, my students championed media literacy

skills by comparing and contrasting comics' portrayal of people living with HIV/AIDS with other media, such as FX's *Pose*, and more traditional sources like students' history textbooks. Queer comics, as windows, provided new content as they facilitated deep discussion and honed critical thinking skills for all students in social studies classes.

Next, our class turned to Marvel's first Gay wedding as a source of curricular "mirrors" for young people. Marvel publicly supported Marriage Equality by marrying Northstar off to his longtime partner Kyle Jindau. Marvel, by 2012, had virtually represented all racial, ethnic, gender, sexual, religious, and generational identities and highlighted the wedding as its diversity panoply. Heroes, anti-heroes, and the regular folx from all across Marvel's most popular comics attended the nuptials thus allowing all students to envision themselves in the rainbow of guests. My students analyzed the images and texts from the wedding and crafted assignments for learners to "find themselves" within the story. Some curricula asked learners to find a character in the crowd that looks like them and then create a backstory for that character. Others challenged students to locate their favorite Marvel hero in the audience and then research the character's history using the "thinking like a historian" paradigm.[6] One team proposed a Socratic seminar on why their chosen character would or would not support Marriage Equality and compared it to their own stance on the subject.

The curriculum-as-mirrors assignments both reflected and reified resistance as a major theme in LGBTQ+ history. As Marvel provides multiple wedding guests' perspectives on gay-marriage-as-resistance, young people can reflect on what resistance means to them. We compared the hypermasculine heroes at the wedding with highschoolers resisting toxically masculine peer pressure at school. One student asked, "what would it mean for a cis-straight-football player to see Wolverine in the front row supporting Northstar and Kyle as they kiss at the end of their vows?" Some students highlighted the parallels between the support of the X-Women and the stories of allyship of GSAs that we had unpacked.[7] One team focused on the students from the X-Men academy who disobeyed their parents' wishes by attending the wedding. We concluded that the character development within the wedding story would speak to students of all gender and sexual identities thus provoking questions about what resistance looks like to them on a daily basis. I had to pull my own college students out of the funhouse of mirrors in Queer comics in order to move onto different topics, so I imagine secondary teachers would fare similarly.

While some Queer comics provide windows and others function as mirrors, all narrative forms of LGBTQ+ history can serve as magical portals for high school students. We defined a magical portal as a "creative way of exploring history that combines historical fact with scaffolded imagination that produces the desired result of joy."[8] That is, high schoolers should play with historical or science fiction in order to provide a Queer (or any historically liberated) person a happy-ending to their historical narrative. I then introduced my students to Somnus, a superhero who can control people's dreams. Somnus, a young, Queer, BIPOC immigrant, visits disenfranchised people's slumber and effectuates visions of a more just and equitable world. My students encountered him on the eve of Stonewall where he spent countless nights projecting the futures of Gay Liberation into the minds of discouraged Queer youth. Somnus does not insert himself into the dreams and instead makes the dreamer the agent of change. My class proposed introducing Somnus at the beginning of the school year as a sort of pedagogical mascot. One team even suggested the saying "What Would Somnus Do (WWSD)?" Students could also create their own superhero that looks and acts like them and travels through their US History curriculum affecting the dreams of folx in any historical context.

Somnus may have provided my students a magical portal, but he definitely serves as my window and mirror. Somnus exemplifies the importance of LGBTQ+ history to social studies teachers as he provides the tools of "critical hope" for youth from historically-oppressed-communities that want social change. Moreover, I see both my younger and current self in him: he is unapologetically Gay; ambiguously not white; has big curly black hair; and wears a disco-inspired costume. I dreamed up a version of Somnus when I started reading comics at age 12, and

30 years later he now exists! Somnus also reflects why I teach. Facilitating resilience, resistance, and joy for my students has always driven my theories and practices. Imagine my shock when Leo asked, "do we need Somnus if we have social studies teachers teaching our histories?" Leo was correct. If young people have a teacher who uses LGBTQ+ history in their classroom, is providing windows, mirrors and magical portals, and using sources like comic books, they do not need Somnus. They already have a hero who inspires their dreams!

Challenge Accepted: Navigating the Obstacles to Teach LGBTQ+ History

Stacie Brensilver Berman

I taught high school social studies at a large public school in New York City for ten years before leaving to enter a doctoral program. It is—and will always be—a highlight of my professional and personal life and one of the greatest learning experiences I have ever had. I loved my school and my students. They were theatrical and creative, smart and inquisitive, and unabashedly themselves. The administration was supportive and encouraged teachers to be innovative in the service of meeting students' needs, which changed significantly over the course of a decade. I began teaching because I love history, and I wanted others to feel the same way. My first principal, a former social studies teacher, encouraged us to connect history to current events on a daily basis; in doing so I learned as much about the ways that we can use the past to awaken us in the present as my students did. By the time I left high school teaching to enter my doctoral program I still wanted my students to be *excited* about history, but, even more, I wanted them to be *inspired* by history to find their voice and understand its power.

This focus on agency was my guiding light as I struggled to decide on a dissertation topic. I wanted to write about something that was present in students' lives, that would help them develop well-informed opinions so they could productively engage with others, and that was not covered in a meaningful way in secondary schools in the United States. It was 2013. Edie Windsor's Supreme Court triumph offered people who identified as LGBTQ+ a new sense of hope. The federal government and advocacy organizations had recently started paying more attention to the impact of bullying on LGBTQ+ youth. More Americans personally knew or recognized media figures who identified as gay (although the same could not yet be said for transgender individuals).[9] Yet, in schools, the silence around LGBTQ+ history loomed large, despite the fact that California passed the FAIR Education Act in 2011, becoming the first state in the country to mandate LGBTQ+-inclusive curriculum in social science classes.[10] This, then, had to be my dissertation topic. Deciding to research and write about efforts to include LGBTQ+ history and the opposition they encountered changed my academic, professional, and personal life and set me on a course that determined my future endeavors.

Through my dissertation work—which included interviews with dozens of people around the country involved in supporting LGBTQ+ history curriculum and individuals in schools who identify as LGBTQ+—and the book project that followed, I developed a more profound sense of the need for inclusive curriculum and formed concrete ideas about what that might entail. This put me in a position to work with groups of teachers in different parts of the country, present at conferences, consult with organizations that promote LGBTQ+ inclusive history resources, and support teachers who wanted to do this important work in the ways that were most effective for them. I encountered some opposition, like the teachers I met at a conference whose reaction was, "Why would anyone ever want to learn *that*?" when I shared the topic of my presentation and the New York City teachers who told me that their students were certainly not mature enough to interact with this information. These challenges were expected and, dare I say, relatively minor. It was an era of increasing acceptance, with new states passing laws mandating the inclusion of LGBTQ+ concepts each year. The number of teachers who attended my conference sessions increased annually, veteran teachers listened more attentively at their school's professional development sessions, and parents whose students identify as LGBTQ+ thanked me for my efforts. I struggled to find teachers to speak to me about the ways in which they included LGBTQ+ history when I conducted oral history interviews for my dissertation (my advisor finally said, "If the point is that few teachers are doing it, doesn't it make sense that you can't find as many as you want?"); five years later teachers sought me out to tell their stories.

Then came the backlash. Amid growing awareness and recognition of racism and systemic inequities, conservative pundits and lawmakers targeted schools, classrooms, teachers, and curriculum, claiming that history instruction and an undue focus on Critical Race Theory—a complex legal philosophy that few social studies teachers actually taught—were the cause of the nation's divisions.[11] By the summer of 2021, educators all over the country knew the term "divisive concepts," which included any topic related to identity. Bills and policies intended to restrict teachers' academic freedom were introduced in forty-four states; according to *Education Week*, laws or state-level policies were enacted in eighteen as of October 2024.[12] Furthermore, this atmosphere created an opening for Florida and seven other states to enact "Don't Say Gay/Trans" laws that explicitly prohibited discussion of LGBTQ+-related topics and concepts in schools.[13] Fortunately (yes, fortunately!), there were two significant unintended reactions to these laws. First, teachers, many of whom were unfamiliar with LGBTQ+ history because of gaps in their own education, became aware that it was missing from their curriculum and began to seek the information and resources they needed to include it. Second, individuals who were already committed to this work—historians, teacher educators, advocates, and curriculum developers—committed to doubling down on their efforts to reach and support teachers.[14] In 2022 when I returned to in-person conferences, over 100 people, triple the number I normally spoke to, attended my session on using primary sources to teach LGBTQ+ history. There were not enough seats to hold them all. I was flabbergasted but also thrilled. I felt like there was hope.

As a teacher educator, at NYU and with teachers around the country, my goal remains the same: provide emerging and practicing teachers with the tools and resources they need to integrate LGBTQ+ in their curriculum. Sometimes, that's relatively easy, like when I work with groups of teachers in liberal-leaning areas who are eager to incorporate this history but lack the knowledge and confidence to do so. I weave LGBTQ+ history through my teacher education courses at NYU so that the students who graduate from the program where I teach feel prepared to do the same. In other instances, it is slightly more difficult; the teachers are excited about or, at least, understand the importance of

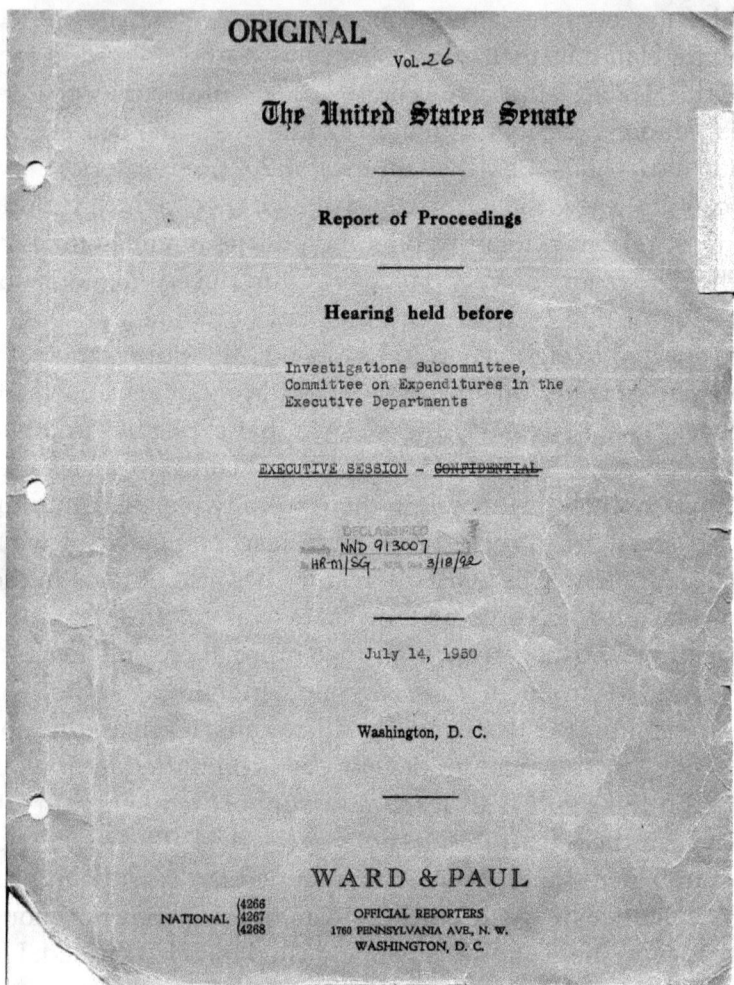

ORIGINAL

Vol. 26

The United States Senate

Report of Proceedings

Hearing held before

Investigations Subcommittee,
Committee on Expenditures in the
Executive Departments

EXECUTIVE SESSION - CONFIDENTIAL

DECLASSIFIED
NND 913007
HR-m|SG   3/18/92

July 14, 1950

Washington, D. C.

WARD & PAUL

NATIONAL {4266 4267 4268}   OFFICIAL REPORTERS
1760 PENNSYLVANIA AVE, N. W.
WASHINGTON, D. C.

FIGURE 3.1a & b
Opening statement of the Hoey Committee (1950), investigating gay employees in the federal workforce. Photos courtesy of the National Archives (photo no. 28748700).

including LGBTQ+ history, but they worry about the responses they might receive from parents, administrators, and community members, even in states and cities with curriculum mandates. In the past three years, more frequently than before, there are significant challenges present. I work with teachers in conservative states with censorship laws who nevertheless want to find ways to integrate this history. I encounter teachers who remain

```
                              EXECUTIVE SESSION - CONFIDENTIAL        2082
                              FILE NO. _____
 VOLUME 26
 BANISTER    1                    Friday, July 14, 1950
    IM
 REC WLC     2                United States Senate,

             3                Investigations Subcommittee,
                                Committee on Expenditures in the
             4                  Executive Departments,

             5                Washington, D. C.

             6      The subcommittee met, pursuant to S. Res. 280, 81st Con-

             7   gress, Second Session, in room 357, Senate Office Building,

             8   Senator Clyde R. Hoey, chairman of the subcommittee, presiding.

             9      PRESENT:

            10        SENATOR CLYDE R. HOEY, Democrat, North Carolina
                      SENATOR JOHN L. McCLELLAN, Democrat, Arkansas
            11        SENATOR KARL E. MUNDT, Republican, South Dakota
                      SENATOR MARGARET CHASE SMITH, Republican, Maine
            12        SENATOR ANDREW F. SCHOEPPEL, Republican, Kansas

            13   ALSO PRESENT:

            14
                      FRANCIS D. FLANAGAN, Chief Counsel
            15        COLONEL EDWARD J. WALSH, Liaison Officer
                      RUTH YOUNG, Clerk
            16
                                   - - -
            17
                 The Chairman.  The subcommittee will be in order.
            18
                 Members of the committee, I have a very brief opening
            19
                 statement which I thought might go into the record.
            20
                 Under S. Res. 280 of the 81st Congress, Second Session,
            21
                 this subcommittee has been directed to undertake an investigation
            22
                 of the alleged employment of homosexuals in the Government
            23
                 service.  As soon as the investigation called for in this
            24
                 resolution was referred to the subcommittee, I directed the staff
            25
                 to begin a study of the various problems involved.
```

FIGURE 3.1a & b
(Continued)

closeted at school for fear that someone in their community will oppose them teaching history. On occasion, in mandated training sessions, teachers resist all efforts and rationales for including this material. Supporting teachers who face seemingly insurmountable obstacles but want to do this work nonetheless is one of the most rewarding aspects of my role. To be clear, I wish it was not something I had to think about at all. Given the reality in which we currently live, though, I am proud to be the person they look to for assistance.

Since 2023, I have had the opportunity to work with teachers who face significant uphill battles but persist in finding ways to make their curriculum more inclusive and representative. I met a Florida teacher at a conference who was recently tasked with revising the school's US history curriculum. Though this teacher had to hide aspects of their personal identity at school, they were nevertheless determined to include primary sources throughout the curriculum that depicted LGBTQ+ experiences over time. I connected with a teacher in Indiana who found ways to modify resources and frame questions in a way that students were introduced to LGBTQ+ history and therefore able to lead discussions that arose from that information. I collaborated with a teacher in Kentucky who found ever more creative ways to leverage state standards to support integrating LGBTQ+ individuals, topics, and themes into their coursework. Their bravery astounds and inspires me; it reminds me that those of us who do not face restrictions need to do all we can to support teachers who do.

Many of the strategies that I offer teachers who face these challenges are based on the ideas and methods I started discussing at professional development sessions almost a decade ago:

♦ Weave LGBTQ+ history into the curriculum organically. It did not happen separately and should not be taught that way. That contributes to the "othering" that is already happening in schools and classrooms.

♦ Let primary sources do the work for you. Most of the sources we use to integrate LGBTQ+ history are and look stunningly similar to the documents we use when we teach every other topic. The Executive Orders, letters, Supreme Court decisions, protest photos, songs, and poetry we see throughout the curriculum are available to teach LGBTQ+ history and fit easily into existing lessons and units (see Figures 3.1a and 3.1b for an example of a government document focusing on LGBTQ+ history).

Using primary sources also situates this information firmly in the historical record.

◆ Be creative and rely on your students. Students want to learn this history and are often angry about the silences in the curriculum. The most effective discussions and lessons are student driven. Provide them with information or a topic to debate and see where they take it (like a teacher I met who lives in a state with a "Don't Say Gay/Trans" law who had her students debate the law). Allow students to choose their own research topics. The mix of teacher innovation and student curiosity is powerful.

As a high school teacher, it meant the world to me to know that something I did or something I taught made a difference for a student. Even now, nearly fifteen years removed from teaching high school, my whole day changes when a former student reaches out to tell me how they applied something they learned in my class. The teachers with whom I work now will have hundreds of students pass through their classes, some of whom will identify as queer, trans, or non-binary or question their gender or sexuality. Integrating LGBTQ+ history into their classes, especially in situations where students know the effort and risk their teacher took to do so, will lead to generations of students—some who likely have little support at home—navigating the world differently because of their social studies experience. I miss teaching high school every day, but it is a privilege to be able to serve teachers and students all over the country in the role I have now.

Teach Queer Joy

Wendy Rouse

As educators, it is our privilege and our responsibility to introduce students to history. This includes introducing them to their own history – to allow them to see themselves in the past. But it also includes introducing them to the history of the people they live side-by-side with in their communities today.

LGBTQ+ people have always existed and will always exist. But they have not always been represented in the history that we teach. Efforts to remedy this have led to the passage of LGBTQ+ inclusive education policies in states such as California, Colorado, New Jersey, Oregon, Illinois, Connecticut, Nevada, and Washington. Educators in New York and California have created resource sets to help teachers begin to incorporate queer history into their curriculum.

In the past, modern terms such as lesbian, gay, bisexual, pansexual, asexual, transgender, non-binary were not always in usage. Today, the term "queer" is often used as an umbrella term to describe non-heterosexual and non-cisgender people in the past who, if they were alive today, might identify as members of the LGBTQ+ community. The term "queer" has been used pejoratively in the past because of its association with homophobia, but was reclaimed by queer activists beginning in the 1980s.

Teachers should incorporate queer history into their curriculum by not only teaching about the long history of the marginalization and oppression of LGBTQ+ people but also by teaching about the persistence of LGBTQ+ people and resistance against inequality. Since the passage of California's FAIR Education Act in 2011 and the creation of a new History/Social Science Framework in 2016, California educators have already begun to make these important changes to their curriculum.

However, as educators continue to revise and refine their teaching, I believe that it is especially crucial to consider even more transformational changes to the curriculum beyond the inclusion of the themes of LGBTQ+ marginalization, oppression, resistance, and persistence. I want to encourage teachers to **teach the history of queer joy.**

Teaching the history of queer joy empowers our students by challenging false narratives that marginalize or dehumanize LGBTQ+ people. This can help counter persistent homophobic and transphobic stereotypes that dismiss LGBTQ+ people as destined to lives of misery and pain. It can be especially empowering for LGBTQ+ students to see examples of people like them in the past who have not just survived, but who have led deeply meaningful and joyful lives.

LGBTQ+ history is full of moments of joy, of celebratory events like the famous pride parades that attest to the importance of community. LGBTQ+ history is also full of incredible love stories such as the story of Edie Windsor and Thea Spyer that stand as evidence of the power of queer joy. These examples allow us to teach the full range of the human experience. It reminds us that learning history can be an affirming and empowering experience.

Here are some practical ideas to help teachers integrate LGBTQ+ history (with a focus on queer joy) into their existing curriculum. These examples are primarily for those teaching middle or high school United States history.

When teaching about the American West, teach about the diversity of individuals who lived in and settled the region. Share the stories of people who, if they were alive today, might identify as two-spirit, transgender, or non-binary. This could include a discussion of We'wha, a notable Zuni potter and weaver who lived in New Mexico, Mother George, a beloved nurse in Idaho, or Albert Eugene De Forest, a prominent actor in the San Francisco Bay Area. Educators might also share the stories of same-sex couples such as miners Jason Chamberlain and John Chaffee, who were known in the California gold country as the wedded couple, or the story of Hannah Clapp and Elizabeth Babcock, who built a home together in Carson City. These examples demonstrate how queer people in the past were loved and respected within their communities.

An examination of the lives of enslaved and formerly enslaved people provides an opportunity to talk about the wide range of family structures/kinship relationships that Black communities created to survive in the era of slavery and Reconstruction. This also allows for conversations about queer families through the stories of people like Minty Caden. Caden was in a relationship with another enslaved woman whose surname she adopted as a sign of her love and commitment. When discussing emancipation and Reconstruction, examine the strategies that Black families (including queer Black families) developed to find one another and rebuild their lives together.

United States history courses introduce students to the variety of domestic arrangements that individuals formed as a result of changes in industrialization and urbanization in the late nineteenth and early twentieth centuries. Define the term "Boston marriages" and explain how these same-sex relationships between women provided alternatives to heterosexual marriage, which was an especially important option for queer women of the era. Discuss the queer history of the suffrage movement and the queer lives of Progressive-era reformers and suffragists such as Jane Addams and Mary Rozet Smith, Lucy Diggs Slowe and Mary Powell Burrill, or Mary S. Malone and Anna Woods Bird.

Students in high school already study the era of the Harlem Renaissance. Diversifying the content around gender and sexuality can help students understand the range of experiences of individuals in this era. The 1920s and 1930s are also full of examples of celebrations of queer joy especially in the poetry, music, and art of the era. Include examples of the popular drag balls and the Pansy craze. Read the poems of Angelina Weld Grimké. Look at the careers of Julian Eltinge or Gladys Bentley and examine the song lyrics of queer singers such as Ma Rainey and Gene Malin. Discuss how theatrical performers and Hollywood stars pushed the boundaries of the gender and sexual norms of their era and brought queer representation to the stage and screen.

Discussions of World War II would not be complete without the inclusion of the contributions of LGBTQ+ people to the war effort. These stories can help complicate and expand our understanding of the experiences of the soldiers and civilians of this era. Talk about the service of people such as Lorraine Hurdle, Vincent Miles, Pat Bond, Robert Fleischer, and José Sarria and the queer community they created in the military. Stories of queer joy abound in this era. Read the letters of Marvyl Doyle and Esther Herbert, who met while serving in the Women's Army Corps during World War II. Share resilient stories of individuals like Jiro Onuma, a Japanese American who met his boyfriend Ronald while he was incarcerated at the Topaz internment camp in Utah.

As your lessons move into the post-world war era, talk about the rich queer community that flourished in mid-twentieth century cities. Connect with the previous units to discuss how thriving queer communities developed in city centers as a result of the effects of urbanization and the development of port cities during World War II. Explore the history of LGBTQ+ nightclubs such as Mona's or famous drag performers such as José Sarria.

In your unit on twentieth-century civil rights movements, introduce students to the history of the homophile and gay liberation movements. Go beyond the Stonewall Riots (1969) to explore even earlier examples of queer resistance in California, such as the Cooper's Do-nuts uprising (1959), the Compton's Cafeteria riot (1966), and the Black Cat Tavern demonstration (1967). There are also numerous examples of queer joy as an act of resistance.

When discussing civil rights movements and women's liberation, share stories of the various demonstrations of queer joy organized by gay liberation activists. Explain how gay and lesbian couples kissed and hugged to protest policies that prohibited same-sex public displays of affection. Discuss the 1968 flower power demonstration at the Los Angeles police station in response to police raids at The Patch, a gay nightclub. Provide examples of gay kiss-ins such as the "demonstration of affection" at the Gold Rail Tavern in New York City or the protest at The Farm bar in Los Angeles in 1970. Share the example of the 1973 lesbian kiss-in at the Los Angeles County Art Museum. Explain that the purpose of these demonstrations was not only to protest exclusionary policies that discriminated against gay people but to fight for the freedom of lesbian and gay couples to express their affection in public in the same way that hetero-sexual couples enjoyed the ability to do so.

The long fight for marriage equality provides ample opportunities to bring in examples of queer joy. From the history of commitment ceremonies to civil unions to federally recognized marriages, LGBTQ+ people have publicly demonstrated and fought for their right to love equally.

It is important for all of us to learn our history – to know where we come from, to feel a sense of belonging, to understand that we are part of something bigger than ourselves – part of a much longer history.

It is especially crucial for LGBTQ+ students to see themselves in history. These examples of queer joy allow them to see themselves as more than simply subjects of history. They can envision themselves as active agents of change. They can see themselves as part of a long history of queer people who have lived joyful and loving lives.

Primary sources and activities related to the events and individuals discussed in this essay can be found in "Teaching LGBTQ History: A Primary Source Set," curated by Wendy Rouse, edited by Don Romesburg and Katharine Cortes, California History-Social Science Project at https://chssp.ucdavis.edu/lgbtq-primary-sources.

Additional Recommended Sources:

◆ Hidden Voices: LGBTQ+ Stories in United States History, New York City Department of Education, Lesson Plans, www.weteachnyc.org/resources/resource/hidden-voi ces-lgbtq-stories-in-united-states-history-lesson-plans-Public-facing/
◆ LGBTQ Lesson Plans, One Archives, www.onearchives. org/lgbtq-lesson-plans/
◆ LGBTQ History Primary Source Sets, GLBT Historical Society, www.glbthistory.org/primary-source-set

*A slightly modified version of this article was originally published on June 9, 2022, on the California History-Social

Science Project blog and is republished here with permission. https://chssp.ucdavis.edu/blog/teach-history-lgbtq-joy

Notes

1 Stacie Brensilver Berman, *LGBTQ+ History in High School Classes in the United States since 1990* (London: Bloomsbury, 2021).

2 Glen A. Larson, "BJ and the Bear Lyrics," ST Lyrics, accessed October 10, 2024, / www.stlyrics.com/lyrics/televisiontvthemelyrics-action/bjandthebear.htm#google_vignette.

3 Shannon D. Snapp, Hilary Burdge, Adela C. Licona, Raymond L. Moody, & Stephen T. Russell, "Students' Perspectives on LGBTQ-Inclusive Curriculum," *Equity & Excellence in Education*, 48 no.2, 2015, p. 257.

4 Snapp, et al., "Students' Perspectives on LGBTQ-Inclusive Curriculum."

5 See Emily Style, "Curriculum as Window and Mirror" in *Listening for All Voices* (Summit, NJ: Oak Knoll School, 1988).

6 Nikki Mandell, "Thinking Like a Historian: a Framework for Teaching and Learning," *OAH Magazine of History* (Bloomington: OAH, 2008).

7 CJ Pascoe, *Dude You're a Fag: Masculinity and Sexuality in High School* (Oakland: UC Press, 2012).

8 I base my "magical portal" paradigm off of Bettina Love's interpretations of Robin Kelley's concept of "freedom dreaming." See *We Want to Do More Than Survive: Abolitionist Teaching and the Pursuit of Educational Freedom* (Boston: Beacon Press, 2019).

9 "Attitudes on Same-Sex Marriage," Pew Research Center, accessed October 10, 2024, www.pewforum.org/fact-sheet/changing-attitudes-on-gay-marriage/.

10 "SB-48 Pupil Instruction: Prohibition of Discriminatory Content," California Legislative Information, last modified July 14, 2011, http://leginfo.legislature.ca.gov/faces/billNavClient.xhtml?bill_id=201120120SB48; Stacie Brensilver Berman, *LGBTQ+ History in High School Classes in the United States since 1990* (London: Bloomsbury, 2021).

11 Sarah Schwartz, "Who's Really Driving Critical Race Theory Legislation?: An Investigation," *Education Week*, July 19, 2021,

www.edweek.org/policy-politics/whos-really-driving-critical-race-theory-legislation-an-investigation/2021/07; Andrew Ujifusa, "Critical Race Theory Puts Educators at Center of a Frustrating Cultural Fight Once Again," *Education Week*, May 26, 2021, www-edweek-org.proxy.library.nyu.edu/leadership/critical-race-the ory-puts-educators-at-center-of-a-frustrating-cultural-fight-once-again/2021/05.

12   Stephen Sawchuk, "Anti-Critical-Race-Theory Laws Are Slowing Down. Here Are 3 Things to Know," *Education Week*, March 26, 2024, www.edweek.org/teaching-learning/anti-critical-race-the ory-laws-are-slowing-down-here-are-3-things-to-know/2024/03.

13   "LGBTQ Curricular Laws," Movement Advancement Project, accessed October 10, 2024, www.lgbtmap.org/equality-maps/curr icular_laws.

14   This trend is evident in 2025, as well, with historians and activists emphasizing the need to focus on LGBTQ+ history despite calls at state and federal levels to prohibit its inclusion and historians affirming their commitment to push back against the so-called "anti-woke agenda"and support teachers who seek to do this work.

References

"Attitudes on Same-Sex Marriage." Pew Research Center. Accessed October 10, 2024. www.pewforum.org/fact-sheet/changing-attitu des-on-gay-marriage/.

Brensilver Berman, Stacie. *LGBTQ+ History in High School Classes in the United States since 1990*. London: Bloomsbury, 2021.

Larson, Glen A. "B.J. and the Bear lyrics." ST Lyrics. Accessed October 10, 2024. www.stlyrics.com/lyrics/televisiontvthemelyrics-action/ bjandthebear.htm.

"LGBTQ Curricular Laws." Movement Advancement Project. Accessed October 10, 2024. www.lgbtmap.org/equality-maps/curricul ar_laws.

Love, Bettina. *We Want to Do More Than Survive: Abolitionist Teaching and the Pursuit of Educational Freedom*. Boston: Beacon Press, 2019.

Mandell, Nikki. "Thinking Like a Historian: A Framework for Teaching and Learning." *OAH Magazine of History*. Bloomington: OAH, 2008.

Pascoe, C.J. *Dude You're a Fag: Masculinity and Sexuality in High School.* Oakland: UC Press, 2012.

Sawchuk, Stephen. "Anti-Critical-Race-Theory Laws are Slowing Down. Here are 3 Things to Know." *Education Week.* March 26, 2024. www. edweek.org/teaching-learning/anti-critical-race-theory-laws-are-slowing-down-here-are-3-things-to-know/2024/03.

"SB-48 Pupil Instruction: Prohibition of Discriminatory Content." California Legislative Information. Last modified July 14, 2011. http://legi nfo.legislature.ca.gov/faces/billNavClient.xhtml?bill_id=201120 120SB48.

Schwartz, Sarah. "Who's Really Driving Critical Race Theory Legislation?: An Investigation." *Education Week.* July 19, 2021. www.edweek.org/pol icy-politics/whos-really-driving-critical-race-theory-legislation-an-investigation/2021/07.

Snapp, Shannon D., Burdge, Hilary, Licona, Adela C., Moody, Raymond L, & Russell, Stephen T. "Students' Perspectives on LGBTQ-Inclusive Curriculum." *Equity & Excellence in Education* 48, no. 2 (2015): 249–265.

Style, Emily. "Curriculum as Window and Mirror." In *Listening for All Voices: Gender Balancing the School Curriculum.* Summit, NJ: Oak Knoll School, 1988.

Ujifusa, Andrew. "Critical Race Theory Puts Educators at Center of a Frustrating Cultural Fight Once Again." *Education Week.* May 26, 2021. www-edweek-org.proxy.library.nyu.edu/leadership/critical-race-theory-puts-educators-at-center-of-a-frustrating-cultural-fight-once-again/2021/05.

4

Voices of Activism: LGBTQ+ History's Power to Create Societal Change

A clear through thread emerges from the essays in this chapter: in an era of backlash, opposition, and division, it is imperative that we teach LGBTQ+ history. This stance evolves from the authors' different professional positions and endeavors, as well as the circumstances and spaces they occupy and their experiences navigating the world. The essays reveal that, with hate and its harmful effects on the rise, incorporating LGBTQ+- history and prompting students to interact with it from different perspectives and through various pedagogies can provide students with the tools and skills they need to challenge the status quo, grow more comfortable with and better understand their own and their peers' identities, and engage in the difficult conversations and discussions they will have outside of the safe space established in that inclusive classroom.

Moreover, these essays, like the historians' in Chapter 1, make clear that support and resources must be available for teachers who seek to bring this information into their classrooms. Though seven states currently have laws mandating the inclusion of LGBTQ+ history, for myriad reasons there is not a direct

DOI: 10.4324/9781032689678-6

connection between legislation and classroom implementation. Book bans and laws that seek to censor information related to LGBTQ+ history and identities are increasingly present and prominent, contributing to teachers' fears and uncertainty about whether or how to integrate this content. These essays urge educational organizations to support teachers and demonstrate ways in which they are currently doing so. Additionally, they remind educators that doing this work, at this time or any other, calls out hate, pushes back against misinformation, and makes all of the places where students learn safer and more representative.

Queer History Over Our Shoulders

Rick Oculto (he/him/his), MSW

The sociology professor, in all earnestness, looked me in the eye and asked if I wanted a security escort back to my car, hinting that it was more than a suggestion. This was around 2002 while speaking at a local Bay Area college about Queer issues. I had been threatened in the classroom by a self-proclaimed "god-fearing man" that could not come to accept the existence of Queer people or our humanity. I declined the escort erring on the side of wanting to demonstrate strength rather than pander to that man's assumption about Queer weakness and walked through the campus towards my car without looking over my shoulder. I have not had to think about that experience as anything more than a distant memory up until 2016, a good decade and a half later, when that same emboldened, hateful rhetoric returned en force. The difference today is that our work to ensure better representation has already been done. The rhetoric has returned but the pillars of disinformation that it stood upon have eroded with a more Queer-informed and Queer-accustomed populace. While the detractors are loud, it is clear that the overall sentiment about Queer issues is positive at best and neutral in the majority. The elucidation of Queer history and more exposure through representation makes the bogeyman made of the issue in the past less viable.

In 2000 California implemented the Student Safety and Violence Prevention Act (AB 537) authored by then California Assemblymember Sheila Kuehl (D) and Carolyn Laub, former Executive Director and founder of the GSA Network. During this period of time there were still questions about whether or not you could talk about Queer topics in the classroom in any capacity. Could Queer teachers talk about their lives? Teachers wondered what they were allowed to say to a student if they came out to them. If they acknowledged the student's identity, then would they be reprimanded or even fired? What if a student was in crisis? Would it be worth the risk? The new law plainly stated that teachers, students, and families had the right to talk about their own lives and that it was fine to talk about Queer issues in the classroom. Still, everyone was nervous. I provided countless training workshops in the Bay Area assuring teachers it was okay. This was the environment that shaped the discourse in the late 90s and early 2000s, in addition to the tragic murder of Matthew Shepard in Wyoming. The shift in public opinion from taboo to topical was palpable.

Motivated by the passage of AB 537, Kuehl and Laub wanted to create more substantial preventative changes and sought out the input of Queer youth through statewide surveys. The Queer youth professionals at the time, myself included, anticipated that the surveys would reveal that the youth wanted stronger legal protections, more resourced clubs, or even better training for their teachers on creating spaces for Queer youth. To our surprise, by a wide margin, the youth wanted better representation in the curriculum. In order to be a part of the world they lived in and to be accepted by their peers they felt that they and their community needed to be spoken about like any other culture by being included and talked about in literature, art, history, and science. They reasoned that if Queer people were seen through these lenses that it would remove the mystery and pervasive misconceptions made about us. Kuehl and Laub took this to heart and created The Bias-Free Curriculum Act (SB 1437), which would have prohibited discrimination based on sexual orientation and gender identity in the curriculum. The bill passed but was subsequently vetoed by Governor Arnold Schwarzenegger. Those who worked on the bill decided to wait for a more receptive administration to avoid another last-minute disappointment and the foundations for the FAIR Education Act (SB 48), introduced and passed by Senator Mark Leno more than half a decade later, were born.

The FAIR Education Act was a less ambitious bill but incredibly effective in its simplicity. In the California Education Code, there was already a provision for including underrepresented groups in history and social science curriculum and FAIR, in addition to other groups, simply added "lesbian, gay, bisexual, and transgender Americans" to the list of groups that needed to be covered in the material. The bill was passed in 2011 and went into effect in 2012. While the actual provision of the bill was modest, its effects were immediately felt as textbook publishers adapted their materials to better reflect the new obligation for representation. About 5 years later, when the state had to adopt new textbooks, one publisher was barred from selling middle school and elementary textbooks in California having failed the review process for being unable to adequately and respectfully include groups from the list, including but not limited to LGBT individuals, women, Asian Americans, and African Americans. While the other publishers still had some issues, their good faith efforts allowed them to sell their books in California and in 2018, the first history and social science textbooks with Queer representation were in pilot programs in classrooms around the state.

It is at this point that I wish I could say that all went well, and Queer inclusive history and social science curriculum is in every classroom in California. However, if you piece together the timeline in the story, I have told it as a constant effort of nearly one and a half decades to get from the conception of the law to its modification, its passage, its elaboration, its implementation, book review, and finally adoption of the curriculum. Not to mention all of the training needed to teach the new material well. This would have been the path without any additional obstacles, but that is not the case. Some districts and schools did not agree with the directive and are using every excuse to forego the responsibility. One school in southern California even caught some of their elementary school teachers ripping out pages that mentioned any Queer issues or events from the new textbooks the district provided them. Some did not have the funds to do it. Competing priorities for what needed to happen in the school from better math textbooks to active shooter trainings meant that the priority of ensuring that there was Queer inclusive curriculum was at the bottom of the priority list. These priorities were present before the pandemic breakout in 2020 and the large push for adoption was supposed to happen that year. Even schools and districts that had people who were dedicated to ensuring that the curriculum was inclusive found that their peers were under-resourced in terms of training and materials. The fact that there were also no systems developed to track the adoption process meant that there was no way to ascertain which schools or districts had adopted and who needed support. In a fun exchange with the state department of education, I wanted to get the number of school districts that had adopted new curriculum so we could prioritize the least resourced and they replied that I should ask a certain expert. I was flabbergasted when they directed me to someone on my own team!

These issues highlight the need for a number of different interventions in order for inclusive curriculum to be effective. First and foremost is line-item funding for the implementation process that includes guidelines from the state for both adoption criteria to be considered as well as training and ongoing consultation. Supportive teachers I have met across the state have said time and time again that the uncertainty of how to use the materials or how to respond to pushback has prevented them and their colleagues from a more robust use of the resources. Intentions set forth from legislation are a good start to motivate Local Education Agencies (LEAs) towards better curriculum, but many of those efforts get hampered by a lack of funding to ensure those efforts come to fruition in a sustainable way leaving districts with a directive without support. Second, data is key to ensuring that practices are consistent and effective. We should be able to, at the very least, have an accurate report of which schools and districts have adopted inclusive textbooks. It would be even better if we could get data on which LEAs have invested in training and how the information is being taught in the classroom. Without this information, we only have anecdotal evidence to inform us about the effectiveness, impact, and breadth of implementation. Finally, the effort for adoption must be a multi-tiered strategy from administration, teachers, and paraprofessionals that span beyond just history and social science. Just like any other social construct that involves climate and behavior, if only one class and one type of education professional in the entire ecosystem of the school talks about Queer inclusion and contributions then its importance is diminished along with its effect. What good is representation if we are only teaching that it matters in one context? It is a losing proposition to have inclusion for inclusion's sake as opposed to recognizing the value of diverse perspectives and finding worth in one another despite differences.

From book bans, bathroom access, sports team segregation, and the constant reports of fiery school board meetings it can sometimes be hard to see what progress has been made, but we cannot take it for granted. I have a friend who is a middle school teacher and runs a youth GSA. As with many of these groups, it was set up as a support system for Queer youth to be able to connect with one another and create a space free of anti-Queer stigma. While many of these groups had been ones that served primarily as mental health support groups, over the years, they have become ones that have leaned more into mobilization and socialization. One day my friend complained that his group has shifted into nothing more than watching Queer themed cartoons together at lunchtime and was considering disbanding the group because it did not feel important anymore. I had to remind him that his situation was a blessing. When I was coordinating the Let's Unite the South Bay GSAs in San Jose in the early 2000s every group that attended was dealing with youth that had to hide their identities at school, members who felt suicidal, kids who got kicked out of their homes, and none of them were younger than high school. In 20 years, these groups have moved from that reality to one where elementary and middle school kids can form a group, do not have to hide their identities, and watch a cartoon with overt and intentional Queer characters and themes. To me, while not the culmination of what I wanted from the progress of this work, this is an astronomical leap in how youth today can be themselves. I told my friend that he should cherish and honor the space that he helped create for those kids because that would have never been an option in the past and its existence now is a testament to his work and the years of progress it took to get there. The youth of the past said that they wanted representation for a better sense of belonging and community and I think they would be glad to see where the kids are today.

We wanted a better future for Queer youth and in this small way, it happened. But the work is not done… and so we continue until our kids can walk across campus without having to look over their shoulders.

It's a Critical Time to Foster LGBTQ+-Inclusive School Climate and Curriculum

Jinnie Spiegler, Anti-Defamation League (ADL)

ADL's timeless mission, which has existed since its founding in 1913, is "to stop the defamation of the Jewish people and to secure justice and fair treatment to all." Today, ADL continues to fight all forms of antisemitism, bias, and hate. We work to prevent and fight hate and extremism, study and call out online hate and harassment, and aim to protect democracy and ensure a just and inclusive society for all.

In my ten years at ADL, one of the most profound lessons I have learned is this: you cannot reduce or end hate and bias by simply confronting, challenging, and disrupting that hate. You cannot prevent it by pointing out over and over again that it is wrong, unacceptable, unethical, and causes harm. It would be nice to think that is enough, but it is not enough.

In addition to calling out bias and hate, we must also highlight, pay attention to, and uplift the complexity, humanity and dignity of the people and community at whom the hate is directed. As Ambassador Deborah Lipstadt, US Special Envoy to Monitor and Combat Antisemitism, stated in a 2023 *New York Times* op-ed, "We need, to borrow an old phrase, to accentuate the positive among our diverse cultures, and shine a light on how Jews, and anyone confronting persecution, live rather than how they suffer"[1].

In the school and education realms, we call this "mirrors and windows." Coined by Dr. Rudine Sims Bishop in 1990, the concept speaks to the importance of young people seeing themselves and others in books. The mirrors represent the core and complex aspects of their identity that are reflected in books and narratives, which helps students feel accepted, included, and valued in society. The windows in books (and other media) show students the lives and experiences that are different than their own, and help students learn about, understand, and empathize with people who belong to other identity groups.[2] Leaning into those mirrors and windows helps young people appreciate themselves and the diversity of others, ultimately helping to foster a more just and inclusive society.

Anti-LGBTQ+ Bias and Hate in the Ecosystem

The LGBTQ+ community is currently facing heightened levels of bias, bigotry, harassment, and injustice. There is a compounded threat and harm to those in the LGBTQ+ community when they also hold other marginalized identities (e.g., Black trans women, gay people who are immigrants and refugees, Jewish queer people).

The myriad ways that this bias, injustice, and hate show up in society is alarming. It impacts young people and their families in direct and indirect ways.

We see it in the anti-LGBTQ+ hate and extremism that is reported in the news on a regular basis and is taking hold across the country. In 2023, in a first-of-its-kind report, ADL and the national LGBTQ+ advocacy organization GLAAD tracked extremist and non-extremist acts of harassment, vandalism and assault (not online) motivated by anti-LGBTQ+ hate. The report identifies more than 350 incidents of harassment, vandalism and assault over an eleven-month period that directly coincided with a disturbing increase in anti-LGBTQ+ rhetoric and legislation. Almost half of these incidents (49%) were perpetrated completely or substantially by individuals associated with extremist groups. Anti-LGBTQ+ incidents often overlapped with other forms of hate, with at least 128 incidents also citing antisemitic tropes and 30 incidents also citing racist tropes.[3]

We see it as we scroll our devices and check our social media feeds. Online hate and harassment surged in 2023, according to ADL's annual Online Hate and Harassment study. In 2023, online hate and harassment rose sharply for adults and teens ages 13–17. Among adults, 52% reported being harassed online in their lifetime, the highest number seen in four years since the study began. Overall, reports of each type of hate and harassment increased by nearly every measure and within almost every demographic group. Given the increase of anti-transgender legislation and

The *Pyramid* shows biased behaviors, growing in complexity from the bottom to the top. Although the behaviors at each level negatively impact individuals and groups, as one moves up the pyramid, the behaviors have more life-threatening consequences. Like a pyramid, the upper levels are supported by the lower levels. If people or institutions treat behaviors on the lower levels as being acceptable or "normal," it results in the behaviors at the next level becoming more accepted. In response to the questions of the world community about where the hate of genocide comes from, the *Pyramid of Hate* demonstrates that the hate of genocide is built upon the acceptance of behaviors described in the lower levels of the pyramid.

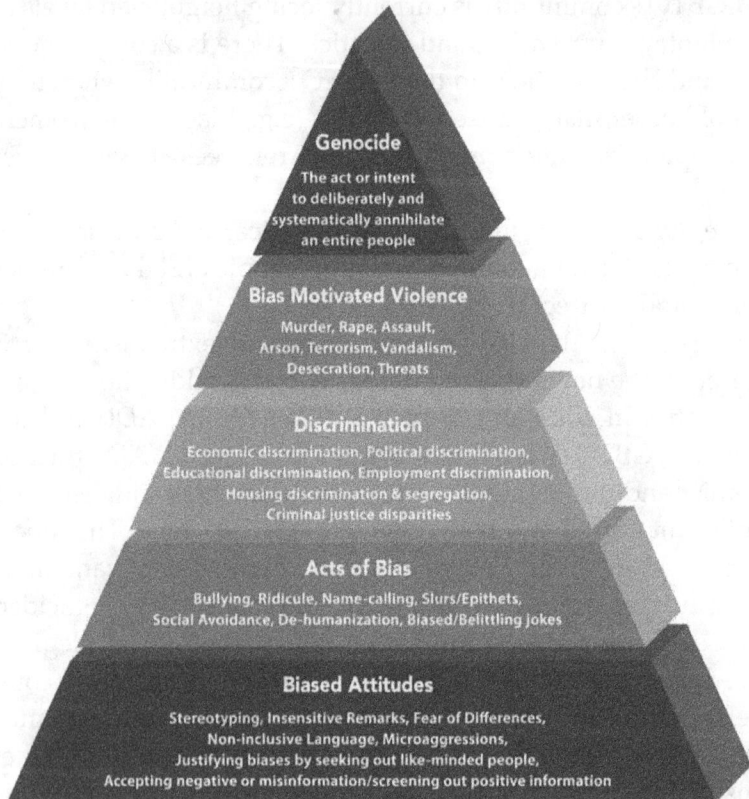

Genocide
The act or intent to deliberately and systematically annihilate an entire people

Bias Motivated Violence
Murder, Rape, Assault, Arson, Terrorism, Vandalism, Desecration, Threats

Discrimination
Economic discrimination, Political discrimination, Educational discrimination, Employment discrimination, Housing discrimination & segregation, Criminal justice disparities

Acts of Bias
Bullying, Ridicule, Name-calling, Slurs/Epithets, Social Avoidance, De-humanization, Biased/Belittling Jokes

Biased Attitudes
Stereotyping, Insensitive Remarks, Fear of Differences, Non-inclusive Language, Microaggressions, Justifying biases by seeking out like-minded people, Accepting negative or misinformation/screening out positive information

FIGURE 4.1
Anti Defamation League's "Pyramid of Hate," detailing bias in society and the harm it causes. © 2021 Anti-Defamation League, www.adl.org. Reprinted with permission.

rhetoric, the study oversampled transgender respondents for the first time, a sampling method to ensure enough responses from a small demographic group. The study revealed that 76% of transgender respondents were harassed in their lifetimes, with 51% of transgender respondents harassed in the past twelve months, by far the highest of any reported demographic category. After transgender respondents, LGBQ+ people experienced the most harassment at 47% over this period. Together, transgender and LGBQ+ people were the most harassed demographic group every year we have conducted this survey.[4]

We see this bigotry and oppression manifesting in the anti-LGBTQ+ bills being proposed and passed in state legislatures across the US These bills aim to restrict the rights, freedom and fair treatment of LGBTQ+ people. Over the past several years, there have been hundreds of bills introduced by state legislatures across the country. Many of those bills have become laws. The laws restrict the rights of LGBTQ+ people and limit their ability to live safely and freely, feel included in school and society, and be treated with dignity, respect, and equity. There are a wide range of laws, with most unfortunately centering around the lives of children and teenagers, families, schools, and educators.[5]

Despite this bias permeating most aspects of society, public opinion polls demonstrate that people in the US continue to be broadly supportive of LGBTQ+ rights and are against discrimination.[6] The opposition voices are in the minority but they are loud, impactful and consequential.

Pyramid of Hate

To help understand how different levels of bias and hate work together, the Pyramid of Hate is an instructive model.[7] A core concept of ADL Education's work, the Pyramid of Hate is a visual representation of the prevalence of bias, hate, and oppression in our society and the escalation and compounding harm that takes place for marginalized communities. Like a pyramid, the upper levels are supported by the lower levels. Unlike a pyramid, the levels are not built consecutively or to illustrate a ranking of each level. In other words, hate and bias do not always follow an upward trajectory. Indeed, biased attitudes and actions can lead to systemic discrimination (legislation) and hate-motivated violence (extremism). But those levels of hate can also move in the opposite direction. When we see so much anti-LGBTQ+ legislation, extremism, and online hate, that can negatively influence broader attitudes and everyday actions—those steps at the bottom of the Pyramid.[8]

All of this leads to a climate and culture that is hostile, unsafe, dangerous, and potentially life-threatening for LGBTQ+ people.

With all this anti-LGBTQ+ hate in the ecosystem and so prominent on most levels of the Pyramid of Hate, as a society we must ask ourselves: *What message are we sending to young people—both those who identify as LGBTQ+ and those who do not? How do they feel about their very existence if some of society's laws are all but saying they should not exist?*

In schools across the country, some children are not allowed to listen to a story read to them that contains mirrors about their own two-Mom or two-Dad families or read books that reflect their sexual orientation or gender identity. Students are being teased, bullied and stigmatized based on their gender identity and gender expression but in some states or districts there are no policies that protect that aspect of their identity. There are gay and lesbian students in schools without GSAs (Genders and Sexualities Alliance) and no acknowledgment of LGBTQ+ people or topics in US history, literature or anywhere in the curriculum. Some transgender and non-binary students attend schools that are not allowed to use their accurate name or pronouns and force them to use a bathroom that does not align with their gender identity.

These students are excluded, disrespected, marginalized, and treated inequitably at every turn. Further, all students are harmed by these non-inclusive policies because they are not exposed to and able to learn about the full experience of the human condition.

LGBTQ+-Inclusive Schools for All Students

Now, more than ever, it is critical that our nation's schools have LGBTQ+-inclusive policies and practices that promote a respectful, inclusive and equitable climate for all students.

Inclusive policies include curriculum and other teaching materials that highlight LGBTQ+ history, people, narratives, struggles and related topics. This helps LGBTQ+ young people feel seen, valued, appreciated and represented ("mirrors") and teaches all students about the LGBTQ+ community—past and present ("windows"). Inclusive policies and practices must be prioritized in order to provide a welcoming environment for LGBTQ+ students, safe from bullying, bias, stigma, stereotyping, and harassment and one that also helps those students feel seen and valued.

Education is a meaningful and essential way that we can make a difference in helping young people, educators, and families understand, challenge, and disrupt hate and bias, particularly anti-LGBTQ+ hate. We know from two decades of research the importance of students having GSAs in their schools, educators that are supportive of LGBTQ+ students, inclusive school policies, classes that include LGBTQ+ topics and positive representations about LGBTQ+ people, history, or events. When those inclusive policies and climate are in place, LGBTQ+ students are less likely to hear homophobic remarks and less likely to feel unsafe because of their sexual orientation and gender identity. They experience lower rates of victimization and are less likely to miss school because of safety concerns and discomfort.[9]

ADL Education provides LGBTQ+-inclusive resources, lesson plans, discussion guides and children's literature to the schools that we serve through our programs and to schools and educators at large.

You can find ADL Education's open-source resources here https://www.adl.org/about/education.

Drag Herstory: Making Learning Fabulous

Lil Miss Hot Mess

I was in high school when I first learned about—and fell in love with—drag.

I had grown up in an era in which gender nonconformity was not exactly the norm, though it was not wholly uncommon either. My child and teen years were filled with countless examples from cartoon characters like Bugs Bunny with blonde hair and painted lips, to films like *Mrs. Doubtfire*, and even then-mayor Rudy Giuliani donning a dress in programs like *Saturday Night Live*. Still, it was not until I found the drag classic *To Wong Foo, Thanks for Everything! Julie Newmar* at the local video store that I began to understand the power of this art form and how much it resonated with me.

It was also in high school that I began to dabble in the drag arts, in a few highly-formative moments. In my junior year, I auditioned for my public school's production of Shakespeare's *A Midsummer Night's Dream*, with a determined focus on the role of Francis Flute, the amateur actor who takes on the cross-dressed role of Thisbe in the play-within-the-play. For the tryout, we were asked to not only prepare a monologue, but also

FIGURE 4.2
Lil Miss Hot Mess Hosting Drag Story Hour at Brooklyn Friends School, 2017.
Source: Photo by Tracy Chow.

a dance. I performed my first drag number: a figure skating-style routine on rollerblades to a homemade mix of Aerosmith's "Dude Looks Like a Lady" and Cyndi Lauper's "Time After Time," complete with costume reveals and an oversized stuffed animal who served as my love interest and dance partner. I got the part and was elated to design a costume of a toga made from a bedsheet and a makeshift wig from dollar-store hair extensions. On the safety of the stage, I was able to find a new way to express myself.

In my senior year, my forays went even further. For a vintage-inspired school dance, a small group of friends and I all decided to go in drag. Ironically, none of us were yet out of the closet—even to each other—though in a few years, three out of four would be. And while our unconventional approach may not have been celebrated, we also managed to get by without too much negative attention: the cover of a themed dress-up dance allowed us just a bit of room to play with over-the-top gender expression without raising too many questions of identity. (At least not to our made-up faces.) Later that year, I once again experimented with drag, this time in my AP English class, for a creative project responding to E.L. Doctorow's novel *Ragtime*. In this satirical retelling, I invented and played a character called Lil Miss Ragtime, who inserted herself into the already historically irreverent narrative through made-up songs and in a "dress" I had fashioned by precariously safety-pinned American flag. While some of the dudes in the class snickered, my teacher praised my boldness and creativity. It would be five or so more years until I found a true drag community and began performing. Still, some might say these were the formative moments in which a drag scholar was born, as they all contributed to my work as both a performer *and* an educator.

Of course, my experience is just that of one person. But I begin with my own biography to highlight the fact that, even in the relatively homophobic and transphobic white suburban environment that I grew up in, and in the era of Y2K, I still found and created a spirit of queerness—and in school no less. Much of my life's work since, through many twists and turns, has been to highlight the artistry and activism of queer and trans communities, and to think about what everyone, regardless of identity, can learn from this expertise to make the world a more just and joyful place. These days, I come to this work from two angles: on the one hand, a drag performer, children's book author, and storyteller with Drag Story Hour; and on the other, a university professor with a background in media and cultural studies. In what follows, I draw on my own experience, as well as scholarly research and creative practice, to propose some ways that drag might help educators and students think differently about teaching and learning—specifically about history and culture. As with all drag, I encourage readers to consider this a provocation, not a prescription: that is a set of ideas to play with, push back on, and ultimately transform into one's own.

Drag Pedagogy

By way of a bit of background, in "Drag Pedagogy: The Playful Practice of Queer Imagination in Early Childhood"[10], Harper Keenan and I theorize the educational opportunities of Drag Story Hour (DSH). In the article, we consider what young children might learn from drag performers, particularly if we move beyond considering drag cultures and LGBTQ+ histories simply as a *subject*, to also consider drag as a *method*. That is, while programs like DSH offer valuable opportunities to educate students about LGBTQ+ people or concepts, we have been more interested in what happens if we read between the lines, to consider what lessons drag might offer for deeper forms of learning: about how we express ourselves, relate to others, and make change in our communities.

Though that article and others we have written since focus primarily on Drag Story Hour and early childhood years,[11] many of our findings resonate with—or with just a little imagination, could be adapted for—educational environments for older children, teenagers, and even adults, as well. To summarize briefly, we identify five overlapping interventions that drag pedagogy can offer:

1) **Fantasy and play** as unscripted, imaginative, and embodied modes of learning that help move beyond rote methods or

predefined learning outcomes to prioritize fluid and emergent forms of knowledge.

2) **Serving style and aesthetic transformations** as ways of giving attention not just to *what* is being communicated but *how*, inviting multisensory approaches to learning and enticing (rather than commanding) engagement.

3) **Inviting strategic defiance** to encourage critical thinking about social norms and cultural expectations, including when and how authority might be challenged (and how teachers might playfully respond to students with sass rather than punishment).

4) **Embracing humor to challenge stigma**, or otherwise finding ways of using laughter to collectively address serious or shameful subjects by poking fun at society (rather than each other) and removing the power they hold over us.

5) **Moving beyond empathy to embodied kinship** by learning not to consume or imitate differences in others, but to notice and celebrate the differences in ourselves so that we can build solidarity and chosen families.

Again, these were conceived for younger children but might equally apply to middle and high school students, not by "reverting" to early childhood, but rather by identifying age-appropriate ways to play, laugh, and ask questions together. Additionally, it is important to make clear that drag pedagogy does not require actual drag performance—teachers and students do not (necessarily) need to don a wig or a feather boa—but should experiment with disrupting some of the routines and expectations of their own classrooms. That said, in this chapter, I focus specifically on how drag pedagogy as an approach can be combined with the study of drag as a historic and contemporary art form, with the potential for fabulous collective learning.

Drag Herstories

Drag pedagogy might be applied to any range of subjects—including math, see Kyne Santos's fabulous *Math In Drag*[12]—however, studying histories of drag performance can offer a unique layer in learning about LGBTQ+ communities and cultures. (And, as drag performers, we do love layers!) Moreover, teaching about the *herstories* or *hirstories* of drag[13] can not only offer helpful case studies, but can provoke students to consider some of the "big questions" about history, including what actually constitutes history, how it is told, and by whom. While it would be impossible to offer anywhere near a complete telling of drag history in this chapter—or in any volume, as there are always more sequins to turn over—here I wish to offer just a few notes on drag as a starting point for anyone diving into this rich topic. For educators looking for additional background resources, I have curated an additional reading list focused on drag histories, ranging from news articles to academic books: www.lil misshotmess.com/drag-syllabus (I recommend previewing for accessibility and appropriateness for students).

Drag resists simple definition, but is rooted in queer and trans communities.

While there are many forms of cross-dressed and gender-playful performances—including traditions like ancient Greek and Elizabethan theatre, Japanese kabuki, or Harlem's ballroom culture—not all are drag per se. (I often think of them as drag's cousins.) This is not to suggest that we police what is or is not drag, but to locate drag's roots explicitly among queer and trans performers and audiences, and the communal sense of fantasy, camaraderie, and joy it produces. This is especially complicated, given that language is always in flux: performers may not have used terms like "drag queen" or "drag king," and many historic figures have used such terms to refer to themselves before language like "trans" was common. It is also important to remember that trans identity and drag performance are not the same, but that many drag performers historically and contemporaneously identify as trans.

Drag has many styles, but always challenges the status quo.

There is not, and has never been, just one way to do drag; instead, there are infinitely diverse approaches. Still, drag generally pushes the boundaries of society's norms. It often starts by disrupting the gender binary and playing with stereotypes of masculinity and femininity, but may also play with other elements of a performer's own culture, including race, class, or religion.[14] Others push the envelope by commenting on mainstream culture and politics, or drawing on nature and science fiction. It is thus important to pay close attention to drag's aesthetics and politics, how it *looks* and *feels,* and the kind cultural work it *does*. How does a performance embody humor, satire, kitsch, melodrama, exaggeration, earnestness, subtlety—or all, none, or beyond the above? It is also worth emphasizing that drag is both local and global: it often has its own local flavors, but can be found in most parts of the world—with plenty of cross-pollination.

Drag not only reflects, but makes history—and it is always evolving.

Finally, the history of drag is not isolated from other events and narratives of the past, but is deeply enmeshed in many key artistic and political movements, including the Harlem Renaissance, vaudeville, hippie and punk countercultures, and many more. Studying drag can not only offer a glimpse into histories that have been left out, but can also explore well-worn accounts from new perspectives. For example, William Dorsey Swann, the first known person to use the phrase "queen of drag" in the late 1800s, was a formerly enslaved person.[15] Or José Sarria, a drag queen, was the first out gay person to run for political office in the US, opening the way for other historic campaigns.[16] Equally momentous, drag performers Sylvia Rivera, Marsha P. Johnson, Miss Major Griffin-Gracy, and Stormé DeLarverie played integral parts in the infamous Stonewall rebellion (with drag king DeLarverie believed to have thrown the first punch), as well as subsequent social movements for lesbian and trans rights, economic and housing justice, and prison abolition.[17] These figures are just starting points to explore drag as an intersectional practice of liberation, especially as its place in politics and culture continues to evolve. It is worth examining how drag's mainstream popularity is in constant flux, and to understand how today's so-called "culture wars" are hardly new.[18]

Drag Pedagogy Through Drag Herstory

As that brief historical recounting of drag demonstrates, there are many angles from which to learn about drag—and like the art form itself, they are sometimes incomplete, ambiguous, or paradoxical. However, fear not: such complexities are ultimately generative and fabulous! They invite opportunities to engage students around drag as a practice that, like many aspects of life, holds many contradictions. I encourage educators (including myself) to tackle these sorts of big questions head-on: *How might drag help us understand changes in language and identities over time? How might we compare different approaches to drag (whether historic, stylistic, geographic, etc.), and what does that tell us about art and politics? What are the opportunities and challenges in engaging artistic forms of activism?* That is, our goal should not be to neatly define drag, but rather to explore what its messiness tells us about other aspects of identity, history, and culture.

In this vein, I now offer just a few ideas for how high school educators might not only teach about the herstory of drag but do so in a way that reflects the creativity of drag pedagogy. My hope is that these serve as an inspiration, with plenty of room for adaptation and improvisation, whether in your own classroom or even in different subjects or educational contexts.

Unpacking Drag Archives & Media

While many aspects of drag culture are ephemeral—either by design or neglect—much has been preserved in a range of formats. In locales with LGBTQ+ focused archives such as the GLBT Historical Society in San Francisco or Lesbian Herstory Archives in New York, many contain fascinating objects and ephemera befitting drag royalty: photographs, flyers, costumes, props, journals, audio and video recordings, and more.[19] And even in places without dedicated queer and trans archives, one might be surprised by what is held in a local university, library, or historical society collection. Moreover, many institutional as well as community-created collections like the Digital Transgender Archive and Drag King History website are expanding to include rich digital collections, inviting public scholars to explore materials remotely. Additionally, there are numerous examples of drag-related media, especially short and feature length documentaries that can offer a near-immersive introduction into drag, especially for teenagers who may be too young to experience it in person.[20]

Working with these materials can provide opportunities for students to learn about archival processes and consider the affordances of primary (and secondary) sources, making history feel all the more tangible. They can also provoke important conversations about how history is constructed, raising questions like: *Who gets to tell their own histories? How do institutions decide what kinds of objects get preserved? How can we create our own archives and media?*

To that last point, educators might engage students in creatively developing their own ways of presenting "found" drag herstories, thinking critically about not just *what* might be shared with public audiences but *how*. For example, students might consider what forms their findings take—a physical or digital exhibition, a zine, a podcast, a social media account, etc.—and how different formats and genres speak to different audiences. Drawing on drag pedagogy, they can be encouraged to think carefully about the aesthetics or tone of their work, including how it may look, sound, or feel different from more "traditional" approaches. They might also explore ways to activate their projects and encourage interactivity: that is, as creators, how would they want audience members to engage with these materials in ways to be more experiential or activate multiple senses? For example, perhaps rather than a traditionally quiet and austere museum, they might create a web exhibition complete with a playlist that encourages attendees to lip-sync along or create a game that explores aspects of drag herstory. What might these creative formats feel like?

Documenting Local Histories

In a similar vein, educators can work with students to actually contribute to existing archives or create their own. As noted above, drag is a highly localized practice, and as such, presents fruitful opportunities to explore *microhistories*, which home in on a particular event, individual, venue, or community in order to explore larger themes.[21] While it may seem like drag only happens in larger cities, this is hardly true: even rural or suburban communities likely have some proximity to performers and events, which can be uncovered through research and invited for partnerships. Additionally, there are a number of drag networks and institutions that exist across the United States (and often other parts of the world), including organizations like the Imperial Court System, Sisters of Perpetual Indulgence, pageant systems like Miss Continental and Miss Gay America, and organizations like Drag Story Hour. Additionally, local LGBTQ+ organizations, community centers, and pride festivals are likely to have existing connections with drag performers (or former performers, event organizers, and patrons).

Educators might guide students in working with local drag artists to document their lives and experiences in a range of ways, exploring many of the themes discussed in previous sections. For example, students could interview drag performers to document their oral histories. Such an experience not only supports students in developing skills like formulating interview questions but also supports cross-generational dialogue. Students might also work with participants to document materials from performers' personal archives (there is nothing like holding a piece of history in one's hand). With the right legwork, they may even be able to help contribute this research to existing institutional archive, or create their own exhibition formats like the ones suggested above. (A caution: all of the above is predicated on working with local performers to establish enthusiastic consent, agree on goals and expectations for collaboration, and discuss age-appropriate content for students.)

Ideally, in the spirit of drag pedagogy, such approaches are not merely focused on the final product, but encourage students to think critically about their processes as well. For example, students might reflect on how learning about history from an interview they conduct themselves differs from learning history from a textbook: *How do the questions they ask differ from those that others have (or have not) asked? Whose stories have been preserved and circulated? What are their ethical responsibilities in sharing other people's stories?* Again, educators should also encourage students to think carefully about how they can creatively share their work, with attention to form, aesthetics, and tone that are aligned with those of the performers they speak to.

Creating Drag Personas & Performances

Finally, drag also offers an opportunity to get even more creative in how history is explored and told by drawing on the tricks of the trade. Inspired by my own attempts at high school literary drag as Lil Miss Ragtime, there are myriad opportunities for educators to work with students to craft their own drag personas, performances, and other creative materials that directly respond to historical events, figures, and themes. Such work can draw on a range of imaginative approaches, including historical and speculative fiction—or what historian Saidiya Hartman calls "critical fabulation"[22]—to creatively construct historically-informed narratives that help fill in gaps in mainstream histories.

With this approach, students might construct drag personas that reflect moments in history: perhaps creating characters tied to particular events, or imagining how drag performers at the time might have used the art form to offer contemporaneous social commentary. Constructing a drag persona can include many creative decisions, including choosing a name, developing a personal backstory and character traits, determining a look and performance style, and more.[23] With each, students can think critically about how history might inform their choices, and how their choices in turn shape how audiences will interpret that history. Educators can also get creative in how students present these personae, perhaps through drawings, scripts, or actual dress up!

Taking it a step further, students could create solo or group performances to explore chosen moments in history, opening up the creative process to include conversations on song choice, choreography, and more. In some cases, students may actually perform their own performances, live or prerecorded. Or, some students and educators might wish to express themselves through other formats (or a combination), including: designing a poster or playbill for a performance, creating a comic strip or storyboard, or writing a "review" of what a performance might have looked like. Again, drag pedagogy reminds us that style is often just as important as substance, as students consider how to balance humor, sincerity, satire, and other tactics to convey their intended messages.

For educators who may be intrigued, but feel they lack the experience to pursue these projects, drag or otherwise, do not worry: there are existing models and resources. In recent decades, there have been many projects that offer high school (and sometimes younger) students opportunities to experience drag, for example, Queens of the Castro in San Francisco and the School of Drag in Tucson. Additionally, these sorts of projects can also be wonderful opportunities to enlist the support of teachers in other areas (e.g., theatre and visual arts), and to involve local drag communities in the design from the start. And most importantly, I offer this reminder: drag, like learning, should not be about perfection. Demonstrating one's own willingness to improvise, take risks, and learn alongside students is equally a part of drag pedagogy.

Conclusion

By way of a conclusion, allow me one confession: most of the above suggestions are not things I myself have tried, or at least not to the fullest extent I dream about here. Which is to say: as much as I hope that educators are willing to have queen-sized dreams and take big swings, I also recognize that we all have to start somewhere, and that often means baby steps. But to paraphrase one of my own drag mentors once reminded me early in my career: "just put on some heels and try it."

On a personal level, writing this essay has offered me a chance to let my imagination run wonderfully wild. And, since I began both reading to children in drag and teaching college students—which, incidentally, started in the same year—my challenge to myself is to try these techniques out in my own classrooms. And, at the same time, to remind myself that, like any drag number, it may flop or be a huge hit; but it is always worth trying. We owe that to our students, and to ourselves.

Ultimately, drag is just one tool among many to change our world, but it is a hell-of-a fun place to start.

Notes

1 Deborah E. Lipstadt, "Want to Fight Antisemitism? Embrace Jewish Traditions." *New York Times*, September 14, 2023, www.nytimes.com/2023/09/14/opinion/antisemitism-jewish-pride.html.

2 Rudine Sims Bishop, "Windows, Mirrors, and Sliding Glass Doors," *Perspectives: Choosing and Using Books for the Classroom* 6, no. 3 (Summer 1990), accessed at https://scenicregional.org/wp-content/uploads/2017/08/Mirrors-Windows-and-Sliding-Glass-Doors.pdf.

3 "Year in Review: Anti-LGBTQ+ Hate & Extremism Incidents, 2022–2023," Anti-Defamation League, June 22, 2023, www.adl.org/resources/report/year-review-anti-lgbtq-hate-extremism-incidents-2022-2023.

4 Center for Technology and Society, "Online Hate and Harassment: The American Experience 2023," Anti-Defamation League, June 27, 2023, www.adl.org/resources/report/online-hate-and-harassment-american-experience-2023.

5 ADL Education, "Anti-LGBTQ+ Bills that are Impacting Children, Families and Schools," Anti-Defamation League, April 27, 2023, www.adl.org/resources/tools-and-strategies/anti-lgbtq-bills-are-impacting-children-families-and-schools.

6 Alison Durkee, "Here's How Americans Really Feel About LGBTQ Issues," *Forbes*, June 5, 2023, www.forbes.com/sites/alisondurkee/2023/06/03/heres-how-americans-really-feel-about-lgbtq-issues/?sh=56c80f122e88.

7 ADL Education, "Pyramid of Hate," Anti-Defamation League, updated August 28, 2024, www.adl.org/resources/tools-and-strategies/pyramid-hate-en-espanol.

8 ADL Education, Pyramid of Hate.

9 Joseph G. Kosciw, Caitlin M. Clark, & Leesh Menard, *The 2021 National School Climate Survey: The experiences of LGBTQ+ youth in our nation's schools* (New York: GLSEN, 2022).

10 Harper Keenan and Lil Miss Hot Mess, "Drag Pedagogy: The Playful Practice of Queer Imagination in Early Childhood," *Curriculum*

Inquiry 50, no. 5 (October 19, 2020): 440–61, https://doi.org/10.1080/03626784.2020.1864621.

11   Lil Miss Hot Mess and Harper Keenan, "Royal Reading: Drag Pedagogy and the Art of Queer Literacy," *Literacy Today*, June 2023; Harper Keenan et al., "Out of the Classroom & Onto the Runway: Queer and Trans Pedagogies in Early Childhood," in *Reimagining Diversity, Equity, and Justice in Early Childhood*, ed. Haeny Yoon, A. Lin Goodwin, and Celia Genishi, 1st edition (New York, NY: Routledge, 2023).

12   Kyne Santos, *Math in Drag* (Johns Hopkins University Press, 2024).

13   David Evans Frantz, Christina Linden, and Chris E. Vargas, eds., *Trans Hirstory in 99 Objects* (Munich: Hirmer Publishers, 2023).

14   Kareem Khubchandani, *Decolonize Drag* (New York: OR Books, 2023).

15   Channing Gerard Joseph, "The First Drag Queen Was a Former Slave," *The Nation*, January 31, 2020, www.thenation.com/article/society/drag-queen-slave-ball; Cari Shane, "The First Self-Proclaimed Drag Queen Was a Formerly Enslaved Man," Smithsonian Magazine, June 9, 2023, www.smithsonianmag.com/history/the-first-self-proclaimed-drag-queen-was-a-formerly-enslaved-man-180982311.

16   Jordan Villegas, "'The Empress Is a Man': The Drag Royalty of José Julio Sarria," *Latina* (blog), May 20, 2021, https://latina.com/the-empress-is-a-man-the-drag-royalty-of-jose-julio-sarria/; Elyssa Goodman, "Drag Herstory: The Drag Queen Who Ran For President in 1992," Them, April 20, 2018, www.them.us/story/joan-jett-blakk-drag-queen-president; Alex Hawgood, "Yass, We Can! Drag Performers Enter the Political Mainstream," W Magazine, October 29, 2020, www.wmagazine.com/culture/drag-performers-politics-maebe-a-girl-marti-gould-allen-cummings.

17   Nichols, "Miss Major On Rioting At Stonewall: 'That Was 3 Nights Of Absolute Terror,'" HuffPost, June 1, 2018, www.huffpost.com/entry/miss-major-on-rioting-at-stonewall_n_5b0c4312e4b0568a880dadbc; Rachel Tashjian, "A Brief History of Stormé DeLarverie, Stonewall's Suiting Icon," GQ, June 27, 2019, www.gq.com/story/storme-delarverie-suiting; Jules Gill-Peterson, "It's Not Enough to Celebrate Transgender Women of Color during Pride. It's Time to Learn Their History," *Washington Post*, June 25, 2021, sec.

Perspective, www.washingtonpost.com/gender-identity/its-not-enough-to-celebrate-transgender-women-of-color-during-pride-its-time-to-learn-their-history.

18 Daniel Villarreal, "Drag Queens Are More Political than Ever. Can They Lead a Movement?," *Vox*, November 5, 2018, www.vox.com/identities/2018/11/5/18056558/drag-queens-politics-activism-lgbtq-rupaul; Mary Emily O'Hara, "GLAAD Report: Drag Events Faced at Least 141 Protests and Significant Threats in 2022," *GLAAD* (blog), November 21, 2022, www.glaad.org/blog/updated-glaad-report-drag-events-faced-least-141-protests-and-significant-threats-2022; Gillian Branstetter, "How the ACLU Tracks Anti-LGBTQ Bills, and How We're Fighting Back," *American Civil Liberties Union* (blog), January 23, 2023, www.aclu.org/news/lgbtq-rights/how-the-aclu-tracks-anti-lgbtq-bills; James Greig, "Inside America's Escalating War on Drag," Dazed, March 2, 2023, www.dazeddigital.com/life-culture/article/58337/1/america-war-on-drag-story-hour-right-proud-boys.

19 For a more comprehensive list, see: Elvis Bakaitis, "LGBTQ / Gender & Sexuality Studies Archival Resources," CUNY Graduate Center's Mina Rees Library, March 6, 2024, https://libguides.gc.cuny.edu/c.php?g=159573&p=1045186.

20 As a starting point, I recommend: Elyssa Goodman, "11 Wig-Incinerating Drag Documentaries to Watch For Pride," Them, June 28, 2019, www.them.us/story/11-drag-documentaries-pride; Harris Kornstein, "Drag Performance on Screen," in *The International Encyclopedia of Gender, Media, and Communication*, ed. Karen Ross (John Wiley & Sons, Ltd, 2020), 1–6, https://doi.org/10.1002/9781119429128.iegmc315; and, for a series of PBS-produced shorts, consider: "Masters of Drag," American Masters (PBS), accessed March 20, 2024, www.pbs.org/wnet/americanmasters/shorts/masters-of-drag/.

21 "What Is Microhistory?," *The MicroWorlds Lab (Duke University)* (blog), accessed March 21, 2024, https://sites.duke.edu/microworldslab/what-is-microhistory/.

22 Alexis Okeowo, "How Saidiya Hartman Retells the History of Black Life," *The New Yorker*, October 19, 2020, / www.newyorker.com/magazine/2020/10/26/how-saidiya-hartman-retells-the-history-of-black-life.

23 For an easily-adaptable worksheet, see: Nino Testa, "My Drag Worksheet," 2023, https://addran.tcu.edu/wgst/community/My-Drag-Worksheet-2.pdf.

References

ADL Education. "Anti-LGBTQ+ Bills that are Impacting Children, Families and Schools." Anti-Defamation League. April 27, 2023. www.adl.org/resources/tools-and-strategies/anti-lgbtq-bills-are-impacting-children-families-and-schools.

ADL Education. "Pyramid of Hate." Anti-Defamation League. Last updated August 28, 2024. www.adl.org/resources/tools-and-strategies/pyramid-hate-en-espanol.

American Masters (PBS). "Masters of Drag." Accessed March 20, 2024. www.pbs.org/wnet/americanmasters/shorts/masters-of-drag/.

Bakaitis, Elvis. "LGBTQ / Gender & Sexuality Studies Archival Resources." CUNY Graduate Center's Mina Rees Library. March 6, 2024. https://libguides.gc.cuny.edu/c.php?g=159573&p=1045186.

Bishop, Rudine Sims. "Windows, Mirrors, and Sliding Glass Doors." *Perspectives: Choosing and Using Books for the Classroom* 6, no. 3 (Summer 1990): https://scenicregional.org/wp-content/uploads/2017/08/Mirrors-Windows-and-Sliding-Glass-Doors.pdf.

Branstetter, Gillian. "How the ACLU Tracks Anti-LGBTQ Bills, and How We're Fighting Back." *American Civil Liberties Union* (blog). January 23, 2023. www.aclu.org/news/lgbtq-rights/how-the-aclu-tracks-anti-lgbtq-bills.

Center for Technology and Society. "Online Hate and Harassment: The American Experience 2023." Anti-Defamation League. June 27, 2023. www.adl.org/resources/report/online-hate-and-harassment-american-experience-2023.

Durkee, Alison. "Here's How Americans Really Feel about LGBTQ Issues." *Forbes*. June 5, 2023. www.forbes.com/sites/alisondurkee/2023/06/03/heres-how-americans-really-feel-about-lgbtq-issues/?sh=56c80f122e88.

Frantz, David Evans, Christina Linden, and Chris E. Vargas, eds. *Trans Hirstory in 99 Objects*. Munich: Hirmer Publishers, 2023.

Gill-Peterson, Jules. "It's Not Enough to Celebrate Transgender Women of Color during Pride. It's Time to Learn Their History." *Washington Post.* June 25, 2021, sec. Perspective. www.washingtonpost.com/gen der-identity/its-not-enough-to-celebrate-transgender-women-of-color-during-pride-its-time-to-learn-their-history/.

Goodman, Elyssa. "11 Wig-Incinerating Drag Documentaries to Watch For Pride." Them. June 28, 2019. www.them.us/story/11-drag-documentaries-pride.

———. "Drag Herstory: The Drag Queen Who Ran For President in 1992." Them. April 20, 2018. https://www.them.us/story/joan-jett-blakk-drag-queen-president.

Greig, James. "Inside America's Escalating War on Drag." Dazed. March 2, 2023. www.dazeddigital.com/life-culture/article/58337/1/amer ica-war-on-drag-story-hour-right-proud-boys.

Hawgood, Alex. "Yass, We Can! Drag Performers Enter the Political Mainstream." W Magazine. October 29, 2020. www.wmagazine. com/culture/drag-performers-politics-maebe-a-girl-marti-gould-allen-cummings.

Hot Mess, Lil Miss, and Harper Keenan. "Royal Reading: Drag Pedagogy and the Art of Queer Literacy." *Literacy Today.* June 2023.

Joseph, Channing Gerard. "The First Drag Queen Was a Former Slave." *The Nation.* January 31, 2020. www.thenation.com/article/society/drag-queen-slave-ball/.

Keenan, Harper, and Lil Miss Hot Mess. "Drag Pedagogy: The Playful Practice of Queer Imagination in Early Childhood." *Curriculum Inquiry* 50, no. 5 (October 19, 2020): 440–61. https://doi.org/10.1080/03626784.2020.1864621.

Keenan, Harper, Lil Miss Hot Mess, LeRoi Newbold, and Lee Iskander. "Out of the Classroom & Onto the Runway: Queer and Trans Pedagogies in Early Childhood." In *Reimagining Diversity, Equity, and Justice in Early Childhood,* edited by Haeny Yoon, A. Lin Goodwin, and Celia Genishi, 1st edition. New York, NY: Routledge, 2023.

Khubchandani, Kareem. *Decolonize Drag.* New York: OR Books, 2023.

Kornstein, Harris. "Drag Performance on Screen." In *The International Encyclopedia of Gender, Media, and Communication,* edited by Karen Ross, 1–6. Wiley, 2020. https://doi.org/10.1002/9781119429 128.iegmc315.

Kosciw, Joseph G., Clark, Caitlin M., & Menard, Leesh. *The 2021 National School Climate Survey: The Experiences of LGBTQ+ Youth in Our Nation's Schools*. New York: GLSEN, 2022.

Lipstadt, Deborah E. "Want to Fight Antisemitism? Embrace Jewish Traditions." *New York Times*. September 14, 2023. www.nytimes.com/2023/09/14/opinion/antisemitism-jewish-pride.html.

Nichols. "Miss Major on Rioting at Stonewall: 'That was 3 Nights of Absolute Terror.'" *HuffPost*. June 1, 2018. www.huffpost.com/entry/miss-major-on-rioting-at-stonewall_n_5b0c4312e4b0568a880dadbc.

O'Hara, Mary Emily. "GLAAD Report: Drag Events Faced at Least 141 Protests and Significant Threats in 2022." *GLAAD* (blog). November 21, 2022. www.glaad.org/blog/updated-glaad-report-drag-events-faced-least-141-protests-and-significant-threats-2022.

Okeowo, Alexis. "How Saidiya Hartman Retells the History of Black Life." *The New Yorker*. October 19, 2020. www.newyorker.com/magazine/2020/10/26/how-saidiya-hartman-retells-the-history-of-black-life.

Santos, Kyne. *Math in Drag*. Baltimore, Maryland: Johns Hopkins University Press, 2024.

Shane, Cari. "The First Self-Proclaimed Drag Queen Was a Formerly Enslaved Man." Smithsonian Magazine. June 9, 2023. www.smithsonianmag.com/history/the-first-self-proclaimed-drag-queen-was-a-formerly-enslaved-man-180982311/.

Tashjian, Rachel. "A Brief History of Stormé DeLarverie, Stonewall's Suiting Icon." *GQ*. June 27, 2019. www.gq.com/story/storme-delarverie-suiting.

Testa, Nino. "My Drag Worksheet." 2023. https://addran.tcu.edu/wgst/community/My-Drag-Worksheet-2.pdf.

The MicroWorlds Lab (Duke University). "What is Microhistory?" Accessed March 21, 2024. https://sites.duke.edu/microworldslab/what-is-microhistory/.

Villarreal, Daniel. "Drag Queens are More Political than Ever. Can They Lead a Movement?" *Vox*. November 5, 2018. www.vox.com/identities/2018/11/5/18056558/drag-queens-politics-activism-lgbtq-rupaul.

Villegas, Jordan. "'The Empress is a Man': The Drag Royalty of José Julio Sarria." *Latina* (blog). May 20, 2021. https://latina.com/the-empress-is-a-man-the-drag-royalty-of-jose-julio-sarria/.

"Year in Review: Anti-LGBTQ+ Hate & Extremism Incidents, 2022–2023." Anti-Defamation League. June 22, 2023. www.adl.org/resources/report/year-review-anti-lgbtq-hate-extremism-incidents-2022-2023.

Part II

How We Can Teach LGBTQ+ History: Practical Strategies

5

Voices from the Field: Incorporating LGBTQ+ History in Middle and High School Classrooms

Stacie Brensilver Berman

As the previous chapters and the historians', teachers', teacher educators', and activists' voices included in them establish, integrating LGBTQ+ history into academic content is not only pedagogically necessary, but potentially life-changing for students and educators. A decade ago, it seemed like more people began to agree, with an increasing number of states mandating–through legislation or revised standards and policies–the inclusion of LGBTQ+ history in K-12 courses. As that progress met with backlash, though, and the number of states seeking to restrict efforts at inclusivity outpaced those intending to promote it, the landscape demanded new forms of advocacy and activism in educational spaces. In the 2022–2023 school year, with laws and policies that restricted or prohibited including LGBTQ+ history in K-12 curricula on the rise, it became even more imperative to directly support teachers who sought to do so.

DOI: 10.4324/9781032689678-8

Among social studies teachers, one unintended consequence of curriculum censorship policies quickly became clear: the uproar over "Don't Say Gay/Trans" laws alerted educators to a topic that many did not include in their curriculum, largely because they did not know this history well enough to meaningfully integrate it into their lessons. The number of teachers attending conference sessions and professional development workshops focusing on LGBTQ+ history increased threefold; there were one hundred more applicants for the National Endowment for the Humanities' 2022 summer institute on LGBTQ+ history than available seats.[1] It made sense to us, at that point, to gather a working group of teachers to plan and teach lessons that organically integrated LGBTQ+ history into topics they already taught in the hope of creating a supportive environment for those teachers and generating work that we could make available to teachers across the country.

Even teachers in states without restrictive laws and policies feel the pressure of working in a national climate where the conversation so often focuses on book bans, parental rights, and limits placed on schools and teachers. A 2023 RAND Corporation survey found that two-thirds of the teachers who responded censor themselves out of fear of parental and administrative pushback.[2] In such an environment, bringing teachers together to share their backgrounds, concerns, triumphs, and challenges as they attempt curricular reform offers a level of support not found when they operate in isolation. Additionally, the teachers in our working group–six at the beginning, four at the end–knew they had social studies teacher educators whose work focuses on making LGBTQ+ history a significant part of the K-12 curriculum available to them throughout this process. Though that is not possible for every teacher seeking to do this work, the lessons discussed in this chapter are a testament to the fact that a diverse set of teachers in different contexts can effectively develop inclusive curricula.

LGBTQ+ history is present throughout social studies classes, even when it is not explicitly referenced or taught. Individuals who would identify as LGBTQ+—a term that did not exist until the twenty-first century–are present throughout history and integral in many of the eras and topics on which history teachers focus. Lessons on the Harlem Renaissance, World War II, civil rights, ancient civilizations, and the Holocaust, among others, impart information in which LGBTQ+ lives and themes are prominent and impactful, even when they are not mentioned. The assumption of heteronormativity buries, but does not eradicate, this history. The teachers with whom we worked, then, took advantage of an opportunity to make their lessons more complete. In doing so, they establish models for their colleagues to similarly develop materials in ways that reveal a history that is too often hidden, rather than starting something new.

The Teachers

Our working group ultimately included four teachers[3] working in different contexts in the 2022–2023 school year. Each of them was invited to join this project based on their prior work towards building more inclusive curricula and/or participation in workshops specifically dedicated to integrating LGBTQ+ history into the lessons they teach. We knew it would be difficult to recruit teachers in more conservative states who might face significant hurdles in their attempts to implement the resources they created for this endeavor, so we instead aimed to assemble a group representing different school settings. We hoped that this diversity would contribute to conversations and reflections on the different goals, challenges, and processes that teachers navigated in their distinct circumstances.

Each teacher joined the working group with specific intentions. Two of them participated in an extended workshop on teaching LGBTQ+ history the summer before and were excited about the opportunity to implement what they learned and participate in further discussions about their practice. One is a veteran teacher who regularly attends professional development sessions aimed at building her practice and including marginalized groups in the curriculum; another was, at the time, an early career teacher with a strong social justice focus in the lessons he planned. Together, they formed a group committed to greater LGBTQ+ representation and more accurate and compelling depictions of historical

Teacher's Name	Years Teaching (as of the 2022–2023 school year)	Location	School Type	Grade Level
Charles Masters	2	New York City	Charter	Middle School
Kiley Hart	10	Upstate New York	Independent/ Boarding	High School
Emma Banks	18	Southern California	Independent	High School
Lia Taylor	31	New York City	Public	High School

FIGURE 5.1
Teachers Participating in the Teaching LGBTQ+ History Working Group, 2022–2023.

events that are traditionally included in United States and world history curricula.

In the 2022–2023 school year, Charles Masters was a second-year middle school teacher at a charter school in New York City. Before he entered the classroom, Charles spent years working in the hospitality industry; he therefore had significant experience anticipating others' needs and establishing a productive environment under a variety of circumstances. Charles's school was committed to diversity and social justice initiatives; earlier in the year students read and analyzed the young readers' edition of Ibram X. Kendi's *Stamped*. Among the student population, nearly half identified as Black or Hispanic/Latino, approximately 40% identified as White, and other students identified as Asian, Hawaiian, or two or more races. More than half of the students identified as male, and 50% of students qualified for free or reduced-price lunch. Charles entered teaching with the belief that students need teachers who share their background and culture and need to learn about joy and resistance among marginalized groups. In fact, he decorated his classroom with photos and posters of influential individuals across the gender spectrum in United States history who identified as Black, Indigenous, queer,

Latinx, and Asian, paying specific attention to the ways in which each person's intersectional identities influenced their historical contributions. Discussing his motivation for participating in this project, Charles said, "I believe it is important that my lessons are inclusive of the community which I serve as an educator."[4] Incorporating LGBTQ+ history aligned with his philosophy, and participating in the working group provided a foundation for him to receive the support and feedback he needed to feel prepared to effectively bring that history into his classroom.

Kiley Hart taught at an independent girls' school in upstate New York where most of the students (approximately 60%) boarded on campus during the academic year. Kiley's student population was different from Charles's. More than a quarter of the students were international, hailing from thirty-six different countries. Among students from the United States, half identified as White, approximately 20% of students identified as Asian or Asian/Pacific Islander, and just over 10% identified as Black or Latinx. Students at Kiley's school applied for admission and paid tuition to attend; approximately 40% received financial aid. Kiley entered her tenth year of teaching in 2022 and, as our working group began, was preparing to teach a Global Queer Studies elective she created after "a few students in [her] US History class reached out to say that they thought LGBTQIA+ history was not represented well in [their] US History classes—and also that we should teach a queer studies class."[5] Kiley participated in a workshop on teaching LGBTQ+ history the during the summer of 2022 and envisioned the working group as an opportunity to "to share some of [her] experiences teaching the course."[6]

Emma Banks attended the same summer professional development workshop as Kiley and left that experience motivated to integrate LGBTQ+ history throughout her year-long curriculum. For Emma, who maintained a strong focus on representation before she participated in the summer workshop and this working group, taking a position at an independent school that she asserted was "very LGBTQ+ friendly" with a substantial number of students who identify as LGBTQ+ motivated her to learn more about this history and develop pedagogical strategies to effectively integrate it in her lessons. Emma's independent school and, by extension, her classes were diverse: slightly more than half of the students identified as male; just under half of the students identified as White; and nearly 20% of students identified as two or more races or Asian. Families pay tuition to cover the cost of their student's education; approximately one-third of the students receive tuition assistance. Emma's students approached LGBTQ+ history believing that queer and transgender identities should be uplifted and celebrated. Part of the work that Emma did in our group, therefore, was figuring out how to help her students understand the struggles that many individuals within the LGBTQ+ population faced historically and continue to navigate in the present.

Lia Taylor was the veteran teacher in our group, with 31 years of experience at the start of 2022–2023 school year. Lia was the only public school teacher in our group, and the only participant teaching a world history survey class. Prior to joining the working group, Lia hadn't developed a lesson or unit that included LGBTQ+ history beyond a few discussion points, and she "hoped by participating in this project that [she] could become more knowledgeable and thereby strengthen the teaching of this history in [her] school." Lia also shared that she was "very concerned about the restrictions being placed on social studies teachers in other states" and therefore more motivated to bring this history into her classroom.[7] The population at Lia's school is diverse: one-third of the students identify as Hispanic or Latino; 20% identify as Black or White, respectively; and approximately 10% identify as Asian or two or more races. The student population is evenly split between male and female, and approximately half of the students qualify for free or reduced-price lunch. By joining this working group, Lia hoped to build upon existing resources and "efforts by various organizations, especially the NYC DOE, to integrate topics and create welcoming, affirming, and culturally responsive schools."[8]

Each of the teachers who participated in the working group, then, were interested in and committed to developing more LGBTQ+- inclusive lessons and resources before joining this project. Their enthusiasm was essential in ensuring that we met our goals during a sometimes tumultuous, post-pandemic school year during which myriad additional challenges arose for each of the teachers. The working group model and the support and flexibility it provided ultimately paved the way for Charles, Kiley, Emma, and Lia's students to engage with materials and have valuable, informative, and affirming discussions about LGBTQ+ history.

The Process

Our goals and plans for this project were largely informed by our experiences planning and working with groups of teachers in the past. Both of us have decades of experience, separately and together, collaborating with teachers working in different contexts and regions to create, implement, and reflect upon lessons and units on significant topics in US history. Prior to this project, we worked with ten teachers from New York, California, Indiana, and Illinois on integrating Critical Race Theory into lessons on race and civil rights throughout the curriculum. We were prepared then to engage with and support a group of teachers who likewise hoped to bring topics for which they might receive pushback into their classes.

Our previous work and the circumstances teachers faced in a post-COVID school environment led us to make certain decisions before we began recruiting teachers to work on the project in order to respect their time and expertise. First, we knew that we would not require teachers to attend full group meetings throughout the project; we would plan meetings to establish expectations for the teachers' work and to reflect on that work at the end of the year. Second, we recognized that it was important for teachers to determine the topics of their lessons or units and to have autonomy over their planning process in order to meet their students' needs. Third, we decided to prioritize including teachers in different locations and to rely on their reflections and observations over focusing solely on New York City and observing the classes in person. Given the different policies and teaching practices throughout the country, geographic diversity was more important to us than onsite observations.

Having made these decisions, we assembled the teachers for the first time over Zoom. Our goals for the first meeting were to give the teachers–all of whom were invited to participate in the project–a chance to introduce themselves and meet their colleagues, establish our goals for the project overall, and provide a timeline along with expectations for the work the teachers would commit to do. There were six teachers at the initial meeting; two eventually exited the project due to time constraints and other personal events. The teachers shared their rationale for participating in this working group, why they believed it was important to include LGBTQ+ history, and their experiences with and efforts to do so in the past. Though we were clear from the start that this project would not require the teachers to attend frequent group meetings–that was a concern for a few of the participants–this initial meeting and the opportunity to share space with like-minded educators offered a sense of comfort that none of the teachers were alone in this endeavor.

The teachers' distinct grade levels and settings meant that they would develop and teach lessons on different topics throughout the school year. We met with each teacher individually as they planned and implemented their lessons, offering feedback and support along the way. In the early planning phases, as the teachers chose topics and eras, we shared resources and background information that they might include in their student-facing materials. As their planning progressed, we listened to ideas about objectives, activities, and methods of assessment, offering guidance and giving the teachers a sounding board to talk through their goals and the lessons' trajectories. Though full working group meetings were not a part of this process, it was important for this to be a collaborative effort. Considering the isolating nature of this work–often teachers who include LGBTQ+ history in their curriculum do so on their own—we wanted the teachers involved with this project to know that their questions would be answered, their concerns addressed, and their efforts met with enthusiastic and encouraging responses. These individual meetings also provided teachers with fewer years of experience overall an opportunity to hone their craft and think deeply about the connections between historical events and groups' experiences.

Each of the teachers shared their lesson plans and student facing materials prior to implementation. This step gave us a sense of what students would learn and the ways that they would engage with the material despite the fact that we were not able to observe most of the classes on the days that the lessons were taught. Access to these plans allowed us to ask specific questions when we checked in with the teachers following their classes and provided common ground as we prompted teachers to reflect on their experiences. Two of the teachers taught their lessons in the middle of the school year and used this opportunity to revise their plans for future use. The others, one of whom did an extended project on queer history with her class and one who taught her lesson at the very end of the school year, shared meaningful reflections but did not have time to revise while this project was ongoing. We were able to observe one of the New York City teachers; watching students interact with the material and being able to provide detailed feedback provided that teacher with the additional support we wish we could have offered to all.

The value of this project was two-fold: the teachers and their students explored and deeply engaged with LGBTQ+ history, and the teachers' work and experiences contributed to materials and guidance that other educators could use in the future. It was imperative, then, for everyone involved in the working group to reflect and share their reactions to this endeavor on multiple occasions. First, we asked all of the teachers to share instinctive reactions at the conclusion of their lessons, usually via electronic communication. We then met with each teacher over Zoom to have more in-depth conversations about the lessons' effectiveness and students' reactions to the material. Lastly, we asked each teacher to reflect in writing, responding to prompts including, "In your opinion, what went well as you planned and taught this lesson(s)/unit(s)?" and "What would you do differently if you taught this lesson(s)/unit(s) again in the future?" Through these multiple rounds of reflection, we gained a comprehensive understanding of what these learning experiences meant to both the teachers and the students and the ways in which their takeaways might be transferable to colleagues across the country.

The Lessons

Each of the teachers came into this project with specific ideas about the topic on which they would focus based on their grade levels, state standards, curriculum, and student population. As a working group, we ultimately produced three lessons on topics with clear connections to LGBTQ+ history: the Newport Scare/Red Scare of 1919, the Harlem Renaissance, and gay men's experiences during World War II and the Holocaust. Kiley, whose queer history elective was her setting for this work, developed a project where students chose events in LGBTQ+ history and planned lessons that they used to teach their peers.[9] All of these educational experiences emphasized the importance of LGBTQ+ history in the context of the events and themes of the time and offered students choices for the ways that they interacted with LGBTQ+ history, making them accessible and engaging for all learners. LGBTQ+ history was woven into each lesson and not emphasized as distinct from other historical events, fulfilling one of the project's main goals and ensuring that, because they fit organically into the curriculum, each of the lessons is replicable in multiple settings.

The Newport Scandal

Emma joined the working group following her participation in a two-week summer seminar on LGBTQ+ Histories in the United States. She was already planning to incorporate LGBTQ+ history in her curriculum and had several ideas about how to do so for the more frequently discussed entry points (the Harlem Renaissance, the Lavender Scare, the civil rights era, etc.). She hoped to be able to develop lessons on less frequently discussed topics and to support her students as they made connections between different moments in US history. To meet this goal, Emma researched and planned lessons on the Newport Scandal, an event that inserts an LGBTQ+ history narrative into lessons on the post-World War I Red Scare and evokes parallels to the Lavender Scare and connections with Franklin D. Roosevelt's rise to power and presidential policies.

The Newport Scandal emerged from actions taken by Assistant Secretary of the Navy Roosevelt and other military officials, including chief machinist's mate Ervin Arnold, to investigate and arrest sailors who engaged in sexual interactions with other men. Arnold, who learned of Newport's gay culture from other sailors while being treated for rheumatism in the Navy infirmary and decided that these "perversions" were "past tolerating,"[10] recruited sailors to befriend and engage with servicemen and civilians suspected of homosexual activity and report their findings. Arnold did so with permission from Assistant Secretary Roosevelt, who "agreed that 'a most searching and rigid investigation' needed to be conducted with the aim of prosecuting those individuals responsible for the spread of degeneracy."[11] Ultimately, Arnold's investigation led to twenty naval officers being arrested and court-martialed; fourteen received 20-30 year sentences for their actions.

The scandal came to light when the investigation targeted a respected minister, eroding its morality-focused justification. The *Providence Journal* revealed the steps that Roosevelt and Secretary of the Navy Josephus Daniels instructed the Navy to take to entrap officers. Both of them attempted to distance themselves from the scandal. A Senate subcommittee investigated, placing most of the blame on Roosevelt. According to Sherry Zane, author of *"I did it for the Uplift of Humanity and The Navy": Same-Sex Acts and The Origins of The National Security State, 1919–1921,* "They hold him morally responsible for the investigation and they say that he should never hold public office again;"[12] Roosevelt ultimately faced few consequences from his role while the men targeted by Arnold's investigation were dishonorably discharged and faced the stigma associated with their actions for decades. Therefore, though the Newport Scandal is not frequently covered in US history classes and curricula, it has deep connections to the Progressive era, the quest for normalcy in the 1920s, the Roosevelt administration, the treatment of LGBTQ+ soldiers in World War II, and the Lavender Scare.

Emma's objective for her lesson on the Newport Scandal was: "Students will examine the repression of 'homosexual' activity among men in the military after World War I, focusing on the Newport Scandal (1919), through an exploration of primary source materials." She began by contextualizing this event in the larger history of civil liberties violations, asking students to recall what they learned about repressions on free speech and political activity during World War I and the Red Scare that began in its aftermath. Emma also reminded students that in times of "social, economic, and political tension" the government often targets people's rights, especially when those rights are used to support dissent or difference. Thus, from the beginning of the lesson, Emma established that students would learn about the ways in which people in power criminalized individuals' private lives, that this moment in LGBTQ+ history is part of a larger national narrative, and that there were connections between this moment in history and others students were aware of or would learn about in the future.

Emma's lesson (Appendix 5A) included three sections: introducing the topic and establishing context; small group work reading and analyzing primary sources; and a full class discussion evaluating the impact of the Newport Scandal and the ways in which gender, sexuality, and class played a role in how it unfolded. She began by providing context on the way that many Americans viewed individuals who identified as LGBTQ+ or engaged in "same-sex intimate encounters"[13] in the early 1900s, including that they were targeted as security risks and seen as threats to the nation's moral order. Emma also informed her students that prohibitions on LGBTQ+ individuals serving in the military were established in 1916 and that these laws provided the foundation for the actions that naval officers took during the Newport Scandal. Students read and annotated documents on "The First Red Scare" and the Palmer Raids; the information in these documents provided students with a sense of the atmosphere in the United States in the aftermath of World War I, setting the stage for them to make connections between the repressive environment created by the Red Scare and the impetus to target anyone whose differences could be viewed as a threat.

Emma followed this introduction by breaking students into groups of five, with each group analyzing and asking questions about a different primary source related to the Newport Scandal. These included Roosevelt's Confidential Memo on the scandal, images and photos of Newport and the soldiers stationed there, a list of arrests and convictions following the scandal, a document from the congressional inquiry into Roosevelt's actions, and the testimony of Dudley J. Marriott, one of the servicemen who "investigated" the scandal. Students engaged in a structured document analysis activity, noting the type of document and its author, purpose, point of view, and context, and shared their findings with their group to create a comprehensive summary of what they read. Together, the class read Roosevelt's draft note to Senator Henry Keyes, who wrote the report condemning his actions, in which Roosevelt stated, "I have had the privilege of knowing many thousands of Harvard graduates. Of the whole number, I did not personally know one whom I believed to be personally and willfully dishonorable. I regret that because of your recent despicable action, I can no longer say that. My only hope is that you will live long enough to appreciate that you have violated decency and truth and that you will pray your Maker for forgiveness."[14] Equipped with the information that they read separately and together, Emma's students embarked on a full class discussion synthesizing what they learned. They considered how social class and differing perspectives on morality and privacy played a role in the events that unfolded during the Newport Scandal and the impact of these events on individuals' lives. She ended the lesson by asking, "Do you think there are any broad social or cultural implications for America of prosecuting or banning queer folks in the military? That is, what does prosecuting or banning queer folk suggest about their place in the nation?" This question allowed students to draw conclusions about the Newport Scandal and make connections to the present.

Emma's lesson demonstrated that teaching LGBTQ+ history gives students the opportunity to meaningfully engage with history and build historical thinking skills in the same way that they do when studying other topics and groups while also learning about events that are often omitted from the curriculum.

Students engaged in source analysis, interacted with text and visual sources, synthesized information, and participated in discussions where they contextualized information and supported their positions. Meanwhile, the focus on the Newport Scandal enriched students' knowledge of the post-World War I era in the United States and set them up to better understand other forms of backlash that emerged in the 1920s. Furthermore, students were introduced to Franklin Roosevelt earlier in the curriculum than usual, establishing his political trajectory and complicating the narrative around a complex, and often overly simplified, figure. Integrating LGBTQ+ history through this lesson on the Newport Scandal accomplished Emma's goal of making her class more inclusive and showed the power of organically incorporating concurrent events.

After teaching the lesson, Emma reported, "Students were FASCINATED to learn about queer folks from [the early twentieth century]. They were excited to engage with the sources we have, especially the primary sources, and curious about what sources we might not have."[15] She also reflected on the differences between her students' lives in a progressive community in the twenty-first century and the attitudes that people faced a century ago, sharing that students were confused about why the sailors' same-sex interactions were a "scandal" at all, and wondering about the disconnect between "navy men claiming to be loathe to engage in homosexual acts while volunteering to do so." Emma stated that her students' reactions "revealed to me that my students struggle to imagine a repressive — even dangerous — context for LGBTQ+ folks."[16] Based on this experience, Emma's resolve to include LGBTQ+ history in more of her lessons deepened.

The Harlem Renaissance

The eighth-grade Humanities curriculum at Charles's school began with Reconstruction and ended with the mid to late twentieth century, depending on the pace of the school year. The school, which promoted diversity and inclusion throughout its practices, emphasized the contributions and triumphs of individuals from marginalized communities throughout the history curriculum. Lessons on the Harlem Renaissance, then, were meant to encompass the celebration of identity that the art, litera-ture, and lifestyles of that era conveyed. For Charles, who joined the working group because he "support[s] ALL beautiful young minds,"[17] the Harlem Renaissance represented a time in history when his students could explore individuals' intersectional iden-tities and the ways in which those identities motivated efforts towards social justice. Those twin goals authentically represented Charles's pedagogical philosophy and allowed him to present the era in a way that was representative of his students.

Harlem emerged as an enclave of African American cul-tural expression in the 1920s as a result of the Great Migration. Approximately 175,000 African American individuals moved from the South to Harlem, "giving the neighborhood the lar-gest concentration of Black people in the world."[18] The Harlem Renaissance,[19] a term that describes the literary and artistic works created by poets, authors, visual artists, musicians, and performers focusing on Black identity and experiences, was, according to Alain Locke, "a 'spiritual coming of age' in which African Americans transformed 'social disillusionment to race pride'."[20] As Henry Louis Gates asserted, the Harlem Renaissance was "surely as gay as it was Black."[21] Musicians like Ma Rainey included implicit and explicit references to queer desire in their lyrics; poets wrote about same-sex interactions, like Countee Cullen's "Tableau"; and "drag balls" were a prominent aspect of Harlem's social scene. Lessons on the Harlem Renaissance, then, can organically include the intersectional identities and expressions of identity of that era.

Charles's lesson (Appendix 5B), titled "The Harlem Renaissance and The LGBTQ+ Movement: Social Justice Contributors," prompted students to delve into the ways in which individuals whom we would now identify as LGBTQ+ contributed to the Harlem Renaissance.[22] He began by establishing the era as one in which people who existed on the margins of society began to advocate for their right to be acknowledged and valued, complicating the narrative by focusing on gender and sexuality in addition to race. Ultimately, in alignment with his school's goal of promoting social justice throughout the curriculum, Charles hoped his students would be able to analyze the ways in which individuals used their platforms and talents to establish their presence and push for acceptance.

Charles began the lesson by introducing students to the foundational ideas of the Harlem Renaissance. At the beginning of the class, he presented a quote from Alain Locke's *The New Negro*, "The younger generation comes, bringing its gifts. Youth speaks, and the voice of the New Negro is heard. Art must discover and reveal the beauty which prejudice and caricature have overlaid. The younger generation is vibrant with a new psychology; the new spirit is awake in the masses... Each generation... will have its creed;"[23] Charles asked students to evaluate the content and purpose of the quote and state their own creed. Next, students watched a video that provided context and information on the Harlem Renaissance from "Black History in Two Minutes" and responded to questions including: 1) What flourished throughout the decade of the 1920s?; 2) What was one of the most important factors that contributed to the Harlem Renaissance?; 3) What is sometimes created in the most repressive times?; and 4) How was art used by Black people during this period? Then, Charles segued into the role of LGBTQ+ history in the Harlem Renaissance, sharing the aforementioned Gates quote and showing students a video on Alain Locke, one of the era's most prominent writers and someone whose writing and personal correspondence indicated queer desires.

Equipped with this introduction, students worked independently and in groups to learn more about specific artists. In groups of three, students read about the writers (Langston Hughes, Countee Cullen, and Alain Locke), entertainers (Jimmie Daniels and Gladys Bentley), and Blueswomen (Ma Rainey, Bessie Smith, and Alberta Hunter) of the Harlem Renaissance. Each member of the group focused on one of those three options, sharing what they learned with their peers in a jigsaw-style activity. Students took notes on what they learned about the different artists and their art, drawing conclusions about the implicit and explicit ways they expressed aspects of their identity, including their sexuality, and how their art helped them share these identities with the wider world. Each group shared their discoveries with the rest of the class, culminating in a discussion of the ways in which artists of the era expressed all of their identities in the work they created and evaluating why the atmosphere of the Harlem Renaissance provided the opportunity for them to do so.

FIGURE 5.2
Photograph of Gladys Bentley. Photo courtesy of the Collection of the Smithsonian National Museum of African American History and Culture.

According to Charles, the "classroom discussion and student facing documents demonstrated the students' high-level of engagement and appreciation."[24] Students participated actively throughout the lesson, drawing connections between artists' rationale behind expressing pride in their race and in their sexuality and discussing their ideas about the greater openness promoted during this time period. Though Charles reminded his students that not everyone was accepting of LGBTQ+ individuals and identities, it was clear that they understood the vibrant intersectionality of the Harlem Renaissance based on the art that emerged from it. Charles began his lesson by addressing the "often-overlooked place of the Harlem Renaissance within queer history." By the end of the lesson, for the students in his eighth-grade class, it was no longer overlooked.

LGBTQ+ Individuals in the Holocaust

Lia joined the working group with the awareness that her "students are very interested in the topic and our GSA has struggled with the lack of information/misinformation that proliferates online about LGBTQ+ issues in general."[25] Though she attended workshops on integrating LGBTQ+ history into the curriculum before our work began, many focused more on the United States than global history. This project offered her a path to delve into the presence of LGBTQ+ topics and themes in the units that she already taught. She found a powerful entry point in her unit on World War II and the Holocaust, exploring the ways that LGBTQ+ individuals, particularly gay men, experienced life in Germany before World War II, becoming targets of the Nazi regime during the Holocaust and struggling for equality in Germany since the end of the war.

Though history classes across the United States include lessons and units on the Holocaust, they rarely focus on the ways in which the Nazis targeted LGBTQ+ individuals and the persecution that LGBTQ+ people faced in Germany after World War II. As historian Andrea Carlo wrote in 2021, "while Holocaust remembrance has become an integral part of our civic duties... LGBTQ victims are often missing from that collective memory."[26] The Nazis began their campaign to eliminate queer life and culture, and therefore, LGBTQ+ people, as soon as they came to power, immediately enforcing Paragraph 175, a German law prohibiting homosexual relationships between men. Carlo asserted, "Weimar-era Berlin came to be labeled as the 'gay capital of the world,' a city where a booming queer nightlife scene was wedded with the budding dissemination of new academic ideas calling for greater acceptance of homosexuality and gender non-conformity"; the Nazis were determined to stem the power of this movement as they sought to solidify their power over German life.[27] Throughout the 1930s the Nazis passed laws criminalizing same-sex interactions and established agencies to enforce them, ultimately arresting over 100,000 men and sending 5,000-15,000 to concentration camps.[28]

Gay men could be easily identified in concentration camps by the pink triangles they were forced to wear, making them targets for additional harassment and exclusion among other prisoners. According to the United States Holocaust Memorial Museum, "pink triangle prisoners were among the most abused groups in the camps. Sometimes pink triangle prisoners were assigned the most grueling and demanding jobs in the camp labor system. They were often subjected to physical and sexual abuse by camp guards and fellow inmates"; they were also at risk for forced castration by camp commandants.[29] The end of the war, meanwhile, did not bring the end of gay men's sentences. Homosexuality remained illegal in Germany with "some Holocaust survivors even being forced to carry out their sentences in prison." An additional 100,000 gay men were arrested between 1945 and 1969; thousands more lived closeted lives or submerged their gay identity.[30] Gay Holocaust survivors' experiences weren't acknowledged until the 1970s.

Lia's lesson (Appendix 5C) aimed to immerse students in this long-silenced history and have them investigate the trajectory of LGBTQ+ life in Germany from the thriving urban enclaves of the Weimar Republic to the oppression and vilification imposed by the Nazis, to the continued criminalization of LGBTQ+ individuals in post-war East and West Germany. The lesson's goals, therefore, were for students to evaluate and analyze primary and secondary source documents to understand:

1. Historical context and culture of Germany in regard to the LGBTQ+ community prior to the rise of the Nazi Regime;
2. Key events and laws enacted by the Nazis during the Holocaust to target gay men; and
3. Lessons learned/struggles to obtain equal rights by the LGBTQ+ community in Germany since the WWII period and Holocaust.

Lia's objectives included students synthesizing the information they gathered from these sources to complete a visual or written reflection on what they learned in this multi-day lesson.

The lesson, which was designed to take two to four days depending on the pace at which students analyzed the assigned primary and secondary sources, began with students reflecting on groups beyond Jewish people that the Nazis targeted during the Holocaust and what they have or have not learned about those groups in previous history classes. Lia then asked

FIGURE 5.3
Prisoners marked with the pink triangle in the concentration camp at Sachsenhausen, Germany, 1938. Photo courtesy of the National Archives (photo no. 242-HLB-3609-25).

students about the ways in which all of these groups' rights and freedoms have been protected since World War II, based on their knowledge of the late twentieth-century and current events. This opening discussion set the stage for the students to interact with information about the Holocaust, particularly focusing on gay men's experiences and the lack of attention paid to their stories.

The class worked in groups, with each group responsible for examining the conditions gay men faced in Germany in different eras. The first group reviewed text and visual sources on life in Germany prior to the Nazis' rise to power, including queer culture during the Weimar Republic. This group was specifically tasked with drawing conclusions about attitudes toward homosexuality in the late nineteenth and early twentieth centuries while considering the divisions within German society during that time. The second group evaluated sources from and about the 1930s and 1940s, including the Nazis' ascendance and the Holocaust. This group engaged with information from the United States Holocaust Museum and stories about and reflections from gay men who were imprisoned during the Holocaust as provided by the Holocaust Memorial Day Trust; they drew conclusions about the impact of Nazi-era laws and imprisonment on gay men and the ways in which their suffering in the camps was similar to and different from other groups. The third group traced the evolution of attitudes and actions towards LGBTQ+ individuals in Germany since World War II, including their continued imprisonment at the end of the war. They examined more recent efforts by the German government to acknowledge gay men's experiences and protests in support of LGBTQ+ rights among German individuals and athletes. Each group designated a presenter upon completing this work; the presenters shared their group's findings, allowing students to learn from each other as they construct a narrative of LGBTQ+ individuals' experiences in twentieth-century Germany. The lesson finished with students reflecting on the ways that incorporating marginalized histories contributes to inclusivity and belonging in the present.

Thinking back on her experience developing and teaching this lesson, Lia said:

> Content that resonated with students included: (1) Understanding why lesbian women were not directly imprisoned/criminalized. (2) Seeing the role of liberal and conservative nationalism on the politics of the time, and how the conservatives/Nazis mirrored similar political debates today. One student noted how cities and urban areas were more liberal in Weimar Germany, just like big cities on the coasts especially in the US today—with more conservative Southern and rural areas being less tolerant. (3) The viciousness of some of the attacks as described in primary sources; the way that victims did not share their stories and/or were not recognized as victims until much later. (4) The lack of officially repealing the laws until the 1990's...and East Germany doing it before West Germany. (5) The reclamation of the Pink Triangle as a symbol of empowerment. (6) The Qatar controversy at the World Cup and the German soccer team's resistance.[31]

Though Lia wished she had more time to implement this lesson in her class–it came at the end of the year when the schedule was interrupted by several planned and unplanned days off– she appreciated that students' experience with this information filled gaps in their knowledge and provided opportunities for them to make connections between the past and present. She also noted that the ways that students approached this lesson aligned with the extent to which they engaged with or felt connected to world events. She recalled, "While most students found the topic interesting, especially students who are members of our GSA, some seemed disinterested... This paralleled similar attitudes, lack of empathy, lack of concern for current events related to political polarization in the country... One student told me personally that he thought this was the most interesting unit we had studied all year, while others failed to complete required preparatory homework."[32] As the working group came to an end,

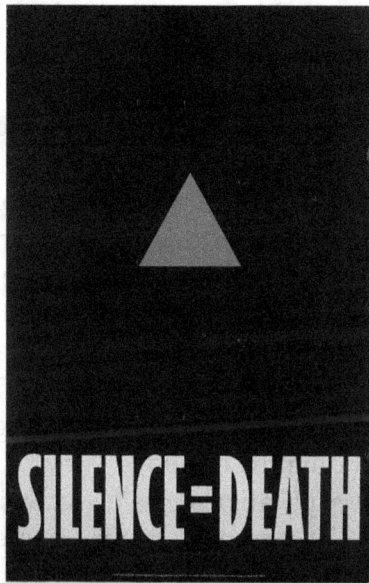

FIGURE 5.4
"Silence=Death" poster designed by ACT UP to protest the United States government's lack of action or acknowledgement during the AIDS crisis in the 1980s. The poster is one of the most recognizable examples of the LGBTQ+ community reclaiming the pink triangle. Image courtesy of ACT UP.

Lia resolved to teach this lesson again and incorporate LGBTQ+ topics throughout her curriculum in an effort to highlight this group's experiences and reinforce the real-world implications of effective historical learning.

Students as Teachers: Developing Lessons on LGBTQ+ History

Unlike the other teachers in the working group, all of whom taught required survey courses, Kiley's class was an elective that specifically focused on global queer history. She therefore had the time and flexibility to dig deeply into events, themes, individuals, and trends significant to LGBTQ+ populations in different parts of the world and ask her students to do the same. The elective, which resulted from students' desire to see queer history better represented in the curriculum, sought to integrate students' interests and contributions in meaningful ways. Among the other lessons and assignments she developed to meet that request, Kiley devised a project in which students selected topics on which the class would focus, planned lessons, and taught their peers. Through this endeavor, the class learned about queer experiences throughout United States history, including eras in which the role and experiences of LGBTQ+ individuals are significant, but unacknowledged.

The project served multiple purposes for Kiley and her students. First, it provided students with an opportunity to work collaboratively on a topic of their choice to enhance their own and their peers' knowledge of a moment in LGBTQ+ history. Second, it enhanced student agency and empowered them to take control of their learning experience. Third, the stated rationale of the project, which was "enhancing our US History materials and extending the coverage of our core textbook, Eric Foner's *Give Me Liberty!*" aligned the project with the derivation and mission of the class: to make history classes more inclusive and representative and fill in the gaps that existed throughout the curriculum relative to LGBTQ+ history. The work that students completed, then, enabled them to grow as learners, historians, and teachers.

Students worked in groups, following a series of steps to complete their projects (Appendix 5D). The first step in the lesson planning process, which students completed in class, included creating a homework assignment to prepare their classmates for the lesson including textbook reading to provide context as well as information on the specific topic that students would learn about the following day. Students then chose three primary sources to share with their peers, with the intention of addressing the omissions that they noticed in their text. Next, they outlined their lesson plan, stating their lesson objective, developing an activity that would support their peers in reaching that goal, and coming up with discussion questions through which the class would synthesize what they learned and form new conclusions. Groups then taught their lessons, with each of the seven groups leading a class on separate days. Lastly, students revised their lesson plans based on their assessment of their effectiveness and reflected on the process. In their written reflections, students responded to the following prompts:

a. What was the goal of your activity? What worked in your activity? What didn't work?

b. What worked in the class discussion of your primary sources? What didn't work? What would you have liked to discuss more?

c. What did you have to revise in your lesson plan between your teaching day and submitting the final version of your lesson?

d. How did your lesson expand your understanding of US History? What did you learn?

e. How was working with a partner?

Kiley's students developed and taught lessons on seven topics, spotlighting the importance of LGBTQ+ history in different eras. The lessons focused on Two Spirit identities, Reconstruction, the Harlem Renaissance, Japanese American internment during World War II, Hollywood in the 1960s, the AIDS epidemic, and LGBTQ+ individuals in the military. Some of these topics, like the Harlem Renaissance and the AIDS epidemic, are more widely covered in classes where teachers integrate LGBTQ+ history. Others, like Reconstruction and Japanese internment, are less often mentioned in relation to LGBTQ+ history and individuals' experiences. The students, therefore, had the opportunity to engage with material that revealed historical facts that they had not encountered previously and filled in the gaps in traditional classroom resources.

As they compiled and taught their lessons, students took on the role of historians and teachers. They explored online archives to locate primary sources, considered the perspectives and intentions of those sources, and led discussions on the significance of the information they presented to the class. The group focused on Reconstruction, for example, shared background information on and photographs of William Dorsey Swann, a formerly enslaved individual who became the "self-named Queen of Drag"[33] and Millie Brown, who was assigned male at birth but lived as a woman in 19th century Milwaukee. The group that investigated and taught about the way that queer individuals experienced internment camps during World War II explored the Jiro Onuma papers housed at the GLBT Historical Society, selecting images and other sources to incorporate into their lesson and further complicate the narrative around this tragic, discriminatory experience. Students interacted with the Hays Code and journalistic accounts of hate crimes perpetrated against actors outed as gay, offering a new perspective on the violence and harassment that grew out of the Red Scare and Lavender Scare. Given the opportunity to create the curriculum they wanted to experience, students relied on the most compelling aspects of social studies education–rich sources, engaging activities, and challenging discussion questions–to design lessons that made history representative and relevant.

LGBTQ+-inclusive history lessons allow students to see the big picture and understand where LGBTQ+ individuals and topics fit into it. As Kiley related, "Pegging the unit to our existing US History textbook, Eric Foner's *Give Me Liberty*, made the project feel really connected to the students' other learning and gave them ownership of expanding it."[34] Each of the lessons focused on a topic or era frequently covered in the US history curriculum but went a step further in terms of the perspectives that the curriculum encompassed. In the students' reflections, they discussed individuals that they had never heard of before this project, like Gladys Bentley, and new revelations, like the historic role of censorship in limiting access to queer people and identities. Students wrote of a renewed commitment to ensure that individuals long erased from history remained in the narrative and the ways in which developing, teaching, and participating in these lessons helped them deepen their overall understanding of LGBTQ+ history. Through this work, then, students were able to situate key events and individuals in context and fulfill the goals of the project and the unit of which it was a part.

The Impact

Despite their different circumstances and topics of instruction, all four teachers had similar reactions to integrating LGBTQ+ history into their classes and its effect on their students. When asked if they would continue teaching LGBTQ+ history, each teacher responded positively; two were already immersed in planning other inclusive lessons and units. Charles, who had not significantly integrated LGBTQ+ history before this project, reported, "It will be a lesson I will continue to use going forward. I will sharpen a few aspects and utilize more student voices in the planning and teaching of the lesson." He believed that it fit well into his Humanities curriculum because "it's important that members of marginalized communities see themselves represented in a history that often negates our/their profound contributions to our human, social, and historical constructs."[35] Lia shared similar sentiments, asserting, "Teaching LGBTQ+ history is a critical entryway into reinstating hope and a sense of the necessity of active citizen participation in nurturing and maintaining our democracy. For these reasons, I will continue to incorporate LGBTQ+ history in my curriculum." Lia found that 60-70% of her students "seemed very unaware of the attacks on LGBTQ+ community, especially transgender people in the US and around the world," and integrating this information into the curriculum helped to address gaps in their historical and current events knowledge.[36]

Emma's recollections spoke to her students' positive reaction to the Newport Scandal lesson and the ways that it supported their historical inquiry. Emma began planning this as part of the final project for the institute she attended the summer before our working group began meeting and she was excited to see how well it went upon implementation. As a result of that experience and her students' positive reaction to this and a prior lesson on Two Spirit individuals, Emma was committed to integrating LGBTQ+ history into lessons on other twentieth and twenty-first century events. Her students learned about Eleanor Roosevelt's relationship with Lorena Hickock, Bayard Rustin's role and marginalization within the Civil Rights Movement, postwar lesbian spaces, the Lavender Scare, and the movement for LGBTQ+ rights in the 1960s and beyond. Kiley, who developed and taught a year-long queer studies course, indicated a similar commitment to this work. According to Kiley, this work reinforced the value of "including giving queer-identifying students an opportunity to see themselves reflected in history and all students an opportunity to see that queer people have always existed, whether they would have labeled themselves as queer in the past." Having taught this elective and seen the ways in which students made meaning of what they learned from their teachers and from each other, Kiley emphatically reported, "I will ABSOLUTELY continue to include LGBTQ+ history in the curriculum!"[37]

The work that all of the teachers did demonstrates that the same strategies and pedagogical tools we use when we teach other topics in US and world history apply when we teach LGBTQ+ history. The teachers used source analysis, text, media and visual sources, research projects, writing exercises, "stations" activities, jigsaws, small group work, and peer-to-peer presentations to deepen students' understanding of the content that they (and, in Kiley's case, her students) taught, replicating the strategies used in other lessons and units. Moreover, the teachers selected and modified the sources that they chose to meet students' needs, ensuring that they maintained a focus on accessibility while introducing a new topic. Educators and historians who advocate for LGBTQ+-inclusive curriculum and previous studies focused on the ways that teachers integrate this content have long maintained that this history can be treated similarly to other topics taught in K-12 classrooms.[38] Each of these lessons demonstrates that an inclusive, representative curriculum aligns with state and national standards, the most up-to-date ideas on effective pedagogical practices, and Universal Design for Learning principles.[39] These lessons demonstrate, then, that there are compelling arguments in favor of including LGBTQ+ history in the face of any opposition teachers might encounter.

At the conclusion of the working group, Emma, Charles, Lia, and Kiley reflected on the impact of including and focusing on LGBTQ+ history. All of them emphasized the connections that students were able to make between these lessons and other topics and moments in US and world history as well as the commonalities that students identified between LGBTQ+ individuals and those from other marginalized groups. Emma's students, for example, had a better understanding of the ways that LGBTQ+ people experienced and became targets during the Red Scare of the 1920s and the McCarthy era having learned about the Newport Scandal before they engaged with documents on the Lavender Scare.[40] They also better understood the world beyond their bubble, including the discrimination that LGBTQ+ individuals face today. Lia's students likewise gained insight into the ways that homosexuality was criminalized in East and West Germany for decades after World War II and laws in place around the world today that target queer and transgender people.[41] Charles's students, meanwhile, were able to apply what they learned about intersectional identities to some of the issues people face in the twenty-first century. These lessons, then, successfully accomplished a major goal of social studies education: providing students with the skills and context to address what they see in the world around them.

The teachers also found this work impactful for their own planning and practices. All believed in the power of LGBTQ+-inclusive social studies curricula when the project began; experiencing its effects over the course of the year–with the lessons described here or in broader scope–confirmed its necessity. As Lia asserted:

> LGBTQ+ people have been one of the most marginalized groups in Western culture—and this stigma was spread with cultural diffusion via Western imperialism, Eurocentrism, and globalization, thus threatening rights of the LGBTQ+ community across the world. Along with all other minority groups that have struggled to achieve equality and inclusion and protection of rights through democratic ideals which also flourished in the modern period, if this history is not taught and discussed—there will be more backsliding and threats to democracy for us all.[42]

Kiley, who created her elective to meet students' needs and address their requests for greater coverage of this history, reflected that the course and the project, which relied on independent work and student agency, empowered students and gave them a greater sense of ownership over their learning. Charles, who conducted his lesson with middle school students, was excited about being one of the first teachers to introduce LGBTQ+ history to his students. Though many of his students were familiar with issues facing the LGBTQ+ community today or personally identified as LGBTQ+, few had the context to make connections between the past and present. For Charles, that made this endeavor particularly worthwhile.

Like Charles, all of the teachers in the working group were motivated in part by wanting to ensure that students who identify as LGBTQ+ felt represented in the curriculum and valued in the educational space they inhabited. They were mindful of the challenges that they might face and the potential for parental or administrative pushback, but, ultimately, serving all of their students took precedence. Emma recalled that "encouraging interaction and discussion proved key"; it paved the way for the LGBTQ+ students in her class to "share their own lived experience freely with their peers, who were respectful." As she succinctly stated, "Teaching LGBTQ+ history is life-saving. Simple as that."[43]

Notes

1 This trend continued in 2024 when there were 125 more applications than seats available at the National Endowment for the Humanities institute.
2 Ashley Woo, Melissa Kay Diliberti, and Elizabeth D. Steiner, "Policies Restricting Teaching About Race and Gender Spill Over into Other States and Localities: Findings from the 2023 State of the American Teacher Survey," RAND, February 15, 2024, www.rand.org/pubs/research_reports/RRA1108-10.html.
3 Teacher names throughout this chapter are pseudonyms.
4 Charles Masters, written correspondence, July 5, 2023.
5 Kiley Hart, written correspondence, June 30, 2023.
6 Kiley Hart, written correspondence, June 30, 2023.
7 Lia Taylor, written correspondence, July 9, 2023.
8 Lia Taylor, written correspondence, July 9, 2023.

9   Full descriptions of the lessons and projects, including resources, lesson plans, and project instructions, can be found in the appendices at the end of this chapter.

10 John Loughery, *The Other Side of Silence: Men's Lives and Gay Identities: A Twentieth -Century History* (New York: Henry Holt and Company, 1998), https://archive.nytimes.com/www.nytimes.com/books/first/l/loughery-silence.html.

11 Loughery, *The Other Side of Silence*.

12 The Editors, ""I did it for the uplift of humanity and the Navy": FDR's Gay Sex-Entrapment Sting,"The MIT Press Reader, January 20, 2020, https://thereader.mitpress.mit.edu/fdrs-gay-entrapment-sting/.

13 Lesson plan, see Appendix 5A.

14 Quoted in Sherry Zane, ""I Did it for the Uplift of Humanity and the Navy': Same-Sex Acts and the Origins of the National Security State, 1919-21," *The New England Quarterly* 91, no. 2 (2018): 279–306.

15 Emma Banks, written correspondence, June 20, 2023.

16 Emma Banks, written correspondence, June 20, 2023.

17 Charles Masters, written correspondence, July 5, 2023.

18 "A New African American Identity: The Harlem Renaissance," National Museum of African American History & Culture, accessed August 29, 2024, https://nmaahc.si.edu/explore/stories/new-african-american-identity-harlem-renaissance.

19 Though this cultural movement is known as the Harlem Renaissance, it encompassed artists in several northern and western cities including Detroit, Chicago, and Los Angeles.

20 "A New African American Identity: The Harlem Renaissance," National Museum of African American History & Culture.

21 "The Queer Harlem Renaissance," Yale University Library Online Exhibitions, accessed August 29, 2024, https://onlineexhibits.library.yale.edu/s/we-are-everywhere/page/the-queer-harlem-renaissance#:~:text=In%20the%20words%20of%20scholar,about%20same%2Dsex%20female%20desire.

22 LGBTQ+ is a modern designation; people in the 1920s would not have known this acronym or labeled themselves as such.

23 Alain Locke, "Enter the New Negro," *Survey Graphic*, March 1925, accessed via https://nationalhumanitiescenter.org/pds/maai3/migrations/text8/lockenewnegro.pdf.

24 Charles Masters, written correspondence, July 5, 2023.

25   Lia Taylor, written correspondence, July 9, 2023.
26   Andrea Carlo, "Why It Took Decades for LGBTQ Stories to Be Included in Holocaust History," Time, April 7, 2021, https://time.com/5953047/lgbtq-holocaust-stories/.
27   Carlo, Why It Took Decades.
28   United States Holocaust Memorial Museum, Washington, DC, "Gay Men Under the Nazi Regime," United States Holocaust Memorial Museum, May 28, 2021, https://encyclopedia.ushmm.org/content/en/article/gay-men-under-the-nazi-regime.
29   United States Holocaust Memorial Museum, Washington, DC, "Gay Men Under the Nazi Regime.
30   Carlo, "Why It Took Decades for LGBTQ Stories to Be Included in Holocaust History"; United States Holocaust Memorial Museum, Washington, DC, "Gay Men Under the Nazi Regime."
31   Lia Taylor, written correspondence, July 9, 2023.
32   Lia Taylor, written correspondence, July 9, 2023.
33   Marjorie Morgan, "From slavery to voguing: the House of Swann," National Museums Liverpool, accessed October 12, 2024, www.liverpoolmuseums.org.uk/stories/slavery-voguing-house-of-swann.
34   Kiley Hart, written correspondence, June 30, 2023.
35   Charles Masters, written correspondence, July 5, 2023.
36   Lia Taylor, written correspondence, July 9, 2023.
37   Kiley Hart, written correspondence, June 30, 2023.
38   Stacie Brensilver Berman, LGBTQ+ History in High School Classes since 1990 (London: Bloomsbury, 2021).
39   "Universal Design for Learning Guidelines version 3.0," CAST, 2024, https://udlguidelines.cast.org.
40   Conversation with Emma Banks, June 15, 2023.
41   Lia Taylor, written correspondence, July 9, 2023.
42   Lia Taylor, written correspondence, July 9, 2023.
43   Emma Banks, written correspondence, June 20, 2023.

References

"A New African American Identity: The Harlem Renaissance." National Museum of African American History & Culture. Accessed August 29, 2024. https://nmaahc.si.edu/explore/stories/new-african-american-identity-harlem-renaissance.

Berman, Stacie Brensilver. *LGBTQ+ History in High School Classes since 1990*. London: Bloomsbury, 2021.

Carlo, Andrea. "Why it Took Decades for LGBTQ Stories to be Included in Holocaust History." *Time*. April 7, 2021. https://time.com/5953047/lgbtq-holocaust-stories/.

Editors, The. ""I did it for the uplift of humanity and the Navy": FDR's Gay Sex-Entrapment Sting." The MIT Press Reader. January 20, 2020. https://thereader.mitpress.mit.edu/fdrs-gay-entrapment-sting/.

Locke, Alain. "Enter the New Negro." *Survey Graphic*. March 1925. Accessed via https://nationalhumanitiescenter.org/pds/maai3/migrations/text8/lockenewnegro.pdf.

Loughery, John. *The Other Side of Silence: Men's Lives and Gay Identities: A Twentieth -Century History*. New York: Henry Holt and Company, 1998. https://archive.nytimes.com/www.nytimes.com/books/first/l/loughery-silence.html.

Morgan, Marjorie. "From slavery to voguing: the House of Swann." National Museums Liverpool. Accessed October 12, 2024. www.liverpoolmuseums.org.uk/stories/slavery-voguing-house-of-swann.

"The Queer Harlem Renaissance." Yale University Library Online Exhibitions. Accessed August 29, 2024. https://onlineexhibits.library.yale.edu/s/we-are-everywhere/page/the-queer-harlem-renaissance#:~:text=In%20the%20words%20of%20scholar,about%20same%2Dsex%20female%20desire.

United States Holocaust Memorial Museum, Washington, DC. "Gay Men Under the Nazi Regime." United States Holocaust Memorial Museum. May 28, 2021. https://encyclopedia.ushmm.org/content/en/article/gay-men-under-the-nazi-regime.

"Universal Design for Learning Guidelines version 3.0." CAST. 2024. https://udlguidelines.cast.org.

Woo, Ashley, Diliberti, Melissa Kay, and Steiner, Elizabeth D. "Policies Restricting Teaching about Race and Gender Spill Over into Other States and Localities: Findings from the 2023 State of the American Teacher Survey." RAND. February 15, 2024. www.rand.org/pubs/research_reports/RRA1108-10.html.

Zane, Sherry. ""I Did it for the Uplift of Humanity and the Navy': Same-Sex Acts and the Origins of the National Security State, 1919-21." *The New England Quarterly* 91, no. 2 (2018): 279–306.

Appendix 5A
Lesson on the Newport Scandal (1919)

Focus Question

In what ways did the US government repress civil liberties during World War I? To what extent were gender and sexuality targeted? To what extent did social class and privilege play a role?

Lesson Objective

Students will examine the repression of "homosexual" activity among men in the military after World War I, focusing on the Newport Scandal (1919), through an exploration of primary source materials.

Standards, Practices, And Skills

Comparison and Contextualization

♦ *Identify and compare similarities and differences among historical developments over time and in different cultural contexts.*
♦ *Connect historical developments to specific circumstances of time and place and broader regional, national, or global processes and draw connections to the present (where appropriate).*

Historical Causation

♦ *Compare causes and/or effects, including between short- and long-term.*
♦ *Analyze and evaluate the interaction of multiple causes and/ or effects.*

Common Core/State Standards:

♦ *CCSS.ELA-LITERACY.RH.9-10.9. Compare and contrast treatments of the same topic in several primary and secondary sources.*

◆ *CCSS.ELA-LITERACY.RH.11-12.1. Cite specific textual evidence to support analysis of primary and secondary sources, connecting insights gained from specific details to an understanding of the text as a whole.*

◆ *CCSS.ELA-LITERACY.RH.11-12.2. Determine the central ideas or information of a primary or secondary source; provide an accurate summary that makes clear the relationships among the key details and ideas.*

◆ *CCSS.ELA-LITERACY.RH.11-12.7. Integrate and evaluate multiple sources of information presented in diverse formats and media (e.g., visually, quantitatively, as well as in words) in order to address a question or solve a problem.*

◆ *CCSS.ELA-LITERACY.RH.11-12.9. Integrate information from diverse sources, both primary and secondary, into a coherent understanding of an idea or event, noting discrepancies among sources.*

Curriculum Placement

This lesson should come after classes and readings on World War I and the Red Scare of 1919 but may come either before or after a discussion of Red Summer. The introductory questions can be revisited during classes on McCarthyism and the Lavender Scare as well as the reaction to the attacks on 9/11.

Lesson Materials

Resource A: Hodges, "The First Red Scare"

◆ Adam J. Hodges, "The First Red Scare," *Oxford Research Encyclopedia of American History.* February 25, 2019. https://oxfordre.com/americanhistory/view/10.1093/acrefore/9780199329175.001.0001/acrefore-9780199329175-e-555.

Resource B: Hochschild, *American Midnight* (excerpt)

◆ Adam Hochschild, *American Midnight: The Great War, A Violent Peace, and Democracy's Forgotten Crisis* (New York: Boston, 2022), pp. 295–96, 297.

Resource C: Roosevelt's Confidential Memo

◆ US Congress, Senate, Committee on Naval Affairs, *Report of the United States Senate, Alleged Immoral Conditions at Newport (R.I.) Naval Training Station*, 67th Cong., 1st sess., 1921.

Resource D: Views of Newport

◆ Images from the Newport Historical Society, https://collections.newporthistory.org/

Resource E: Arrests & Convictions

◆ US Congress, Senate, Committee on Naval Affairs, *Report of the United States Senate, Alleged Immoral Conditions at Newport (R.I.) Naval Training Station*, 67th Cong., 1st sess., 1921.

Resource F: Congressional Inquiry

◆ US Congress, Senate, Committee on Naval Affairs, *Report of the United States Senate, Alleged Immoral Conditions at Newport (R.I.) Naval Training Station*, 67th Cong., 1st sess., July 1921.

Resource G: Testimony of Dudley J. Marriott

◆ As quoted in Sherry Zane, "'I Did it for the Uplift of Humanity and the Navy': Same-Sex Acts and the Origins of the National Security State, 1919-21," *The New England Quarterly* 91, no. 2 (2018): 297–298.

Resource H: Roosevelt's Letter to Senator Keyes (unsent)

◆ As quoted in Sherry Zane, "'I Did it for the Uplift of Humanity and the Navy': Same-Sex Acts and the Origins of the National Security State, 1919-21," *The New England Quarterly* 91, no. 2 (2018): 304–305.

Introduction (5–10 minutes)
Although President Woodrow Wilson proclaimed that World War I was meant to "make the world safe for democracy," during the war years the United States government inaugurated the most intense repression of civil liberties the nation had ever known. Social, economic, and political tensions during the war raised questions that would trouble the nation again during the McCarthy era and in the aftermath of the terrorist attacks of 2001: What is the balance between security and freedom? Does the Constitution protect citizens' rights during wartime? To what extent is dissent equated with a lack of patriotism?

◆ Ask students to recall what they know about repressions on free speech and political activity during World War I:
  ◆ What social and cultural changes (including issues surrounding economic class) occurred before and after the war?
    ◆ *SAMPLE ANSWERS: industrialization, urbanization, immigration, immigration restrictions, Great Migration, labor organizing, socialist movement, constitutional amendments, the suffrage movement, the Espionage and Sedition Acts, prosecution of Eugene V. Debs, loyalty oaths for teachers, Palmer raids, "slacker raids," and the IWW raid. Depending on the placement in the curriculum, also review the events of Red Summer.*

◆ What groups were targeted by the US government?
  ◆ *SAMPLE ANSWERS: immigrants, labor movement, women in the suffrage movement, critics of capitalism, suspected draft dodgers, etc.*

Modeling (10 minutes)

◆ Distribute the readings on the First Red Scare and Palmer Raids.
◆ Model annotating the reading to identify the following and asking students to draw on their prior knowledge:
  ◆ *To what extent was the Red Scare fueled by political concerns? And economic concerns?*
◆ Explain that LGBTQ+ Americans, as well as anyone engaged in same-sex intimate encounters, were also targeted during this period and seen as a security risk because of "sexual perversion." Such ideologies and identities as communism and "homosexuality" were seen as "unpatriotic" as well as a threat to the social, cultural, and economic order.
◆ Tell students that the punishment of LGBTQ+ soldiers in the military was first written into military law in 1916. The first prosecutions of gay service members were just after World War I in Newport, Rhode Island, the scandal to be studied today.
◆ All LGBTQ+ folks were banned from the US military beginning in 1943 when being gay was classified as a mental illness. Since 2011, openly gay, lesbian, and bisexual individuals have been permitted to serve in the military. Acceptance for LGBTQ+ folks in the military expanded with the lifting of the transgender ban in 2021.

Group Activity (20 minutes)

◆ Divide the class into groups of five. Each student should analyze one document, take notes, and answer the questions.

◆ Once everyone in the group has completed the assigned document, students should share their findings with each other within the group. Each person should first summarize the source (detailing the type of document, its author(s), purpose, point of view, and context), then answer the questions. Everyone should take notes.

◆ The entire class should reconvene to read together the final document (Roosevelt's draft note to Senator Keyes). Everyone should answer those questions in a group discussion.

Class Discussion / Wrap Up (5–10 minutes)

As a full class discussion, consider the questions:

◆ To what extent might class be relevant in our analysis and understanding of the Newport Scandal?

◆ What are the concerns and complications about using these sources? Whose stories do we have and how are they preserved? What perspectives might be missing?

◆ Do you think there are any broad social or cultural implications for America of prosecuting or banning queer folks in the military? That is, what does prosecuting or banning queer folk suggest about their place in the nation?

(This will be the final formative assessment.)

Teacher's Notes:

◆ *Share with students that Jeremiah Fowler and his father, a family of jewelers in Providence, Rhode Island, wrote repeatedly to the President and pushed for the case to be considered.*

◆ *Make sure students note that the length of the incarceration without charges was extraordinary: The men were held in dismal conditions on a derelict ship without access to legal aid.*

♦ *Explain that fourteen men were sentenced to up to 20 years, the sentences being longer because they were convicted of crimes because "US was then in a state of war." We do not know what happened to them after.*

Formative Assessment: Exit Ticket

Walter Benjamin once wrote "Nothing that has ever happened should be regarded as lost to history." To what extent is that true or not of LGBTQ+ histories and class in America? Students should write a short reflection, focusing on how class can determine what sources are available to historians. Other questions to consider include:

♦ Whose stories do we have and how are they preserved?
♦ What are the concerns and complications about using these sources?
♦ What perspectives might be missing? How might it be possible to fill in those gaps? Might it be impossible?
♦ Can sources tell us everything about the past? Why or why not? Should all perspectives be given equal consideration and weight?

Appendix 5B
The Harlem Renaissance

Do Now Directions (5 minutes):

1. Read the following quote by Alain LeRoy Locke:
   The younger generation comes, bringing its gifts. Youth speaks, and the voice of the New Negro is heard. Art must discover and reveal the beauty which prejudice and caricature

have overlaid. The younger generation is vibrant with a new psychology; the new spirit is awake in the masses ... Each generation ... will have its creed.

2. Answer the following questions:
   a. What is the *content* of this quote?
   b. What do you think the *purpose* of this quote is? What message is Alain Locke trying to convey?
   c. What is *your creed*?

Mini Lesson (10 minutes)

1. Students watch "The Harlem Renaissance" video from Black History in Two Minutes or So (www.youtube.com/watch?v=9gboEyrj02g).
2. After the video, students will discuss the following questions:
   a. What flourished throughout the decade of the 1920s? (Black writing, art, and music)
   b. What was one of the most important factors that contributed to the Harlem Renaissance? (the migration of Black people from the South to urban areas)
   c. What is sometimes created in the most repressive times? (extraordinary art)
   d. How was art used by Black people during this period? (as a means to help people gain broader political and civil rights)
3. Define the term "Harlem Renaissance" with students, checking that they understand it as both an artistic and an intellectual movement focusing on Black Americans' identities.
4. Share Henry Louis Gates' quote and ask students what it might mean.

Independent Work (10 minutes)
Directions:

1. In a group of three, choose the category you will read (Writer, Entertainer, Blues Woman) and an artist within that category on whom you will focus.
2. Read the information on the artist that you chose.
3. Share what you learned with the rest of your group, taking notes in your graphic organizer as everyone in the group shares.
4. Groups will share themes that emerged from their discussion once all groups complete their work.

Resources:

◆ Writers:
   ◆ "Alain Locke (1885–1954)," National Museum of African American History and Culture, accessed October 13, 2024, https://nmaahc.si.edu/alain-locke.
   ◆ "Countee Cullen (1903–1946)," National Museum of African American History and Culture, accessed October 13, 2024, https://nmaahc.si.edu/countee-cullen.
   ◆ "Langston Hughes (1901–1967)," National Museum of African American History and Culture, accessed October 13, 2024, https://nmaahc.si.edu/langston-hughes.
◆ Entertainers:
   ◆ "Gladys Bentley (1907–1960)," National Museum of African American History and Culture, accessed October 13, 2024, https://nmaahc.si.edu/gladys-bentley.
   ◆ "Jimmie Daniels (1907–1984)," National Museum of African American History and Culture, accessed October 13, 2024, https://nmaahc.si.edu/lgbtq/jimmie-daniels.

- Blues Women:
  - "Alberta Hunter (1895–1984)," National Museum of African American History and Culture, accessed October 13, 2024, https://nmaahc.si.edu/lgbtq/alberta-hunter.
  - "Bessie Smith (1895–1937)," National Museum of African American History and Culture, accessed October 13, 2024, https://nmaahc.si.edu/lgbtq/bessie-smith.
  - "Ethel Waters (1897–1977)," National Museum of African American History and Culture, accessed October 13, 2024, https://nmaahc.si.edu/ethel-waters.
  - "Gertrude "Ma" Rainey (1886–1939)," National Museum of African American History and Culture, accessed October 13, 2024, https://nmaahc.si.edu/ma-rainey.

Questions for Students/Graphic Organizer:

Writers	
1. In your own words describe in detail what you learned about the writer you chose.	
2. Describe what type of writer your artist was during the Harlem Renaissance.	
Entertainer	
3. In your own words describe in detail what you learned about the Entertainer you chose.	

Writers	
4. Describe what type of Entertainer your artist was during the Harlem Renaissance.	
Blueswoman	
5. In your own words describe in detail what you learned about the Blueswoman you chose.	
6. Listen to a song from your Blueswoman and describe what it was about.	
Exit Ticket	
7. Write down the two other LGBTQIA+ artists you learned about today.	
8. Write down something you learned about the artists.	
Reflection	
9. What reflections or questions do you still have?	

Homework

Choose another artist and in your own words write a detailed paragraph on what you learned.

Appendix 5C

LGBTQ+ Individuals' Experiences During and After the Holocaust

Homework (*Assigned 2-3 days before in-class activity*)

1. Open this Web Link (uploaded on Google Classroom) www.hmd.org.uk/learn-about-the-holocaust-and-genocides/nazi-persecution/
2. Review the general introduction and the links for the specific groups of people that were targeted by the Nazis, in addition to Jewish people.

   Take a few notes on what you think is important to remember for group work tomorrow about these various targeted groups. Be sure you have written a few notes about each group. You will turn this in with your group work.
   ♦ The Roma genocide
   ♦ 'Asocials'
   ♦ Black people
   ♦ People with Disabilities
   ♦ Freemasons
   ♦ Gay people
   ♦ Jehovah's Witnesses
   ♦ Non-Jewish Poles and Slavic POWs
   ♦ Political opponents and trade unionists
3. Review these sources regarding LGBTQ+ persecution today. Write down 10 facts you learned about global persecution that you did not know and 10 facts about US related concerns.

   Global Overview:
   https://features.hrw.org/features/features/lgbt_l
       aws/index.html
   www.bbc.com/news/world-43822234

US Issues:
www.aclu.org/issues/lgbtq-rights
www.americanprogress.org/article/state-lgbtq-
   community-2020/

Lesson Plan

Aim: Evaluate and analyze primary and secondary source documents to:

1. Understand the historical context and culture of Germany in regard to the LGBTQ+ community prior to the rise of the Nazi Regime.
2. Key events and laws enacted by the Nazis during the Holocaust to target gay men.
3. Lessons learned/struggles to obtain equal rights by the LGBTQ+ community in Germany since the WWII period and Holocaust.

Objective: Students will work in small groups to discuss and analyze documents in order to understand the historical context, causes, key events, and effects of the persecution under the Nazi regime. They will document their research as they work and then synthesize key learning into a visual or written reflection on their findings.

Standards
Common Core Reading Standards for Literacy in Social Studies 1 & 2

1. Cite specific textual evidence to support analysis of primary and secondary sources, attending to such features as the date and origin of the information. Read closely to determine what the text says explicitly and make logical inferences from it, and cite specific textual evidence

when writing or speaking to support conclusions drawn from the text.

2. Determine central ideas or themes of a text and summarize the key supporting details and ideas.
3. Analyze in detail a series of events described in a text; determine whether earlier events caused later ones or simply preceded them.
4. By the end of grade 10, read and comprehend history/social studies texts in the grades 9-10 text complexity band independently and proficiently.

C. Common Core Writing Standards for Literacy in Social Studies

1. Write routinely over extended time frames and shorter time frames for a range of tasks, purposes, and audiences.
9. Draw evidence from informational texts to support analysis and reflection.

D. Common Core Speaking and Listening Standards Comprehension and Collaboration

1. Initiate and participate effectively in a range of collaborative discussions (one-on-one, in groups, and teacher-led) with diverse partners on grades 9-10 topics, texts, and issues, building on others' ideas and expressing their own clearly and persuasively.
   a. Come to discussions prepared, having read and researched material under study; explicitly draw on that preparation by referring to evidence from texts and other research on the topic or issue to stimulate a thoughtful, well-reasoned exchange of ideas.
   c. Propel conversations by posing and responding to questions that relate the current discussion to broader themes or larger ideas; actively incorporate others into the discussion; clarify, verify, or challenge ideas and conclusions.

2. Integrate multiple sources of information presented in diverse media or formats (e.g., visually, quantitatively, orally), evaluating the credibility and accuracy of each source.

Prior Knowledge: Students have explored a basic chronology of the unification of Germany into a nation state in the 1800's and ways that its first government initiated some reforms that reflected Enlightenment ideals and democracy at the time. They also will have learned the general history of the Jewish people and the development of anti-Semitism in Europe up to the time of and during the Holocaust using class lectures and a video from the US Holocaust Memorial Museum and a field trip to the Museum of Jewish Heritage. Some students have also completed an independent research project on the topic since October 2023. They have explored how in the aftermath of WWII many efforts were sought to prevent the violation of human rights that had ensued via mechanisms such as the creation of the UN, Universal Declaration of Human Rights, Nuremberg Trials, and creation of the concept of genocide and "never again."

Do Now:

1. Students will share what they know and learned from prior evening's homework about other people targeted by the Nazis for persecution after they gained power besides Jews. Students may mention: Political Activists, Members of the LGBTQ+ community, Catholics & Other Minorities, Roma, etc. They will reflect on what they have learned about the persecution of Jews during the Holocaust versus what they have generally learned over the years about these other targeted groups. Students will have been asked to review different groups on this website: www.hmd.org.uk/learn-about-the-holocaust-and-genocides/nazi-persecution/.

2. Students will discuss whether all of these groups, including Jews, have all of their rights protected as per the Universal Declaration of Human Rights and other goals in the aftermath of WWII. Hopefully, students will share examples organically of incidents of anti-semitism, attacks on political activists, other minorities, and the LGBTQ+ community. Concerns about rising hate will generally be discussed.

Procedure:

1. Explain after general discussion that we will be doing a group activity to explore what happened to gay men during the Nazi regime with the hope of understanding more about this less told history and to help context-ualize current efforts for remembering this past his-tory in order to have an impact on our lives today. As author Jake Newsome writes in his book *Pink Triangle Legacies*, "The incorporation of marginalized histories into the mainstream understanding of the national past can contribute to a more inclusive experience of national belonging in the present" (p. 216).
2. Watch the short overview video: https://youtu.be/Qlj5 kQQYOWo.
3. Students will then be broken up into three small groups to review documents that discuss life for the LGBTQ+ community, particularly focusing on gay men, (1) before the Nazis, (2) events during the Nazi time in power, and (3) the ongoing struggle for equality & justice in the aftermath of WWII. Advise students that if they finish their group's work before time is up, they can also explore the other groups' investigations.
4. After completing the group activity, a selected presenter will share out what the group's findings were.
5. **Final Wrap Up: Students will reflect on the below goal:**
   a. Think back to one of the original aims of this lesson which was to understand how "the incorporation

of marginalized histories into the mainstream understanding of the national past can contribute to a more inclusive experience of national belonging in the present."

6. Avenues for future action will be discussed in light of the current rise of discrimination.

Resources and Questions:

Group 1: Before the Nazi Era

Read overviews of Germany at the end of the 19th Century and beginning of the 20th Century.

◆ Facing History & Ourselves, "Visual Essay: Free Expression in the Weimar Republic"- www.facinghist ory.org/resource-library/visual-essay-free-expression-weimar-republic

◆ www.bl.uk/20th-century-literature/articles/on-the-edge-of-the-volcano-culture-in-weimar-germany

Questions:

A. What was cultural life like generally as expressed through the arts during the Weimar Republic?

B. What conclusions can you draw about the time period in relation to attitudes about homosexuality?

C. How do the sources illustrate "schisms that divided German society in the 'golden 1920s'"?

Group 2: During the Nazi Era

Review these sources and answer the questions that follow:

◆ Timeline of Events from *Pink Triangle Legacies* https:// cornellpress.manifoldapp.org/read/pink-triangle-legacies-coming-out-in-the-shadow-of-the-holocaust/section/7ca358f4-96c4-4b50-adef-a4e32a3efd9a

◆ General Article https://encyclopedia.ushmm.org/cont
  ent/en/article/gay-men-under-the-nazi-regime
◆ Case Study: Split stories among group members
  ◆ Pierre Seel www.hmd.org.uk/wp-content/uplo
    ads/2020/09/Pierre-Seel-life-story.pdf or www.
    hmd.org.uk/resource/pierre-seel/
  ◆ Rudolf Brazda www.hmd.org.uk/wp-content/uplo
    ads/2013/06/rudolf_brazda.pdf or www.hmd.org.
    uk/resource/rudolf-brazda/
◆ More Here wjakenewsome.com/stories/

Questions:

A. What was Paragraph 175 and how was it enforced by
   the Nazis?
B. How did Nazi leaders like Rohm view homosexuality?
C. How did the Nazi policies and persecution change
   during these periods: 1933-34, 1934-1936, and 1936-1945?
D. What was the pink triangle used for?
E. How do the personal testimonies more profoundly illustrate the persecution that was experienced by gay men
   during the Nazi era?

Group 3: After the Nazi Era
Review these sources

◆ Documenting and Memorializing Gay Experiences,
  USHMM Encyclopedia- https://encyclopedia.ushmm.
  org/content/en/article/gay-men-under-the-nazi-reg
  ime
◆ Appendix B & C *Pink Triangle Legacies*- https://cornellpr
  ess.manifoldapp.org/read/pink-triangle-legacies-com
  ing-out-in-the-shadow-of-the-holocaust/section/eeed9
  0a6-a163-4fdc-a325-55c8011995ce and https://cornellpr
  ess.manifoldapp.org/read/pink-triangle-legacies-com
  ing-out-in-the-shadow-of-the-holocaust/section/43538
  3d8-4b9a-440f-af60-88e34cf23653

- ◆ Article by Jake Newsome- https://nursingclio.org/
  2017/04/20/pink-triangle-legacies-holocaust-memory-
  and-international-gay-rights-activism/
- ◆ Recent Protests- www.facinghistory.org/resource-libr
  ary/german-national-team-showing-support-lgbtq-rig
  hts and www.timesofisrael.com/german-players-cover-
  mouths-to-protest-lgbt-armband-ban-at-world-cup/
- ◆ Memorials- www.atlasobscura.com/places/homom
  onument and www.archdaily.com/984342/homomonum
  ent-the-importance-of-a-representative-space-in-the-city

Questions:

A. When was enforcement of Paragraph 175 ended in both East and West Germany? How/why did this policy's continued use lead to the burying of the history, fear of sharing experiences, and impacts of the Nazis on the LGBTQ+ community?

B. When did the German government acknowledge LGBTQ+ victims of the Holocaust and thus allow the group to become eligible for compensation?

C. How has the effort to memorialize these victims progressed? Where are some of the monuments located?

D. What is the significance of the use of the Pink Triangle after WWII by the LGBTQ+ community?

Extension: Project

Directions: Jigsaw Groups to include members from the other diverse Research Groups. Within the new groups, students will create a few slides, a poster, or a written reflection collectively to answer the prompts below. All group members should contribute, and information from at least 5 of the sources from this activity should be included/cited:

- ◆ How does this investigation into the persecution of gay men during the Holocaust illustrate how Nazi persecution and intolerance was able to dominate and become policy despite many liberal political views and trends existing in the time period?

♦ What can be learned from this history about standing up to ongoing persecution of the LGBTQ+ community around the world today?

♦ How can historical knowledge help motivate us to take action to promote tolerance and equality today? Why is action critical given the goals of the Universal Declaration of Human Rights and the rise of discrimination and hate crimes across the world?

Appendix 5D
Lesson Planning Project

Queering US History: Expanding the Curriculum

Task:

You and your partner will be responsible for leading a 40- to 50-minute class on LGBTQ+ US History. Your goal here is to improve the US History curriculum at our school by enhancing our US History materials and extending the coverage of our core textbook, Eric Foner's *Give Me Liberty!*

Please note: you may draw on our course book, *Queer Studies: Beyond Binaries*, while preparing your lesson or choosing a homework assignment, but using *Queer Studies* is not required.

Prep Time:

You will have the whole class on Thursday and Friday to choose a topic and plan your lesson. You will be responsible for assigning homework to your classmates for the day of your lesson.

Lesson Plan:
On the day of your presentation, I will expect you to share a typed lesson plan with your instructor (and your classmates if you'd like). The lesson plan should include these items:

1. A section from *Give Me Liberty!* that provides context to the historical era being studied.
2. A homework assignment of roughly 30-45 minutes that students can use to prepare for the lesson.
3. Excerpts from at least three primary sources that fill in the gaps from *Give Me Liberty!*
4. A detailed outline of the lesson, including a sentence identifying your goal for the lesson: What do you want the class to better understand or be able to do by the end of the lesson?
5. An activity that supports your goal. An "activity" requires that we do something interesting. (A Google Slides presentation by itself is not an activity.)
6. A set of discussion questions that will help us shift out of your activity and into a broader discussion.

Grading:
Please note that you will receive a grade for your revised lesson plan and presentation in the unit grade category. Your reflection will be graded in the "short essay" category.

Grading for the lesson plan (equivalent to a unit project grade):
Note that all lesson plans should be typed and include the following: an agenda, a specific activity, a clearly defined goal, discussion questions, three primary sources, and a preparatory homework assignment.

The grade will be determined according to the following rubric:

◆ Quality of the homework assignment that prepares students for the lesson (10 points)

- ◆ Clarity of goal and the central question of the lesson (10 points)
- ◆ Length of lesson–needs to be 40- to 50 minutes (10 points)
- ◆ Relevance of context from *Give Me Liberty!* and tailoring of a lesson to students of US History (10 points)
- ◆ Quality of the activity–it should be student centered, thought-provoking, support the lesson's goals, be facilitated with energy and enthusiasm (15 points)
- ◆ Quality of 3+ primary sources: how well do they enhance *Give Me Liberty!* and relate to the essential question of the lesson? (20 points)
- ◆ Quality of the discussion questions–they should relate to the primary sources and topic of the lesson (15 points)
- ◆ Citation of sources in Chicago style, including primary sources as well as any secondary sources and source banks consulted (10 points)

Reflection (equivalent to an in-class writing or short essay):
After you teach and revise your lesson plan, I will ask you to submit a reflection. Your reflection should be roughly 300-500 words long (roughly 1-2 pages, double spaced). It should address these questions:

a. What was the goal of your activity? What worked in your activity? What didn't work?
b. What worked in the class discussion of your primary sources? What didn't work? What would you have liked to discuss more?
c. What did you have to revise in your lesson plan between your teaching day and submitting the final version of your lesson?
d. How did your lesson expand your understanding of US History? What did you learn?
e. How was working with a partner?

Timeline	Groups/Topic
Day 1	1 **Harlem Renaissance (Entertainment)**
Day 2	2 **Reconstruction (1880s)**
Day 3	3 **AIDS epidemic** (Stigma) 1980s/1990s
Day 4	4 **1960s Hollywood (censorship)**
Day 5	5 **Japanese American internment WWII**
Day 6	6 **—LGBTQ+ in the US military** (WWII, Clinton, Obama)
Day 7	7 **—Two-Spirited (Colonialism/chapter 2)**
Day 8	Revision time/finish reflections

Good Places to Look for Primary Sources:

◆ Primary Source Sets from GLBT Historical Society
◆ Additional digital materials from the GLBT Historical Society
◆ ACT UP Oral History Project
◆ LGBTQ Religious Archives
◆ We Who Feel Differently
◆ University of North Carolina, Southern Communities: Listening for a Change: History of Gay Men and Transgender People in the South
◆ Anti-Defamation League, Unheard Voices: Stories of LGBT History (excerpted transcripts plus background essays and assignment ideas)
◆ GLBT History Center, San Francisco -- more than 500 interviews w/ Bay Area residents. Includes Berube's WWII interviews (transcripts)
◆ Buffalo Women's Oral History Project (interviews by Kennedy and Davis done in the 1970s and 80s)
◆ Veterans History Project, Library of Congress -- includes 19 interviews collected by the San Diego LGBT Community Center
◆ The Gay Center, Stonewall Oral History Project -- approximately 80 video and audio taped interviews

remembering the Stonewall Riots and organizing before and after the uprising
♦ NYC Trans Oral History Project – community-based project collecting videotaped interviews with Trans and nonbinary New Yorkers
♦ Queer Newark Project – approximately 30 interviews with people from Newark, NJ
♦ Southwest Virginia LGBTQ+ History Project – Approximately 50 interviews with transcripts

Conclusion

In a 2017 interview, Lyndsey Schlax, who developed and taught the first LGBTQ+ history elective in a California public school after the passage of the FAIR Education Act, stated the following when asked what advice she had for other teachers hoping to integrate LGBTQ+ history into their classes: "Be ready to fight, because it's worth it."[1] Schlax, who received overwhelmingly positive feedback from the students enrolled in her semester-long class in the years that she taught it, also encountered pushback from parents and administrators and, as a result of the media coverage her class received, threatening letters from people outside the school community.[2] She knows, therefore, what it means to fight for inclusive curriculum and how worthwhile that tenacity can be. Circumstances in 2025 are different from 2017. Though opposition to teaching LGBTQ+ history existed in 2017 it was not yet codified to the extent that it would be five years later; moreover, parental rights organizations, key players in the push for curriculum censorship following the COVID-19 pandemic, did not yet have the foothold they would gain. Nevertheless, Schlax's words continue to ring true. Efforts to integrate LGBTQ+ history and provide students with information, context, and representation are most certainly worth it.

As the previous chapters establish, teaching LGBTQ+ history is a grassroots movement that requires committed teachers, diverse sources of support for those teachers, and access to

DOI: 10.4324/9781032689678-9

resources, especially for individuals who have not had opportunities to interact with this history in their own schooling or teacher preparation. Despite the challenges that exist for educators all over the United States who seek to do this work, which must and should be acknowledged, we are also in an era when that support and those resources are available and accessible; in fact, as opposition to inclusive curriculum has increased, so have the number of people and organizations who seek to counter it. Each of the essays, from historians, teachers, teacher educators, and activists, describes ways in which students and educators can find the support they need in likely and unlikely places, be that supportive administrators, like-minded colleagues, organizations like GLSEN and GSA Network, local librarians, and university faculty who embrace and promote LGBTQ+ history instruction. Teachers can find student and educator testimony, blog/vlog posts, editorials, and commentary online that demonstrate the impact of integrating LGBTQ+ history and how it can change people's lives and perspectives. Though it would be ideal for every teacher to have a trusted colleague in close physical proximity, the essays demonstrate that those intangible forces, most importantly remembering why one intends to teach LGBTQ+ history in the first place, can be impactful and sustaining.

Furthermore, the number of resources available to teachers has increased significantly over the past ten years. In 2013, when we first immersed ourselves in this work, there were few history-focused lessons that teachers could easily find online; almost all of them focused on same-sex marriage or Don't Ask, Don't Tell. In 2025, though, advocacy organizations, government agencies, and educational platforms offer high quality, history-centric resources that teachers can access and use in their classrooms. Moreover, when some existing resources were censored in response to Executive Orders targeting gender, historians and advocates mobilized to ensure that these resources found new homes and others remained accessible and available to teachers. The lessons, sources, and activities focus on a variety of topics from LGBTQ+ experiences during Reconstruction, to the role of gender in the women's suffrage movement, to the intersectional struggle for civil rights in the twentieth century, among other topics (Appendix A). The lessons featured in Chapter 5 are a wonderful starting point for teachers exploring their options around integrating LGBTQ+ history; the additional sources available online can help to continue that process. Additionally, the discussion of the teachers' process and their reflections on the impact of their lessons can be instructive for other educators as they consider how to use the variety of sources they might find outside these pages. In that way, the teachers whose work is represented here are a source of support to colleagues far beyond their schools.

LGBTQ+ individuals, as several of the essays remind us, have always existed. The language has changed over time—the soldiers embroiled in the Newport Scandal would never have heard the term LGBTQ—but these identities and experiences did not emerge in the twentieth or twenty-first century. Omitting that information from classrooms and curricula leaves students with the impression that there is no historical relationship between lives in the past and present, and denies students necessary opportunities to connect with history and contextualize the world around them. LGBTQ+ history, as the previous chapters passionately argue, belongs in classrooms, textbooks, national conversations, and spaces that students voluntarily occupy. In an age of misinformation and disinformation, the knowledge that students receive from trusted sources who understand how to convey information in ways that students can access and comprehend (their teachers!) can be life changing, especially, but not only if, they personally identify as LGBTQ+. Learning this history can inspire agency and activism, demonstrate the myriad ways in which students can use their voices, create safe spaces at school, address incidents of hate and violence, and change the way students conceptualize discussions and debates in the wider world. Teachers contend with an overwhelming number of expectations and responsibilities on a daily basis but at the heart of their jobs is the goal of preparing students to succeed, and hopefully thrive, outside school walls. Teaching LGBTQ+ history is an integral part of that.

The path might be rocky. There might be obstacles and challenges along the way. It's worth it.

Notes

1   Lyndsey Schlax, oral history interview with Stacie Brensilver Berman, January 12, 2017, Brooklyn, NY.
2   Lyndsey Schlax, oral history interview with the Stacie Brensilver Berman, January 12, 2017, Brooklyn, NY.

Appendices

Appendix A: LGBTQ+ History Resources

The following list offers additional suggestions for LGBTQ+ history resources including lesson plans, activities, primary sources and source sets, and visual and media sources. This list is not exhaustive, and new materials are developed and posted by these and other organizations on a regular basis. These resources can be used as published or modified to meet students' needs. We hope that this can be a valuable foundation for teachers beginning to do this important work.

- ♦ **Anti-Defamation League, LGBTQ+ Pride Month and Education Resources**: www.adl.org/resources/tools-and-strategies/lgbtq-pride-month-and-education-resources
- ♦ **California History Social Science Project, LGBTQ+ History Through Primary Sources**: https://chssp.ucdavis.edu/lgbtq-primary-sources
- ♦ **Docs Teach (National Archives), The Long Struggle for LGBTQ+ Civil Rights**: www.docsteach.org/activities/teacher/the-long-struggle-for-lgbtq-civil-rights
- ♦ **GLBT Historical Society, Primary Source Sets**: www.glbthistory.org/primary-source-sets
- ♦ **GLSEN, Activities**: www.glsen.org/activity-list?program=All&type=92&topic=All&issue=All&grade=All
- ♦ **Learning for Justice, Lessons**: www.learningforjustice.org/classroom-resources/lessons

- **Library of Congress, Resources**: www.loc.gov/lgbt-pride-month/resources/#:~:text=LGBTQ%20Activism%20and%20Contributions%2D%2D,contributions%20to%20US%20cultural%20life.
- **New York City Public Schools, Hidden Voices**
  - **Guide:** www.weteachnyc.org/resources/resource/hidden-voices-lgbtq/
  - **Lesson Plans**: www.weteachnyc.org/resources/resource/hidden-voices-lgbtq-stories-in-united-states-history-lesson-plans-Public-facing/
  - www.youtube.com/playlist?list=PLatVP29hm_7Hhf_G6C-ZhulXgOzkOVfo6
- **New York University, A Broader Spectrum: LGBTQ+-Inclusive Resources for Middle and High School US History Classes**: https://docs.google.com/document/d/1ZDvEx8pc5K2ZQkd-AOEuyp6Heqj_b-V4KSCq6HD3QRU/edit?usp=sharing
- **ONE Institute, LGBTQ+ History Lesson Plans**: www.oneinstitute.org/lgbtq-lesson-plans/
- **Social History in Every Classroom (SHEC), Military History and the LGBTQ+ Community**: https://shec.ashp.cuny.edu/exhibits/show/lgbtq-military-history

Appendix B: Resources for Learning and Teaching About LGBTQ+ History

As the contributors express in their essays, LGBTQ+ history is a field with deep historical roots and unlimited potential. Many of us working and invested in this discipline have our own historical "origin stories"—moments where we encountered another scholar, author, or filmmaker's work on an aspect of LGBTQ+ history that opened our minds, enlightened us, introduced us to new ideas and information, answered our questions, or provided a personal and/or academic path forward that did not previously exist. In addition to the advice, lesson plans, and strategies in the main chapters, we thought that readers might also find inspiration in the works that follow:

Bettina Aptheker:
I came into lesbian identity through feminist writings and the Women's Liberation Movement. The two writers who were most important to me were Adrienne Rich and Audre Lorde. They were poets, but both wrote extensive prose essays and books. Rich's book, *On Lies, Secrets & Silence* transformed my thinking because she interpreted literature and Social Justice through a lesbian-feminist lens. For example, her chapter on Emily Dickinson "Vesuvius at Home: the Power of Emily Dickinson" read her work through understanding that she was in love with her sister-in-law. The chapters, "When We Dead Awaken: Writing as Re-vision," "Vietnam and Sexual Violence," and "Women and Honor: Some Notes on Lying," spoke to me, and my students over many years, in deeply powerful political and personal ways.

The other book of great importance as I came into a lesbian and feminist consciousness was by the Black poet laureate of New York Audre Lorde, *Sister/Outside: Essays & Speeches*. The essays that meant the most to me, and to my students, were "Poetry is Not a Luxury," "The Transformation of Silence into Language & Action," "Uses of the Erotic: The Erotic as Power," and "The Master's Tools Will Never Dismantle the Master's House." The essay on the erotic was a whole new way of thinking about the erotic as both a sexual expression and, most importantly, as a way of measuring the satisfaction with and direction of one's life. Breaking silence was a recurring theme in her work. And women and girls are silenced and also silent about many, many experiences and aspects of their lives. "The Master's Tools" was a powerful meditation on how to develop new ways of thinking not relying on the white, male canon. Lorde's work is consistently infused with an anti-racist and Black feminist consciousness.

Finally, one of the most important, early transgender reflections will be found in the book by Leslie Feinberg, *Stone Butch Blues*. This is a fictional autobiography that scores of my students found riveting and transformative. Feinberg was one of the first transgender activists, a revolutionary communist, and married to the Southern-born poet, Minne Bruce Pratt (whose anti-racist, lesbian feminist works were and remain of profound influence).

Stacie Brensilver Berman:
Reading George Chauncey's *Why Marriage?* changed my academic and professional life. As a doctoral student, I knew that I wanted to research and write about including content in social studies classes that would help all students feel seen and represented. My advisor, Robby–now my co-author–handed me Chauncey's book and told me to read it and come back the next day. Overnight I realized how much I didn't know about LGBTQ+ history and the need for this history to be in the curriculum. I will forever credit that conversation and Chauncey's nuanced discussion of the struggle for same-sex marriage rights with opening my eyes and illuminating a path.

Robert Cohen:
Fifty years ago, an undergraduate seminar taught by radical historian Jesse Lemisch introduced me to LGBTQ+ history. In 1972, Jesse had written a *New York Times* review essay praising Martin Duberman's powerful book on Black Mountain College—*Black Mountain: An Exploration in Community*—for its critical stance on that supposedly progressive artistic community's authoritarian tendencies, especially its homophobia. Though I was a history major, Duberman's book was my first exposure to the work and critical sensibility of a gay historian, or anything relating to the LGBTQ+ experience in the US, which had never been mentioned in any prior history class I had taken. Along with Duberman's work, Blanche Wiesen Cook's grand three volume biography of Eleanor Roosevelt, and especially her account of ER's affair with Lorena Hickok, had a major impact on me, as did Blanche's critical writings on supposedly liberal biographers who engaged in lesbian denial. More recently, Bettina Aptheker's brilliant *Communists in Closets* opened a window on to the American Left and the failure of its historiography to confront its homophobia. All of which suggests that historical writing and teaching on the

LGBTQ+ experience has to overcome not only obstacles from the bigoted right-wing, but from a tradition of Left-liberal ignorance and indifference.

Daniel Hurewitz:

I would say that a big book for me was the first edition of Eric Marcus' *Making History*. That book, especially in that edition, told individual activists' stories, in their own voices, and arranged in chronological order. It gave me a powerful feeling of all the people who had been loving & fighting & making change before me: it helped me feel like I was part of a lineage that I could join and take my own place within.

The other powerful texts were the GLSEN surveys that made so explicit the power of one teacher to make a difference. Understanding that power, in a fundamental way, inspired me to want to help educate more teachers to use their power that way.

Lil Miss Hot Mess:

The first thing that comes to mind is *The Celluloid Closet* - first the documentary, and then the book, to which I might also add the documentary *Disclosure* as a trans-specific corollary. Though focused on film history, they're incredibly helpful in thinking about questions of visibility and representation (which have been so central to LGBTQ+ movements) and speak to larger themes in LGBTQ+ history more broadly. https://supportlgbtqeducat ion.com/.

J.B. Mayo, Jr.:

LGBTQ+ history has to be taught because real people, ordinary and extraordinary, struggle with their sexual identities. We go through so much pain, anxiety, joy, pleasure, etc. all because many in society believe that we should remain quiet and ashamed of who we love. But when we tell our stories, positive change can happen. Therefore, I chose these three books as points of inspiration for the essay that I contributed. These three books actually helped ME in my coming out process: Reichen Lehmkuhl's *Here's what we'll say: Growing Up, Coming Out, and the US Air Force*

Academy; Greg Louganis's *Breaking the Surface*; and Scott Peck's *All-American Boy: A Memoir*.

Justin Martinez:
For the first, Judith Butler's *Gender Trouble* was fairly revolutionary for me as I began studying queerness. I first read this during my undergrad, and her discourse surrounding the disruption of heteronormative and hegemonic norms fundamentally shifted the manner through which I think about not only gender but all identities. In many ways, this text completely deconstructs our social perception of self and others. It is an important read for all identity work, specifically with regard to queer identities.

This next one is fiction, but it was the first time I truly saw myself in a text. Madeleine Miller's *Song of Achilles* recounts the *Iliad* from the perspective of Patroclus. While fantastical and mythical, often the Greeks find themselves at the helm of "Ancient" Western History and dominate classical discourses. Consequently, centering Patroclus in this narrative and writing the story of the Trojan War as a queer love story between Patroclus and Achilles is not only empowering but also revolutionary when considering the historical weight we associate with the Greeks. Overall, this was a great read that shifted my own thinking on history and inspired me to find more ways to include LGBTQ+ narratives in an accessible manner.

John Palella:
This is a tough one for a good reason, so many! I have these three moments, one in undergrad, one during my MA at NYU, and one during my PhD where three different books helped inform my trajectory. First was John D'Emilio and Estelle B. Freedman's *Intimate Matters: A History of Sexuality in America* in a family history course in undergrad that showed me that Queer history and the histories of sexuality existed. Second was in Lisa Stulberg's "Diversity & Professional Life" course at NYU I read Audre Lorde's *Sister Outsider* which taught me intersectionality and the third during a doctoral-level course on Latin American

historiography I read James Green's *Beyond Carnival* which helped me do better at global LGBTQIA histories.

Wendy Rouse:
There are honestly so many important queer history books to choose from it is really hard to narrow it down to just a few. In thinking about teaching, I like the topical histories such as Allan Berube's *Coming Out Under Fire* and David K. Johnson's *The Lavender Scare*. These books are helpful in understanding how the government in WWII and the post-war era systematically discriminated against LGBTQ+ people by launching investigations into their lives and attempting to purge them from federal employment. However, the stories in the books also reveal the creative strategies that LGBTQ+ people developed to subvert the system, survive, and thrive. These books are important for understanding the significance of the homophile movement and gay liberation eras that followed as well as the present struggle for LGBTQ+ equality.

Jinnie Spiegler:
The text that has been most influential in my thinking about why LGBTQ+ history needs to be taught in schools is GLSEN's National School Climate Survey. I think I have been reading it since they started doing the survey in 1999! The data and narrative of the survey has really informed my thinking because of two big takeaways-- and the details are important, too. One, LGBTQ+ students face so much harm in school (bullying, exclusion, discrimination, offensive and biased language, harassment, physical attacks, etc.) that impacts their ability to attend, participate and thrive in school. It's critical that information is shared with educators and school leaders about this. The second big takeaway revealed from the survey is that things like teaching LGBTQ+ history, supportive educators, inclusive policies and more makes a huge difference in LGBTQ+ students' feeling safe and wanting to come to and attend school.

References

Aptheker, Bettina. *Communists in Closets: Queering the History 1930s-1990s*. New York: Routledge, 2022.

Berube, Allan. *Coming Out Under Fire: The History of Gay Men and Women in World War II*. Chapel Hill: University of North Carolina Press, 2010.

Butler, Judith. *Gender Trouble: Feminism and the Subversion of Identity*. New York: Routledge, 1990.

Chauncey, George. *Why Marriage?: The History Shaping Today's Debate over Gay Equality*. New York: Basic Books, 2004.

Cook, Blanche Wiesen. *Eleanor Roosevelt, Volume 3: The War Years and After, 1939–1962*. New York: Penguin Books, 2016. (Volume 1, published in 1993, and Volume 2, published in 200, are also available.)

D'Emilio, John and Estelle B. Freedman. *Intimate Matters: A History of Sexuality in America*. Chicago: The University of Chicago Press, 2012.

Duberman, Martin. *Black Mountain: An Exploration in Community*. Boston: EP Dutton, 1972.

Epstein, Rob and Friedman, Jeffrey, dirs. *The Celluloid Closet*. 1995; New York, NY: Sony Pictures Classics.

Feder, Sam and Scholder, Amy, dirs. *Disclosure*. 2020; New York, NY: Netflix. Streaming.

Feinberg, Leslie. *Stone Butch Blues*. Ithaca, NY: Firebrand Books, 1993.

GLSEN. "The 2021 National School Climate Survey." Accessed October 30, 2024. www.glsen.org/research/2021-national-school-climate-survey

Green, James. *Beyond Carnival: Male Homosexuality in Twentieth-Century Brazil*. Chicago: University of Chicago Press, 1999.

Johnson, David K. *The Lavender Scare: The Cold War Persecution of Gays and Lesbians in the Federal Government*. Chicago: University of Chicago Press, 2004.

Lehmkuhl, Reichen. *Here's What We'll Say: Growing Up, Coming Out, and the US Air Force Academy*. New York: Carroll & Graff Publishers, 2006.

Lorde, Audre. *Sister Outsider: Essays and Speeches*. Berkeley, CA: Crossing Press, 1984.

Louganis, Greg [with Eric Marcus]. *Breaking the Surface*. New York, Random House, 1995.

Marcus, Eric. *Making Gay History: The Half Century Fight for Lesbian and Gay Equal Rights*. New York: HarperCollins Publishers, Inc., 2002.

Miller, Madeline. *Song of Achilles*. New York: Ecco Press (Harper Collins), 2011.

Peck, Scott. *All-American Boy: A Memoir*. New York: Scribner, 1995.

Rich, Adrienne. *On Lies, Secrets & Silence*. New York: Norton, 1978.

Russo, Vito. *The Celluloid Closet: Homosexuality in the Movies*. New York: Harper & Row, 1981.

Appendix C: Contributors' Advice to Teachers in 2025 and Beyond

Olive Garrison:

Teaching LGBTQIA+ history and affirming LGBTQIA+ youth in classrooms requires courage, intentionality, and a deep commitment to our students' dignity. I have seen the pain that accompanies isolation. Like many others, I grew up searching textbooks for someone like me and found only silence. That silence told me that people like me did not matter. It is a message no student should ever receive.

For teachers navigating today's politically charged environment, my advice is to focus on the power of stories—stories that connect, challenge, and ultimately transform. Start with the curriculum. Sometimes, the hardest part is just starting. I remember the first time I included Alan Turing in a lesson. I was nervous, anticipating backlash, but my students were deeply engaged. Afterward, two students lingered behind to tell me, "You're the first teacher to ever talk about someone like us." That moment reminded me that teaching LGBTQIA+ content is not just about history—it is about survival. It's about telling students, "You exist. You matter."

In today's climate, bringing current events like Project 2025 or political transphobia into the classroom can feel fraught, but it is also an opportunity to empower students to think critically. I suggest framing discussions around media literacy: Who benefits from this rhetoric? What fears are being leveraged? How does this shape public opinion?

This work is never easy, and it can feel lonely, especially in regions where hostility toward LGBTQIA+ content is visceral and unrelenting. But we do not do this alone. Collaborate with colleagues, seek support from your local union, and draw strength from each other. Every lesson that includes LGBTQIA+ voices is a step toward justice. Every story shared is an opportunity to increase our nation's capacity for empathy.

Ultimately, teaching LGBTQIA+ history is about dignity— ours and our students'. It is about standing in the gap and saying, "We will not let these stories be erased." In doing so, we create a future where every student can look in the mirror and see themselves reflected in the world.

Daniel Hurewitz:
Leaning into the AP or state standards as a framework of requirements can be helpful. "This is part of the AP curriculum as defined by the College Board," can go a long way to defuse the tension.

Secondly, I think embracing a curriculum approach that is consistently comparative and multi-dimensional can really create a protected space to include queer stories. As a practice that can mean: discussing the Civil War by looking at its impact on five very different individuals, including a woman who passed as a man to fight; discussing Jazz Age changes through five different cultural icons, and including Countee Cullen or Ma Rainey in the mix; framing the 1960s-70s as a larger "minority rights revolution" and asking students to compare goals, tactics and outcomes for multiple movements, including Black civil rights, second wave feminists, Native American activists, and gay liberationists. In each of those cases, the queer story is included, but is not in the spotlight alone; instead, it joins a larger set of changes, of which it is just one example. I think that gives it and the teacher some cover, as it were.

Additionally, I suspect that anti-trans and anti-queer cases and policies will be on the political agenda and in the news for the next few years. In a similar way to the framework above,

I would strive to build in a regular "news round-up" day in class, to talk about the historical framework for three or four big news stories of the month. I would make a concerted effort to occasionally incorporate queer stories into the mix.

Finally, it bears repeating what the GLSEN research showed. In order for a teacher to have an impact, they don't need to devote a class or an hour to queer topics. They could make a difference by simply referencing queer individuals from the past in a quick but non-stigmatizing way. Those tiny moments of normalization had a real effect. And if larger actions feel too risky, those smaller ones can be just as profound.

Lil Miss Hot Mess:
I think it is important for teachers to be able to remind administrators and parents that youth have a right to know about the diversity of the world around them, and to reiterate that LGBTQ+ people/cultures are not new but are part of every community – albeit with different nuances and flavors. One strategy in areas facing a lot of opposition might be to give students greater latitude in the kinds of projects they do – that is, not necessarily "teaching" LGBTQ+ subjects, but creating space for students to explore these themes. Or, to really frame the historical aspects: to look to other moments of political repression – against LGBTQ+ people or otherwise – as a comparison to contemporary debates.

John Palella:
I am working with my preservice teachers on teaching LGBTQIA+ history using state standards as shields for teaching the topic. I am privileged to do that in that I am in a blue state. I think teachers in red states should find standards that require them to discuss protest, social change, activism, etc. as the window into teaching the content and to protect themselves. I also caution teachers to be careful not to set up an environment in their classrooms where they think they are doing something positive but accidentally set up a forum for the other students to say transphobic and homophobic statements. I caution teachers to be cognizant about the class norms they have set up. For example, if they do not have

as a class rule that students cannot make disparaging remarks about specific identities, it may be problematic to address the issues without first doing so. I also encourage teachers to use journals, big posters/silent conversations, barometers, etc., to gauge students' understanding and feelings before diving into this. Finally, it is important for teachers to consider what they know about the intersectional identities of their students and the methods that they have used to gather that information.

Wendy Rouse:
In our present moment, we are witnessing a resurgence of homophobic and transphobic rhetoric and policies targeting LGBTQ+ rights. It is vital that we understand the present era in light of the broader context of history. There is a long history of marginalization and oppression of LGBTQ+ people. However, we also know that there has also been a long history of resistance and resilience in queer history. We have been here before, and we have grown stronger in spite of it.

You are no doubt experiencing the direct impact of the homophobic and transphobic policies of the Trump administration and MAGA movement in your own school and district. The effect of this bigotry is impacting teachers and students in schools across the nation. If you widen your perspective even further, you can also see the individuals and coalitions who are resisting and fighting back: parents, teachers, students, and allies speaking out at school board meetings, launching protests and recall campaigns, running for school board and organizing visible demonstrations of LGBTQ+ pride.

As educators, we know how important visibility is for members of marginalized groups to be able to see positive representations of themselves in the history curriculum. It is perhaps even more important for individuals not in those marginalized groups to be able to step outside their worldview to understand the experiences of other people in their communities.

I know this moment feels overwhelming for educators on the frontlines of this cultural battle and especially for LGBTQ+ educators. But please remember that just by doing what you do best, by teaching inclusive histories that reflect the diverse range of identities in your classroom, you are standing on the right side of history.

Jinnie Spiegler:

For educators in red states or states with laws that prohibit the teaching of what is deemed "divisive topics," (i.e., LGBTQ+ topics, race and racism, etc.), it can feel like no topics are safe. If a middle school teacher is discussing bullying with their students, identity-based bullying of LGBTQ+ students has to be mentioned and explored. If a kindergarten teacher reads a story about families and asks children to talk about their families, children of same-sex couple families must be able to participate. LGBTQ+ history, like the histories of all marginalized people, is part of US history and must be woven in not only to be accurate but also to help LGBTQ+ students feel seen, valued, included, and important. During these challenging times, it is also especially urgent to teach students about propaganda and mis- and dis-information. This can be part of studying current events, media literacy, elections, or other topics.

Index

pink triangle 191, 194–5; prisoners
wearing *192*; use in "Silence =
Death" poster *195*
Plutarch 1
Pratt, Minnie Bruce 237
Project 2025 19, 242
Public Universal Friend 105

queer curriculum 103; *see also*
LGBTQ+ history

Rainey, Gertrude "Ma"132, 187, 188,
215, 243
RAND Corporation 18–19, 174
Reconstruction 132, 186, 197, 228, 231
Red Scare (1919) 182–4, 198, 201, 207,
210; *see also* Newport Scare
Rich, Adrienne 69, 99, 236
Rivera, Sylvia 157
Romesburg, Don 7–8, 49–54
Roosevelt, Eleanor *50*, 199, 237
Roosevelt, Franklin D. 183, 185–6,
208, 209, 211
Rouse, Wendy 130–5, 240, 245–6
Rustin, Bayard 2, 199

Sacred Band of Thebes 1–2
Safe Schools movement 51
San Francisco Unified School District
51
Santos, Kyne 155
Sarria, José 133, 157
Savage, Dan 58
Schaefer, Valorie 100
Schlax, Lyndsey 230
Schniedewind, Nancy 70
Schwarzenegger, Arnold 141
Slater, Sandra 55–9
Smith, Bessie *50*, 188, 215
social justice in curriculum 187–8, 236
Somnus (character) 121–2
South Carolina 3
Spiegler, Jinnie 146–51, 240, 246
State of the American Teacher 18–19,
202
Steuben, General Friedrich Wilhelm
von 84
Student Safety and Violence
Prevention Act 140–1

Stulberg, Lisa 239
suicide and queer youth 23, 26, 58,
101
Swann, William Dorsey ("Queen of
Drag") 157, 197

Taylor, Lia *176*, 178, 190–95, 199–201;
lesson 225–9
Tennessee 12
Texas 16, 24
Thornton, Stephen 22–3
Title IX 19
transphobia 2, 19, 24, 26, 101, 242;
bias and hate 147–9; and Trump 5,
245
Trevor Project 23
Trump, Donald 5, 12, 19, 245
Turing, Alan 102, 242
Two Spirit Identities 131, 197, 199, 228

Universal Design for Learning 200
Utah 3, 133
U.S. Holocaust Memorial Museum
191, 193, 220

WNET 65
Walker, Dr. Mary Edwards 103, *104*
Warner, Gracie 20
Washington 52
Weld, William 51
Whitman, Walt *50*
Williams, Juan 5
Willingham-Jaggers, Melanie 10
Wilson, Rodney 52, 87
Wilson, Torey 52
Wilson, Woodrow 209
Windsor, Edie 123, 131
World War I 206, 207, 209, 210, 182–4,
186
World War II and gay men 132–3,
182; history of 190–95, 197; *see also*
Holocaust; Nazi persecution of
LGBTQ+ persons

Young, Jeremy 24

Weld, William 51

Zane, Sherry 183, 208, 209

For Product Safety Concerns and Information please contact our EU
representative GPSR@taylorandfrancis.com
Taylor & Francis Verlag GmbH, Kaufingerstraße 24, 80331 München, Germany